THE LANGUAGES
OF THE
SEAT OF WAR IN THE EAST

THE LANGUAGES

OF THE

SEAT OF WAR IN THE EAST

WITH A SURVEY

OF THE

THREE FAMILIES OF LANGUAGE,
SEMITIC, ARIAN, AND TURANIAN

By

Max Muller, M.A., Ph.D.

GYAN

Published by

Gyan Publishing House
5, Ansari Road
Daryaganj, New Delhi-110002
Phone: 011-47034999, 9811692060
E-mail: books@gyanbooks.com

Distribution Network
gyanbooks.com
India, USA, Canada, UK, Australia, France

ISBN : 978-81-212-6623-9 (PB)
First Published, 1855

2nd Impression 2022

Printed at: Gyan Press, Delhi.

THE LANGUAGES OF THE SEAT OF WAR IN THE EAST
Author: Max Muller

THE LANGUAGES

OF THE

SEAT OF WAR IN THE EAST.

WITH A SURVEY

OF THE

THREE FAMILIES OF LANGUAGE,

SEMITIC, ARIAN, AND TURANIAN.

BY

MAX MÜLLER, M.A., PH. D.

TAYLORIAN PROFESSOR OF EUROPEAN LANGUAGES AND LITERATURE
AT THE UNIVERSITY OF OXFORD.

SECOND EDITION,

WITH AN APPENDIX ON THE MISSIONARY ALPHABET,

AND

AN ETHNOGRAPHICAL MAP, DRAWN BY AUGUSTUS PETERMANN.

1855.

PREFACE.

TO SIR CHARLES TREVELYAN, K. C. B.

My Dear Sir,

Conscious as I feel of the many defects of this Essay on the languages of the seat of war, I wish to plead no other excuse for its publication than the kind encouragement you gave the writer, and the hope held out to him that others would make allowance for the circumstances in which it was written. These pages were commenced in answer to a communication from yourself; but they have expanded into what is too long to be called a letter, and too short and superficial to deserve the name of a book. Indeed, had you not given me leave to print your letter, I should not know how to defend myself against the charges of precipitancy and presumption. This, which gave the first impulse to my undertaking, will serve as the best introduction; and, at the same time, will explain the objects which I have kept in view.

"My Dear Sir, *"20th March, 1854.*

"I have informed all our young Commissariat Officers under orders for the East that, besides perfecting themselves in French and Italian, they will be expected to learn at least one *Eastern* language, so that there may be among them men who will be able to communicate freely with the inhabitants of each province in their own language; and I have supplied them, as far as I have been able, with elementary books in these languages, and, with your help, with a few brief instructions to give the first direction to their efforts.

"But something more than this ought to be attempted. We cannot tell how far and how long this remarkable intervention of the Western nations in Eastern affairs may lead us; and I know, from my Indian experience, that a knowledge of the native languages is an indispensable preliminary to understanding and taking an interest in native races, as well as to acquiring their good will and gaining influence over them. Without it, officers charged with important public affairs, feeling themselves at the mercy of a class of interpreters whose moral character is often of a very questionable kind, live in a state of chronic irritation with the natives, which is extremely adverse both to the satisfactory transaction of business, and to the still more important object of giving to the people of the country a just impression of the character and intentions of our nation.

"It is, therefore, extremely desirable that the attention of all our young officers who are, or are likely to be, employed in the East, not only in the Commissariat, but also in the military and naval services, should be directed to the study of the languages which are spoken in the northern division of the Turkish empire, and the adjoining provinces of Russia.

"If you agree with me in this, you will at once feel that there is a call upon you to help in this good work. What I would suggest is, that you should prepare a treatise showing,

"1st. What are the languages spoken in that part of the world, giving a general idea of their territorial limits, and of the classes of people by whom they are spoken;

"2ndly. The family to which they belong, and their general character and structure, and the alphabets by which they are expressed; and

"3rdly. The best elementary and other books in the respective languages, and where they are to be procured as far as you are aware.

"I find some interesting notices in your article in the 'Edinburgh' on Comparative Philology, of the differences between ancient and modern Greek. An expansion or even a reprint of these would be an obvious aid to our young men fresh from school or college who would be disposed to apply themselves to the study of modern Greek.

"The Russian language should be included in your sketch; and you should show, as far as you are able, what is the extent and nature of the difference between it and the Bulgarian, Servian, and other neighbouring Slavonian dialects.

"You will, no doubt, be able to tell us what is the language of the Tatar population of the Crimea, and of the leading tribes of the Circassians, including that of the redoubtable Shámil.

"I have only two further suggestions to make —

"1st. That whatever you do should be done quickly. Every part of this great effort, including this important literary adjunct, is under war pressure; and

"2ndly. That you should tell us *at once* what you *now* know, leaving the rest to be perfected hereafter as you have opportunity.

"You might conclude the Treatise with an admission of the incompleteness of the sketch, and an invitation to those who will have an opportunity of investigating the different languages on the spot to communicate the result of their researches for the purpose of enriching a second edition of the Treatise.

"Yours sincerely,

"C. E. Trevelyan.

"To Professor Max Müller."

To this I need here add but few remarks. It will be seen that on many of the languages spoken at the seat of war our information is very scanty, and that some of the most important problems of Comparative Philology, in connection with these languages, must wait for their solution until new and trustworthy materials have been collected to illustrate the grammar of the dialects spoken along the Black and the Caspian Seas. Here, then, is a field open where an officer with taste and talent for languages, may do great service, and employ his leisure hours in a manner that will be of practical use to himself, while advancing also the science of ethnology. Some of the greatest discoveries in Comparative Philology have been made by English officers; and the names of Sir A. Burnes, Colonel Rawlinson, and many others, show that these scientific pursuits are not incompatible with a conscientious discharge of the highest political and military functions. If attended by a native servant, a Circassian, an Albanian, or a Kurd, the officer should endeavour to master his language. He might ask him first for a number of words, afterwards for the paradigms of declension and conjugation, and attempt to write them down. It is by no means an easy task to collect the grammar and dictionary of a language from the mouth of a native. Yet it has not unfrequently been effected, and he who would make himself the author of a good

Circassian or Kurdian grammar would leave his name on a monument even more lasting, perhaps, than military achievements.

In writing down an Oriental language by ear, it will be essential, however, that a certain system should be observed in representing foreign sounds by Roman letters. Eastern dialects contain certain sounds that have in English no corresponding letters. These must receive alphabetical expression. Again, in English the same sound is frequently written in two different modes, as in ravine, been; boat and note; date and gait; while many vowels and consonants have more than one power, as in ravine and pine; date and hat; through and cough.

Now, without some agreement that, in transcribing foreign languages, every letter shall always represent but one sound, it will be impossible to say what power, for instance, an *i* might have when used in a list of foreign words. A traveller again, who would allow himself to express the sound of i, as heard in ravine, promiscuously by i, ee, ea, or y, would soon find himself unable to pronounce the words thus written down from oral communication.

This inconvenience has been long felt, and chiefly by missionaries, to whom the reduction to writing of the languages spoken by savage tribes has been always an essential duty. An English missionary would be inclined, if he heard the sound of i (as in ravine), to express it by *ee*; a French missionary by i; and translations of the Bible, printed according to the English and French systems of spelling, would take an appearance so different that a native who had learned to read the one would not be able to understand the other.

Many attempts have been made to remedy this defect, and to settle a uniform system of expressing the pronunciation of foreign dialects. All that is required is to fix on certain letters to express sounds which do not exist in English, and to restrict all other letters to but one phonetical value. This may seem a comparatively easy task, yet uniformity, without which all other results are nugatory, is so difficult to attain between different nations, societies, or individuals that the realization of a common alphabet is still far distant. I give in an appendix (page XV) an abstract of an alphabet, lately the subject of several conferences in London, which the chief Societies have since resolved to submit to not less than five hundred of their missionaries, who will test it in the course of the next few years, and then report on its merits and defects. It is based on the principle of *analogy,* so ably advocated by Sir William Jones, and adopted by Professor Wilson in his Glossary of Indian Terms. The differences between Sir William Jones and Professor Wilson, and between both and the Missionary Alphabet arise from the different application of this principle. The chief cause of difference has been the difficulty of agreeing upon certain new types, whether accented or otherwise modified, or again of procuring these novel types even when agreed upon. It has therefore been the leading principle in framing this Missionary Alphabet to avoid altogether the necessity of new types, and thus to remove the greatest, if not the only obstacle in the way of uniformity.

It may be remarked that most of the grammars and dictionaries recommended in this Essay, as likely to afford assistance to the student of languages, are written by Germans, Frenchmen, Danes, or Russians. This is not owing to any national predilections on my part. On the contrary, I believe that where grammars written by Englishmen can be procured, they will generally be found the most useful and practical. But their number is at present comparatively small from the paucity of Oriental scholars in this country.

It is undoubtedly high time that something should be done to encourage the study of Oriental languages in England. At the very outset of this war, it has been felt how much this branch of studies — in emergencies like the present so requisite — has been neglected in the system of our education.

A man-of-war is built in less time than an Oriental scholar can be launched ready to converse with natives, and capable of procuring supplies, gathering information, translating proclamations, writing circulars, carrying on parleys, assisting at conferences, and, finally, of wording the conditions of a treaty of peace. In all other countries which have any political, commercial, or religious connections with the East, provision has been made by government or otherwise to encourage young men to devote themselves to this branch of studies. Russia has always been the most liberal patron of Oriental Philology. In the Academy of Petersburg there is a chair for every branch of Oriental literature; and there are schools in that city, at Kasan and elsewhere, where the chief languages of the East are taught. Scientific expeditions are sent out to different parts of the world, travellers supported and encouraged, and their works, grammars or dictionaries, printed at the expense of Government. This no doubt is done in the interest of science, but at the same time other interests are served. If Philology owes much to Russia, ever since the days of the Empress Catherine, Russia knows that she owes something to her linguists for her diplomatic successes, and this more especially in the East.

Other countries also, less immediately connected with the East, find it expedient to encourage Oriental learning.

The French Academy has always counted among its members the chief representatives of every department of Oriental Philology; and for more practical purposes, the Government has founded a school, "L'école pour les langues Orientales vivantes", where Hindustani, Persian, Arabic, Armenian, Chinese, and Turkish are taught by the most eminent professors. At Vienna there is an Oriental seminary; and the Imperial Press possesses the richest collection of Oriental types in the world. More Oriental works are brought out there than at any other press in Europe, and, as the Government makes no profit, the expense of printing is about one fourth of what it is in England. Denmark sends regular scientific missions to the East, with a view to encourage the study of Oriental languages; while Prussia finds it expedient to give similar encouragement to young Oriental scholars employed afterwards with advantage, as consuls and interpreters in her service.

In England alone, where the most vital interests of the country are involved in a free intercourse with the East, hardly anything is done to foster Oriental studies. The College of Haileybury, hitherto most liberally supported by the East India Company, is the one exception. It is felt, however, particularly at the present moment, that the country requires a larger supply of men than can be accommodated at Haileybury; and those possessing a thorough knowledge not only of Sanskrit, Hindustani, and Telugu, but of Persian, Arabic, Turkish, Armenian, and even Chinese. But it is unnecessary to found academies, schools, seminaries, or imperial printing offices, in order to encourage the study of Oriental. languages in this country. All that is required is to remove the disabilities under which Oriental scholars have hitherto laboured. I speak only of the two Universities, Oxford in particular. For here a classical scholar, a student of modern history and law, a mathematician, and a lover of physical science, may gain honours, exhibitions, fellowships, and preferment. Why not a student of Oriental languages? If a man, after passing his Moderations, is now allowed to devote his last year at College to more special subjects — the classics, astronomy, geology, or French history, and can thus obtain his degree and the highest honours, why should the Schools be closed to one who has made Hebrew, or Arabic, or Sanskrit, or Persian, the subjects of special study? A knowledge of these languages will be useful to the clergyman whether at home or abroad. A knowledge of Sanskrit — the basis of Comparative Philology — will be an advantage to the classical scholar, and even a judge who is sent to India will not find occasion for regret if he has read the laws of Manu in the original language, and acclimatized his mind to that intellectual atmosphere in which he is henceforth to live and to act. But even from a merely educational point of view, a knowledge of Oriental languages is not less beneficial to the mind than French history or than botany. A new language is the key to a new literature, to a new system of thought, to a new world of feeling. It widens our views of the powers and destinies of the human race, and allows us an insight into the government of the world universal. Nay, there is hardly any branch of classical, mathematical, or physical studies so rich in lessons of morality, of history, and of religion.

The foundation of a fifth school, a School of Languages (excluding Greek and Latin) at the University would, it is my belief, give a sufficient stimulus to this branch of studies. We have large endowments for Oriental Professorships, and their number might easily be increased. If a few exhibitions were added; if honours could be gained in Hebrew, Arabic, Sanskrit, or Persian; if fellowships were awarded to distinguished linguists, and travelling fellowships founded for those who desire to gain a practical knowledge of Oriental languages; if Oxford men were enabled to compete for Indian appointments — fellowships, which, after twenty years of useful activity, yield a pension of a thousand a year — if some consular and diplomatic appointments in the East were given to the University; and if the Press would procure Oriental types sufficient, and afford the opportunity of publishing works in all the chief Eastern languages — these changes effected, and I believe we should soon see England take in Oriental Philology the lead to which she is at present indifferent.

These are suggestions thrown out in a very hurried manner; but I may be permitted the hope they will be taken up by men conversant with the resources and requirements of the University, and careful for the interests of the country at large.

I remain, my dear Sir,

Yours sincerely,

MAX MÜLLER.

SIR ROBERT TAYLOR'S INSTITUTION,
OXFORD, *May 16, 1854.*

In publishing the second edition I have little to add beyond the expression of my thanks for the kind reception which these pages have met with. It will be seen that I have availed myself of some valuable remarks contained in the reviews with which this little Essay has been honoured in England, France, Germany, Sweden, and India. Errors have been here and there set right; although in a work so discursive I am sensible, that others may probably yet remain undetected; and a few additions have been made. A statement by Professor Pott on the origin of the Albanian Language (kindly sent me by that eminent scholar), has been inserted, with some remarks for which I have to thank the Hon. H. Stanley, H. M. Secretary of Legation at Athens. And for some corrections in phraseology I am indebted to my friend Mr. Palgrave of Exeter College.

It was impossible in this second edition to change the original plan of my essay, or make it a complete survey of the three great families of language. But I have learned with much pleasure that, beyond its immediate object, it has been found useful as an introduction to Ethnological study, and has gained the approbation of many of the highest authorities in Comparative Philology.

Oxford, March, 1855.

M. M.

PROPOSALS

FOR

A MISSIONARY ALPHABET,

SUBMITTED TO

THE ALPHABETICAL CONFERENCES

HELD AT THE RESIDENCE OF CHEVALIER BUNSEN IN JANUARY 1854.

PROPOSALS

FOR

A MISSIONARY ALPHABET.

THE signs which we use to express the sounds of our own language, were originally invented in the East. They were adopted by the Greeks and Romans, and have now become, under various forms, the alphabet of the civilized nations of Europe. The twenty-two signs which originally constituted this ancient Alphabet, were not sufficient to express the numerous sounds which can be formed by the organs of the human voice, and which the different nations of Asia and Europe have, in various proportions, allowed to enter into the formation of their languages and dialects.

Two ways were open to remedy this defect. New signs could be invented to represent new sounds, or one and the same letter might be allowed to represent different sounds. The first plan has been adopted with great reserve, and the number of new signs, whether entirely new, or formed by modification and composition, which the Greeks, the Romans, the Slavonic and Teutonic nations have added to the so-called Phenician Alphabet, is comparatively small, while, if we look to the modern languages of Europe, we shall find that in them there are but few letters which are restricted to but one pronunciation, a fact which in no language is felt more painfully than in English. Here one can hardly say that letters, which were originally intended to represent the sound of language, still answer this their original purpose. In pronouncing "thigh", we do not pronounce any one of the five letters according to their proper and original power. The spelling of words is no longer phonetic, but traditional. To call it etymological, would be a false compliment, since it is neither scientific nor systematic. The spelling which in English, as in all other languages, corresponded at some time or other, to the sound of words, has become stationary at various periods in the history of the English language, and it was entirely a matter of chance whether the form, fixed upon by literary tradition, preserved more of the etymology or of the pronunciation.

A reform is needed for the spelling of most modern European languages, and it is extraordinary, that the art of writing, though belonging to the arts in which our times have achieved the greatest improvements, should have been allowed to remain in the same state in which it was three thousand years ago, with no alterations except for the worse.

Whatever may be done in course of time by the different nations of Europe to ameliorate their own systems of writing, it is clear that, with the defects peculiar to each, none could claim in its present state to be used as a standard system; and it would be wrong to smuggle any one of these imperfect systems of writing into those languages of Africa, Australia or America which have not yet been reduced to alphabetical writing. The Missionary who brings the notion of an alphabet, together with more exalted ideas of religion, of law, of arts and sciences to the savage tribes of Africa, will be to them what Cecrops or Cadmus were to Greece. He must therefore not think of the present only, but of the future; he must see in his helpless converts the ancestors perhaps of mighty nations. He ought to remember that the seed which he sows in the mind of these people will bear fruit a thousand fold: that it will yield many harvests, beside that of religion. Whatever objections may be urged against the adoption of a more rational and scientific alphabet for the languages of ancient Europe do not apply to the dialects of the new world of Africa or Australia. If our own case be hopeless, theirs is not, and what with us may remain the scientific alphabet of the student, can with them at once be carried into general practice. Nothing is more simple than what Mr. Ellis has well called the Alphabet of Nature; nothing more complicated than the Alphabet of Tradition. The following is an abstract of a scientific alphabet which was framed with a particular view to assist Missionaries in translating the Bible into the languages of savage and illiterate tribes; but it may be equally useful to the traveller and the philologist in collecting for scientific purposes the dialects of people which are little known and have not yet had their proper place assigned to them in the classification of languages. All strange and complicated types, all diacritical marks which embarrass the printer and dazzle the reader have been avoided, and the chief principle in arranging it has been the principle of all Missionary labours, to obtain the greatest results by the smallest means. Practical experience has shown that this Missionary Alphabet answers the purpose for which it was intended, its employment may therefore be recommended till it is superseded by a more perfect and more convenient system. A fuller account of the whole problem of alphabetical writing may be found in a very able Essay by Mr. Ellis, The Alphabet of Nature; and in the second volume of Chevalier Bunsen's Outlines of Universal History, applied to Language and Religion, Appendix D., The Universal Alphabet and the Conferences regarding it held at the Residence of Chev. Bunsen, in January 1854. My own proposals for a Missionary Alphabet are there printed after the interesting account of the Standard Alphabet by Professor Lepsius.

For the practical solution of the problem, "*How to establish one uniform system of notation which shall be acceptable to the scholar, convenient to the missionary, and easy for the printer,*" we must consider three points: —

I. *Which are the principal sounds that can be formed with our organs of speech, and therefore may be expected to occur in any of the dead or living dialects of mankind?*

This is a physiological question.

II. *How can these principal sounds, after proper classification, be expressed by us in writing and printing without obscuring their physiological value, and without creating new typographical difficulties?*

This is a practical question.

III. *How can this physiological alphabet be applied to existing languages, and*

III. a. *to unwritten dialects;*

Here the chief point is to catch the proper sound of the language as we hear it spoken by different individuals, to determine the character of every vowel and consonant, and to distinguish most carefully between accidental varieties of pronunciation, such as occur in the language of different individuals, and the general and permanent pronunciation of words. Much depends here on a good ear, and this can be acquired by practice. In expressing the sounds of a new language by the signs of the physiological alphabet, the missionary should be guided entirely by ear, without paying any regard to etymological considerations, which are too apt to mislead even the most accomplished scholar.

III. b. *to written languages;*

In transcribing languages possessed of an historical orthography, and where, for reasons best known to the archæologist, one sign may represent different sounds, and one sound be expressed by different signs, new and entirely distinct questions are involved, and capable of solution by archæological and philological research alone. We shall, therefore, discuss this part (III. b.) separately, and distinguish it by the name of **Transliteration**, from the usual method of **transcribing** as applied to unwritten tongues.

I.

Which are the principal Sounds that can be formed with our Organs of Speech, and therefore may be expected to occur in any of the dead or living Dialects of Mankind?

On the first point, which must form the basis of the whole, we have the immense advantage that all scholars who have written on it have arrived at results almost identically the same.* We are here still in the sphere

* In a very able article by Professor Heise, in Hoefer's Zeitschrift für Wissenschaft der Sprache, iv. 1. 1853, the following authorities are quoted: —

Chladni, Über die Hervorbringung der menschlichen Sprachlaute, in Gilbert's Annalen der Physik. vol. lxxvi. 1824.

A. J. Ribbeck, Über die Bildung der Sprachlaute. Berlin, 1848.

K. M. Rapp, Versuch einer Physiologie der Sprache. Stuttgardt, 1836.

H. E. Bindseil, Abhandlungen zur Allgemeinen Vergleichenden Sprachlehre. Hamburg, 1838.

J. Müller, Elements of Physiology. London, 1842. vol. ii. p. 1044.

One of the earliest and best works on this subjectis.

W. Holder, Elements of Speech: an Essay of Inquiry into the natural Production of Letters. London, 1669.

An excellent account of the researches of the most distinguished physiologists on the human voice, and the formation of letters, is found in Ellis, "The Alphabet of Nature;" a work full of accurate observations and original thought.

Three very important essays have lately been published on the Alphabet, one by Professor R. Lepsius, "Das allgemeine linguistische Alphabet," Berlin 1855; the other by Professor Wilson in his learned introduction to his "Glossary of Indian Terms," London 1855; and a third by Wallin, "On the sounds of Arabic and their representation," printed after the death of this eminent Orientalist, in the Journal of the German Oriental Society, vol. IX, p. 1—69. Wallin was one of the few, if not the only of physical science, where facts are arranged by observation, and observation may be checked by facts so as to exclude individual impressions and national prejudice. The classification of vowels and consonants proposed by modern physiologists is, so far as general principles are concerned, exactly the same as that contained in Sanskrit grammars composed in the fifth century before Christ, and appended to the different collections of the sacred writings of the Brahmans, — the four Vedas. These grammatical treatises, called Prâtisâkhyas, exist in manuscript, and have not hitherto been published. The classification established by physiologists, as the result of independent research, will receive the most striking confirmation by a translation of these writings, now more than two thousand years old. But, on their own account also, these phonetic treatises deserve to be published. Their observations are derived from a language (the Vaidik Sanskrit) which at that time was studied by means of oral tradition only, and where, in the absence of a written alphabet, the most minute differences of pronunciation had to be watched by the ear, and to be explained and described to the pupil. The language itself, the Sanskrit of that early period, had suffered less from the influence of phonetic corruption than any tongue from which *we* can derive our observations; nay, the science of phonetics (Sikshâ), essential to the young theological student (who was not allowed to learn the Veda from MSS.), had been reduced to a more perfect system in the schools of the Brahmans, in the fifth century before Christ, than has since been anywhere effected. Our notions on the early civilisation of the East are of so abstract a nature that we must expect to be startled occasionally by facts like these. But we now pass on to the general question.

European, who spoke Arabic so well that he was taken for an Arab by the Beduins. His account of the Arabic alphabet is therefore invaluable, and will necessitate many alterations in the systems of Arabic transliteration hitherto proposed.

Consonants and Vowels.

If we regard the human voice as a continuous stream of air, emitted as breath from the lungs and changed by the vibration of the chordae vocales into vocal sound as it leaves the larynx, this stream itself, as modified by certain positions of the mouth, would represent the vowels. "The vowels," as Professor Wheatstone says, "are formed by the voice modified, but not interrupted, by the various positions of the tongue and the lips." In the consonants, on the contrary, we should have to recognise a number of stops opposing for a moment the free passage of this vocal stream. Hence the vowel is called by the Arabs motion (حركة), while the consonants are called barriers or edges (حرف).*

The consonants must again be divided into Mutae, full stops, and Semi-vocales, half-stops; the latter including the liquids, sibilants, and nasals. The Mutae prevent for a moment all emission of either voice or breath (k, g, t, d, p, b). The Semi-vocales allow a mere breathing to be heard in its various non-vocal modifications (h, y, l, r, w; *h, s,* s, sh, f; n, m). This distinction which the Greeks expressed by ἄφωνα and ἡμίφωνα, is easily tested, for we find that we can breathe while pronouncing h, y, l, r, w, s, sh, f, n, m; but a continued attempt to pronounce k, g, t, d, p, b, would end in suffocation. The consonantal stops, against which the waves of the vowels break themselves more or less distinctly, are produced by barriers formed by the contact of the tongue, the soft palate, the palate, the teeth, and the lips with each other. While English grammarians maintain that consonants cannot be pronounced without vowels, Arabic grammarians declare that vowels cannot be pronounced without a consonant. The former view is true if by vowel is meant not only vocal sounds, such as a, e, i, o, u, but also the Semi-vowels, including liquids, sibilants, and na-

* Wallin, On the Arabic Alphabet, in the Journal of the German Oriental Society, vol. IX, p. 2.

sals. The latter opinion may be defended, if we extend the name of consonant to what the Greeks call spiritus asper and lenis, for no vowel can be pronounced without at least that initial, slightly consonantal, element which we have in hear and ear.

Consonants.

Gutturals, Dentals, and Labials.

According to an observation which we find already in Vaidik grammars, the principal consonantal stops in any language are: —

the guttural (k),
the dental (t),
the labial (p).

The pure *guttural* sound, without any regard as yet to its modifications (whether tenuis, media, aspirata, nasalis, liquida, flatus), is produced by stopping the stream of sound by means of a contact between the root of the tongue and the throat, or, more usually, the soft palate, or the velum pendulum. The throat is called the passive, the root of the tongue the active organ, of the guttural.

The pure *dental* sound is produced by contact between tongue and teeth. Here the teeth are called the passive, and the tip of the tongue the active organ.

The pure *labial* sound is produced by contact between the upper and lower lip; the upper lip being the passive, the lower the active organ.

All consonants, excluding liquids and sibilants or flatus, are formed by a complete contact between the active and passive organ. As the removal of this complete contact causes the voice to burst out with greater force, these consonants have sometimes been called explosive.

Formation of the Tenuis.

If the voice is stopped sharp by the contact of the organs, so as to allow for the moment no breath or sound to escape, the consonant is called *tenuis* (ψιλόν), or hard (k, t, p). Arab grammarians remark very justly that the articulation of these consonants cannot be prolonged, but is instantaneous. They compare them with the point in geometry. (Wallin, p. 11.)

Formation of the Media.

If the voice is stopped less abruptly, so as to allow a kind of breathing to continue after the first contact has taken place, the consonant is called soft, or according to classical terminology, media (μέσον) or middle (g, d, b). The soft consonant does not arrest the sound at once, but allows it to be heard during a moment of resistance.

The difference between a hard and soft consonant is best illustrated by a speaking-machine. "The sound p," as Professor Wheatstone says, "was produced by suddenly removing the left hand from the front of the mouth, which it had previously completely stopped; the sound b, by the same action; but instead of closing the mouth completely, a very minute aperture was left, so that the sound of the reed might not be entirely stifled." This coincides fully with the description given by Mr. Ellis. "In pronouncing ba," he says, "the vowel is uttered simultaneously with the act of relieving the lips from contact, or rather *before* they are quite released. If we separate them before the vowel is uttered, allowing the breath to be condensed during a very brief space of time, the sound pa is heard. There is a similar distinction between ab and ap: in the former the effect of the voice remains throughout the consonant, and we may feel a slight tremor of the lips while it is being produced; in the latter the vowel, properly so called, entirely ceases before the contact is completed."

Formation of Liquids. *

If there is only an approach or a very slight contact

* Although it is usual to call these letters semi-vowels, yet it seems better to keep that name as a general title of all non-mute

between the organs, and the breathing is slightly stopped or compressed as it reaches the point of contact, the consonants are called liquid half-consonants or semi-vowels. They are soft like the mediae, owing to the process of their formation here described ('h, y, r, l, w).

At the end of words and before a tenuis the liquid semi-vowels are frequently pronounced as a flatus, or they become evanescent. In the Dutch dag, we have the nearest approach to a guttural liquid, though in truth a guttural liquid is not to be distinguished from a guttural flatus lenis except in theory. If a Saxon pronounces the same word, he changes the d into t, and the guttural liquid into the guttural flatus asper, like ch in loch. In other parts of Germany, the final guttural is sounded as media or as tenuis, while in the English day the guttural liquid semi-vowel has become evanescent. The same process explains the French sou instead of sol, and vaut instead of valet. In Sanskrit no liquid semi-vowel is tolerated at the end of words or before a tenuis. In Arabic the guttural liquid ع, 'hain, if final, is frequently changed into the guttural flatus asper ح, or followed by a slight vocal breathing. (See Wallin, p. 46, p. 50, N. 2, and 54, N. 1.)

Professor Wheatstone's researches prove that a distinguishing mark of the liquid semi-vowels consists in their having no corresponding mutes. This applies not only to y, r, l, but also to w and 'h.

Formation of Sibilants (flatus).

If there is no contact at all, and the breath passes between the two organs without being stopped, still not without giving rise to a certain friction on passing that point of contact where guttural, dental, and labial con-

consonants. In this sense ἡμίφωνα was used by the Greeks, and it comprised liquids (ὕγρα), nasals, and sibilants.

sonants are formed, we get the sibilants, or the "winds," as they are more properly called by Hindu grammarians. These are, the pure breathing, without even a guttural modification, commonly called spiritus asper and lenis; the deep guttural flatus, sharp, as in loch, mild as in the German tage; the original palatal flatus, sharp as in the German ich, mild as in the German täglich; the assibilated palatal flatus, sharp as in sharp, mild as in pleasure; the sharp and soft s for the dentals; and the sharp and soft f for the labials. The sibilants or flatus are distinguished from all other consonants by this, that with them a breathing is freely emitted, while all other consonants offer more or less impediment to the emission of sound or breath. A candle applied to the mouth will at once show the difference between the labial flatus asper, as in find, and the consonantal stops, such as p, b, or even the liquid semi-vowel, as heard in wind. The b will produce no disturbance in the flame; the p shows its explosive nature by displacing the flame for a moment; the w affects the flame considerably, and the f generally extinguishes it.

As we distinguished between tenuis and media in the consonants, we must admit a twofold intonation for the flatus or the sibilants also. A flatus or sibilant cannot be modified exactly in the same manner as a consonant produced by contact; but, by an analogous process, it may become either asper or lenis, sharp or soft. We are best acquainted with this distinction in the primitive and unmodified breathing which necessarily precedes an initial vowel. The spiritus asper and lenis in Greek are modifications of that initial breathing which is inherent in every vowel sound at the beginning of a word or of a syllable. It comes out freely as the spiritus asper in Homer and ὅρος, frontier, while it is tempered and to our ears hardly audible in 'Aristotle and ὄρος, hill. We can more easily perceive what is meant by the Spiritus lenis inherent in every unaspirated initial vowel, if we pronounce blacking and black ink. In blacking, the vowel i is introduced by the second half of the preceding k, in *black ink*, the i is ushered in by the spiritus lenis. This spiritus lenis is the Hamzeh of the Arabs, which stands to the spiritus asper ﻩ in the same relation as ع to ح, غ to خ, ز to س, و to ف. The Hamzeh cannot be called an explosive letter. Its sound is produced by the opening of the larynx, but there is no previous effort of closing the larynx which alone could be said to give in an explosive character. It has well been compared with the more involuntary *nictus oculi*, which is perhaps the original meaning of Hamzeh. (Wallin, p. 64.) In ancient languages the spiritus asper is frequently represented by the flatus of another class, such as s and f, and the spiritus lenis by a liquid semi-vowel, as, for instance, the Digamma Æolicum w, or the y.

If, instead of allowing the pure pectoral breathing to be heard as in *hand*, we cause it to assume a harsher sound, by elevating the root of the tongue against the uvula and thus narrowing the passage of the breath, we have what may be called a guttural flatus asper, as heard in *loch*. The corresponding sonant or mild flatus is of rare occurrence, but it may be heard in some parts of Germany in words like *tage*.

The Arabs do not form their guttural flatus so high in the throat as the German ch in *loch*, at least not regularly (see Wallin, p. 35); but they admit between the pure and almost uninterrupted breathing of ﻩ, h, and the point of guttural contact where k is formed, two intermediate stations, where by compressing the passage of the throat, two guttural flatus are formed, the ح and خ, with their corresponding sonant representatives, ع and غ. The ح is formed so low in the throat, that here a contact and explosion would be impossible; hence there is no tenuis corresponding to ح as little as to ﻩ. The خ is formed higher in the throat, and occasions, it is said, a friction between the root of the tongue and the lowest part of the palate. It is not, however, the German ch, and according to Mr. Eli Smith should be defined as a breathing whose sound is modified by a tremulous motion of the epiglottis, and not by its striking against the palate as in the German ch in loch.

In none of these there stages, that of the ه, the ح, and خ, is it possible to distinguish between the flatus lenis and the corresponding liquid, unless we admit the opinion of some Arabic grammarians who look upon the ا as a liquid semi-vowel, distinct from the آ (see Wallin, p. 3, N. 1, 22, 24); a view which may be true in theory, but is of no practical importance.

The fourth degree of flatus, after the spiritus asper and the two Semitic guttural breathings ح and خ, would be the European guttural ch as in loch. Next to it would follow the palatal flatus as heard in ich; and after this the assibilated palatal flatus as heard in sharp, corresponding in place with the palatal tenuis and liquid; as heard in church and yea.

The dental flatus, as a tenuis, or rather as a flatus asper, is heard in sin and seal; while the media or flatus lenis is rendered by the English z, as in zeal and breeze.

The sharp labial flatus is the pure f, which the Greeks could not pronounce, and which we hear in find and life. The flat corresponding sound is heard in vine and live. This also is a difficult letter to pronounce, and is therefore avoided by many people, or changed into b, as Scaliger said,

> "Haud temere antiquas mutat Vasconia voces,
> Cui nihil est aliud vivere quam bibere."

Strictly speaking, and in accordance with our own definitions, every consonant at the end of a word, unless followed by a slight exhalation such as is heard in drug, loud, sob, must become a tenuis. Now, if we take words where the final consonant is a flatus asper but where, by the addition of a derivative syllable, the flatus ceases to be really final, we shall see distinctly how the flatus asper and lenis interchange. The sharp dental flatus is heard in grass and grease. Here the s is really final, although an e is put at the end of grease. If we form the two verbs, to graze and to grease, we have the corresponding flat s, the common German s. Exactly the same grammatical process applied to the labial flatus changes life into live, *i. e.* the sharp labial flatus into the flat, and it accounts for the Arabic انقَعْ ånqa'h and بِعْث bi'ht being pronounced انقَحْ, ånqa'h and بِحْث, bi'ht. (Wallin, p. 46.)

Some languages, as, for instance, Sanskrit, acknowledge none but sharp sibilants; and even a media, if followed by a flatus is changed in Sanskrit into a tenuis.

Formation of Nasals.

If, in the three organs, a full contact takes place and the vocal breathing is stopped, not abruptly, but in the same manner as with the sonant letters, and if afterwards the breathing be emitted, not through the mouth, but through the nose, we get the three full nasal consonants ng, n, and m, for the guttural, dental, and labial series. A speaking-machine leaves no doubt as to the manner in which a tenuis may be changed into a narisonant letter. "M," as Professor Wheatstone says, "was heard on opening two small tubes representing the nostrils, placed between the wind-chest and the mouth, while the front of the mouth was stopped as for p."

In most cases the peculiar character of the nasal is determined by the consonant immediately following, In ink, the n is necessarily guttural; and if we try to pronounce it as a dental or labial, we have to stop after the n, and the transition to the guttural k becomes so awkward that, even in words like to in-cur, most people pronounce the n like a guttural. No language, as far as I know, is fond of such incongruities as a guttural n followed by any but guttural consonants, and they generally sacrifice etymology to euphony. In English we cannot pronounce em-ty, and therefore we pronounce and write emp-ty. In the Uraon-Kol language, which is a Tamulian dialect, enan is *I*, and the possessive prefix is in, *my*. But in the Journal of the Asiatic Society of Bengal we find im-bas, *my father;* but ing-kos, *my child.* Cicero alludes to the same where he speaks of the n adulterinum. He says, that cum nobis was pronounced like cun nobis.

At the end of words and syllables, however, the three nasal sounds, guttural, dental, or labial, may occur independently; and as it is necessary to distinguish a final m from a final n (ἀγαϑόν, *bonum*), it will be advisable also to do the same for a final guttural nasal, as the French bon, Lundi, or the English to sing. It is true that in most languages the final guttural nasal becomes really a double consonant, *i. e.* n + g, as in sing; still, as the pronunciation on this point varies, it will be necessary to provide a distinct category, and afterwards a distinct sign, for the guttural nasal.

In some languages we meet even with an initial guttural nasal, as in Tibetan nga-rang, *I myself.* Whether here the initial sound is really so evanescent as to require a different sign from that which we have as the final letter in "rang", is a question which a native alone could answer. Certain it is that in the Tibetan alphabet itself both are written by the same sign, while Csoma de Körös writes the initial guttural n by ň, the final by ng; as ňa-rang.

We have now, on physiological grounds, established the following system of consonants:

	Mutae.		Semivocales.			
	Tenues.	Mediæ.	Liquidæ.	Flatus sibilantes: asperi.	lenes.	Nasales.
Gutturales:	k (kirk)	g (go)	’h (dag)	‘h (loch)	’h (tage)	n (sing).
Dentales:	t (town)	d (do)	l (low)	s (seal)	z (zeal)	n (sin).
Labiales:	p (pint)	b (bring)	w (win)	f (life)	v (live)	m (sum).

Spiritus asper: ‘ or h (hear).
Spiritus lenis: ’ (ear).

Formation of Aspirates.

According to Sanskrit grammarians, if we begin to pronounce the tenuis, but, in place of stopping it abruptly, allow it to come out with what they call the corresponding "wind" (flatus, wrongly called sibilans), we produce the *aspirata,* as a modified tenuis, not as a double consonant. This however, is admissible for the tenuis aspirata only, and not for the media aspirata. Other grammarians, therefore, maintain that all mediæ aspiratæ are formed by pronouncing the mediæ with a final 'h, the flatus lenis being considered identical with the spiritus: and they insist on this principally because the aspirated mediæ could not be said to merge into, or terminate by, a hard sibilant. Accepting this view of the formation of these aspirates, to which we have no corresponding sounds in English, we may now represent the complete table of the chief consonantal sounds possible in any dialect, as follows: —

	Tenuis.	Tenuis aspir.	Media.	Media aspir.	Liquidæ.	Flatus sibilantes.		Nasales.
Guttural:	k	k*h*	g	g*h*	'h	ʻh	'h	ng
Dental:	t	t*h*	d	d*h*	l	s	z	n
Labial:	p	p*h*	b	b*h*	w	f	v	m
					Spiritus:	h	'—	

It should be remarked that in the course of time the fine distinctions between k*h*, g*h*, and ʻh, between *ph*, b*h*, and *f,* become frequently merged in one common sound. In Sanskrit only, and in some of the southern languages of India, through the influence of Sanskrit, the distinction has been maintained. Instead of Sanskrit t*h* we find in Latin the simple t; instead of d*h*, the simple d, or, as a nearer approach, the f (d*hu*ma = fumus, &c.). The etymological distinction maintained in Sanskrit between d*h*ā, *to put, to create*, and dā, *to give,* is lost in Persian, because there the two initial sounds d and d*h* have become one, and the root dā has taken to itself the meaning both of creating and giving. Whatever objections, therefore, might be raised against the anticipated representation of the tenuis and media aspirata by means of an additional *h* or h, they would practically apply only to a very limited sphere of languages. In Sanskrit no scholar could ever take kh for k + h, because the latter combination of sounds is grammatically impossible. In the Tamulic languages the fine distinctions introduced into their orthography have hardly found their way into the spoken dialects of the people at large.

Modifications of Gutturals and Dentals.

From what has been said before on the formation of the guttural and dental sounds, it must be clear that the exact place of contact by which they are produced can never be fixed with geometrical precision, and that by shifting this point forward or backward certain modifications will arise in the pronunciation of individuals, tribes, or nations. The point of contact between the lips is not liable to the same changes, and the labials are, therefore, the most constant sounds in all dialects.

A. *Dialectic Modifications of Gutturals and Dentals.*

Where this variety of pronunciation exists only in degree, without affecting the nature and real character of a guttural or dental consonant, we need not notice it. Gutturals from a Semitic throat have a deeper sound than our own, and some grammarians have made a new class for them by calling them pectoral letters. The guttural flatus asper, as heard in the Swiss ach is deeper, and as it were more pectoral, than the usual German ch: but this is owing to a peculiarity of the organs of speech; and whatever letter might be chosen to represent this Swiss ch in a phonetic alphabet, it is certain no European. but a Swiss could ever pronounce it. This Swiss ch is, according to Wallin, pag. 21, the same as the Arabic خ, for none of the Arabic gutturals, neither ه, ح, or خ, corresponds to the German ch.

But although there is a distinction between the ch as heard in l o c h, and the خ and ح of the Arabs, as described above, yet it is not necessary to admit more than one type of the guttural flatus asper. In a European throat this flatus asper will sound like the German ch. In a Semitic throat both ح and خ will differ from this ch, but it will be sufficient to have one sign for the simple guttural flatus of a Semitic organ, the ح; and to mark the خ diacritically as in the Arabic alphabet. Sanskrit grammarians sometimes regard h as formed in the chest (urasya), while they distinguish the other gutturals by the name of tongue-root letters (*g*ihvāmūlīya). These refinements, however, are of no practical use; because, in dialects where the guttural sound is affected and diverted from its purer intonation, we generally find that the pure sound is lost altogether; so that the two hardly ever co-exist in the same language. The Swiss who pronounces his ch avoids the common German ch in l o c h. The Arab who pronounces ح and خ, entirely ignores the German ch.

The same applies to the so-called Linguals of the Sanskrit and the Arabic alphabets. It is true that there is a difference between the Sanskrit ट and the Arabic ط. In the former the tongue is more contracted than in the latter, but both are produced by contact between the tongue, more or less contracted, and the palate. Their difference is so slight that here again an organ which is able to form the Sanskrit lingual is generally unsuccessful in the formation of the Arabic lingual. In Hindustani therefore where owing to the mixture of Arabic and Sanskrit words, both letters occur, no difference is made between the two. (Wilson, Indian terms, p. XVI.) It will be seen that native Arabic grammarians, though admitting 17 places of articulation, assign the same place or passive organ to ت, د, and ط. The distinction between Arabic dentals and linguals has therefore been avoided altogether in our system of transliteration, and we have preferred to regard the superlative degree of explosiveness in the ط,

as well as in the low guttural ق, and the Ethiopic pait, as the characteristic peculiarity of these letters, and endeavoured to indicate it in our transcription.

B. *Specific Modifications of Gutturals and Dentals.*

1. *Palatals as Modifications of Gutturals.*

But the place of contact of the gutturals may be pushed forward so far as to lie no longer in the throat, but in the palate. This change has taken place in almost all languages. Latin cantus is still canto in Italian, but in English chant. In the same manner, the guttural tenuis in the Latin vocs (*vox*) has been softened in Sanskrit into the sound of the English ch, at least where it is followed by certain letters. Thus we have:

vach + mi, *I speak,*
but vak + shi, *thou speakest,*
vak + ti, *he speaks.*

The same applies to the media. Latin largus is Italian largo, but English large. The Latin guttural media g in jungo is softened in Sanskrit into the sound of the English j. We have Sanskrit yuga, Latin jugum; but in the verb we have:

yunaj + mi, *I join.*
yunak + shi, *thou joinest.*
yunak + ti, *he joins.*

Wallin in his paper "On the pronunciation of Arabic", gives the following description of an analogous change of k into *k*. "Certain tribes particularly among the most genuine Beduins in Negd and ʿIrâk, among the more-southern ʿEneré-Nomads, and in the neighbourhood of Jerusalem, pronounce k (ك) like ksh, a peculiarity which in ancient times was pointed out as belonging to the tribe of Rabîᶜ. Another pronunciation, though of individuals rather than of tribes, is that which gives to k the sound of ks, and this also is mentioned by ancient authors as a distinguishing feature of the tribe of Bakr.

Again by changing the k to t, the sound of k lapses into tsh and ts. The sound of sh and s, however, is so slight and coalesces so entirely with the k and t, that the ear perceives but a single sound, nay that it is difficult to say whether we hear tsh, ts, or ty." — Likewise the guttural media varies in different Semitic dialects between the sound of g and j. It is only in Egypt, Hejáz, and in Southern Arabia that it retains its pure guttural sound; elsewhere it has become palatal.

The identity of many words in Latin and Sanskrit becomes palpable at once, if, instead of writing this modified guttural, or, as we may now call it, palatal sound, by a new type, we write it by a modified *k*. Sanskrit chatvar, or as some write tschatwar, does not look like quatuor; but Lithuanian keturi and Sanskrit *k*atvar speak for themselves. Sanskrit cha or tscha does not look like Latin que; but Greek κε and Sanskrit *k*a assert their relationship without disguise. Although, therefore, we are forced to admit the palatals, as a separate class, side by side with the gutturals, because most languages retain both sets and use them for distinct etymological and grammatical purposes, still it will be well to remember that the palatals are more nearly related to the gutturals than to any other class, and that in most languages the two are still interchangeable.

That the pronunciation of the palatals may vary again, like that of the gutturals, hardly requires to be stated. Some people imagine they perceive a difference between the English palatal in church, and the Italian palatal in cielo, and they maintain that no Englishman can properly pronounce the Italian palatal. If so, it only proves what was said before, that slight modifications like these do never co-exist in the same language; that English has but one, and Italian but one palatal, though the two may slightly differ. Thus even if we invented a special letter to represent the Italian palatal, no one except an Italian would be able to pronounce it, not even for his life, as the French failed in "ceci" and "ciceri" at the time of the Sicilian Vespers. All consonants, therefore, between gutturals and dentals, should be called palatals. That palatals have again a tendency to become dentals, may be seen from words like τέσσαρες instead of Sanskrit *k*atvaras or Lithuanian keturi.

Frequently the pronunciation of the palatals becomes so broad that they seem, and in some cases really are, double consonants. Some people pronounce "church" (kirk) as if it were written "tchurtch." If this pronunciation becomes sanctioned, and we have to deal with a language which has as yet no historical orthography, it must be left to the ear of the missionary to determine whether he hears distinctly two consonants, or one only though pronounced rather fully and broadly. If he hears distinctly the two sounds t + ch, as in pitching, or t + sh, as in the German rutschen, he should write both, particularly if in the same language there exists another series of letters with the simple palatal sound. This is the case, for instance, in Tibetan and its numerous dialects. If, therefore, the missionary has to deal with a Bhotîya dialect, which has not yet been fixed by the Tibetan alphabet, the simple palatals should be kept distinct from the compound palatals, tsh, dsh, &c. In the literary language of Tibet, where the Sanskrit alphabet has been adopted, an artificial distinction has been introduced, and the compound sounds, usually transcribed as tsh, tsh*h*, and dsh, are distinguished by a diacritical mark at the top from the simple palatals, the sound of which is described as like the English ch in church, and j in join. How this artificial distinction should be rendered in transliteration, will have to be considered under III. *b*. If we have once the palatal tenuis, the same modifications as those described above give us the palatal media, the two aspirates, the nasal, the liquid, and the sibilant.

The sound of the tenuis is given in the English church; of the media, in join. The liquid we have in the pronunciation of yea. The nasal again hardly exists by itself, but only if followed by palatals. We have it in inch and injure. Where the Spaniards use an ñ, they write a double by a simple sound; for the sound is the nasal followed by the corresponding semi-vowel, ny. The French express the same sound in a different manner. The French besogne, if it occurred in an African language, would have to be expressed by the missionary as bezonye.

As to the palatal flatus or sibilant, we must distinguish again between its sharp and mild sound. The sharp sound is heard in sharp, or French chose. The mild sound is less known in English, but of frequent occurrence in French; such as je, and joli, very different from the English jolly. It is a sound of frequent occurrence in African languages.* The difference between the sharp and mild palatal flatus may best be illustrated by a reference to the modern languages of Europe. A guttural tenuis in Latin becomes a palatal tenuis in English, and a palatal sibilant in French; cantus, the chant, le chant. Here, the palatal being originally a tenuis, the initial sibilant in French is asper or sharp like the English sh in she. A guttural media in Latin becomes a palatal media in English, and a palatal sibilant in French; elegia, the elegy, l'élégie. Here the sibilant sound of the French g is the same as in genou or je; it is the mild palatal sibilant, sometimes expressed in English by s, as in pleasure.

It should be remarked, however, that the proper, and not yet assibilated sound of the palatal flatus asper is not the French ch as heard in Chine, but rather the German ch in China, mädchen, ich, or g in könig. Both sounds are palatal according to our definition of this term; but the German might be called the simple, the French the assibilated palatal flatus. Ellis calls the former the "whispered guttural sibilant," and remarks that it is generally preceded by a vowel of the i class. The corresponding "spoken consonant" also, or the flatus lenis, was discovered by Ellis in such words as the German kȫn'ge.

* See the Rev. Dr. Krapf's "Outline of the Elements of the Kisuáheli Language:" Tübingen, 1850, page 23.

2. *Linguals as Modifications of Dentals.*

While the pure dental is produced by bringing the tip of the tongue straight against the teeth, a peculiarly modified and rather obtuse consonantal sound is formed if the tongue is curled back till its tip is at the root, and the roof of the mouth then struck with its back or undersurface. The consonants produced by this peculiar process differ from the dentals, both by their place and by their instrument, and it has been common in languages where these peculiar consonants occur to call them "linguals." Although this name is not quite distinct, the tongue being the agent in the palatals and dentals as well as in these linguals, still it is preferable to another name which has also been applied to them, Cerebrals — a mere mistranslation of the Sanskrit name "M*u*rdd*h*anya."* These linguals vary again in the degree of obtuseness imparted to them in different dialects, a difference which evades graphical representation. All letters that cease to be pure dentals by shifting the point of contact backward from the teeth, must be considered as linguals; and many languages, Semitic as well as Arian, use them for distinct etymological purposes. As with the palatals, we have with the linguals also a complete set of modified consonants. The lingual tenuis, tenuis aspirata, media, media aspirata, and nasal have no corresponding sounds in English, because,

* "M*u*rddhanya," being derived from "m*u*rddhan," *head* or *top*, was a technical name given to these letters, because their place was the top or highest point in the dome of the palate, the οὔρανος of the Greeks. The proper translation would have been "Cacuminals." "Cerebrals" is wrong in every respect; for no letter is pronounced by means of the brain, nor does "m*u*rddhan" mean brain. It is not advisable to retain this name, even as a technical term, after it has been proved to owe its origin to a mere mistranslation. It is a word which has given rise to confused ideas on the nature of the lingual letters, and it ought therefore to be discarded from philological treatises, though the mistranslation and its cause have hitherto failed to attract the observation of either Sanskrit or comparative grammarians. Even native grammarians in India have been imposed upon by this name, and the author of one of the best Bengali Grammars says, "the letters of the third division, though called cerebral in Sanskrit, are in Bengali expressed from the middle or hinder part of the palate."

as we shall see, the English organ has modified the dental sounds by a forward and not by a backward movement. The liquid is the lingual r, produced by a vibration of the curled tongue in which the Italians and Scotch excel, and which we find it difficult to imitate. The English and the German r become mostly guttural, while, on the other hand, the Semitic guttural flatus lenis fricatus the '*h*ain, takes frequently the sound of a guttural r. It might be advisable to distinguish between a guttural and a lingual r; but most organs can only pronounce either the one or the other, and the two therefore seldom co-exist in the same dialect.

The lingual sibilant is a sound peculiar to the Sanskrit; and as, particularly in modern Indian dialects, it interchanges with the guttural tenuis aspirata, its pronunciation seems to have partaken of a certain guttural flatus.

There is a peculiarity in the pronunciation of the dental tenuis aspirata and media aspirata, which, though it exists but in few languages, deserves to be noticed here. In most of the spoken idioms of Europe, although a distinction is made in writing, there is hardly any difference in the pronunciation of t aud t*h*, or d and d*h*. The German thun, to do, the French théologie, are pronounced as if they were written tun, téologie. In the Low German and Scandinavian dialects, however, the aspiration of the t and d (according to Grimm's law, an organic aspiration) has been preserved to a certain extent, only the consonantal contact by which they are produced takes place no longer between the tongue and the inside of the teeth, but is pushed forward so as to lie really between the tongue and the edge of the teeth. This position of the organs produces the two well-known continuous sounds of th, in think and though. There is a distinct Runic letter to express them, þ; and in later MSS. a graphical distinction is introduced between þ and ð, tenuis and media. The difference between the tenuis and media is brought out most distinctly by the same experiment which was tried for s and z, for f and v. (page 27.). We have the tenuis in breath, but it is changed into media in to breathe.

We may consider these two sounds as dialectical varieties of the real *th* and d*h*, which existed in Sanskrit, but which, like most aspirated sonant and surd consonants, have since become extinct. To many people the pronunciation of the English th is an impossibility; and in no dialect, except perhaps the Irish, does the English pronunciation of the th coexist with the pure and simple pronunciation of *th* and d*h*. Still, as their sound is very characteristic, approaching almost to a sibilant flatus, it might be desirable to mark it in writing, so that even those who do not know the peculiar accent and pronunciation of a language, should be able to distinguish by the eye the English sound of the th from the original *th* and d*h*.

The principal consonantal sounds, without any regard as yet to their graphic representation, may now be classified and defined as follows. Where possible, the approximate sound is indicated by English words.

	a. Tenuis.	*b.* Tenuis aspirata.	*c.* Media.	*d.* Media aspirata.	*e.* Nasalis.	*f.* Liquida.	*g.* Flatus (sibilans). asper.	lenis.
1. Gutturals	kite	– –	gate	– –	sing	dag (*Dutch*)	hear, loch, Germ.	ear. tage.
2. Palatals	church	– –	join	– –	*Fr.* signe	yet	ich, Germ. sharp,	täglich. Fr. *je*.
3. Dentals	tan	(breath)	dock	(breathe)	not	let	grass,	graze.
4. Linguals	– –	– –	–	– –	– –	run	–	–
5. Labials	pan	– –	bed	– –	mill	will	life,	live.

Vowels.

The Physiological Scale of Vowels.

If we recall the process by which the liquids were formed in the three principal classes, and if, instead of stopping the vocal sound by means of that slight remnant of consonantal contact or convergence which characterized the formation of the liquid semi-vowels, we allow the full volume of breath to pass over the point of contact and there to vibrate and sound, we get three pure vowel sounds, guttural, palatal, and labial, which can best be expressed by the Italian *A, I, U,* as heard in psalm, ravine, flute.

Formation of the Labial Vowel.

Let us attempt to pronounce the labial liquid, the English w in win, and, instead of stopping or compressing the breathing as it approaches the labial point of contact, emit it vibrating and vocalised, through the rounded aperture of the lips, and we have the vowel u.

Formation of the Palatal Vowel.

The same process which changes w into u, changes the palatal liquid y into i. Let us pronounce the y in yea without any vowel after it, and it will be seen that it requires only the removal of that stoppage of sound which takes place between tongue and palate, before the vowel i, as in ravine, can be heard distinctly.

Formation of the Guttural Vowel.

Let us pronounce the spiritus lenis as in *a*rm, or the guttural liquid as heard in the Dutch dag or the Hebrew 'hain, and, if we try to replace this liquid gradually by the vowel a, we feel that what we effect is merely the removal of that stoppage which in the formation of the liquid takes place at the very point of guttural contact.

The vowels, as was said before, are formed by the voice modified, but not interrupted, by the various positions of the tongue and the lips. "Their differences depend," as Professor Wheatstone adds, "on the proportions between the aperture of the lips and the internal cavity of the mouth, which is altered by the different elevations of the tongue."

Succession of Vowels, natural and artificial.

The organic succession of vowel sounds is the same as for consonants, — guttural, palatal, labial. a, i, u. Professor Willis*, has described an interesting experiment as to the scale of vowels in the abstract. The gradual lengthening of a cylindrical tube joined to a reed organ-pipe was found to produce the following series of sounds:

i,	e,	a,	aw,	o,	u.
beat,	bait,	bath,	bought,	boat,	boot.

But as these pipes are round and regular, while the construction of the pipe formed by larynx, throat, palate, jaws, and lips is not, the succession of vowels given by these pipes cannot be expected to correspond with the local succession of vowels as formed by the organs of speech.

Kempelen states that if we pay attention to the successive contraction of the throat only, we shall find, that the aperture of the throat is smallest if we pronounce i, and that it gradually increases as we go on to e, a, o, u; while if we pay attention to the successive contraction of the lips, which is quite as essential to the formation of the vowels as the contraction of the throat, the scale of vowels is a different one. Here the aperture of the lips is largest if we pronounce the a; and it gradually decreases as we go on to the e, i, o, and u.

Hence, if we represent the opening of the lips by Roman, and the opening of the throat by English figures, taking the smallest aperture as our unit, we may, according to Kempelen, represent the five vowels in a mathematical progression:

i = III. 1. e = IV. 2. a = V. 3. o = II. 4. u = I. 5.

It has been remarked by Professor Purkinje, that the conditions for the formation of some of the vowels, par-

* Transactions of the Cambridge Philosophical Society, vol. iii. paper 10. 1828—29.

ticularly of a and e, as heard in far and name, have not been quite correctly stated by Kempelen. The production of both these sounds depends principally on the form of the cavity of the throat between the root of the tongue and the larynx; in both cases this space is large, but largest in the pronunciation of e. The size of the opening of the mouth is the same in the two cases; not different, as Kempelen states. The position which he ascribes to the lips in pronouncing o is unnecessary.*

As to the experiments of Professor Willis, they show that, if we look on the instrument by which the vowels are formed as a vibrating membranous tongue, with one tube prefixed, and another added below the tongue, the shortest length of the tube gives i; the longest, u; and an intermediate one, a. But as the human organ of speech is not a regular tube, we must insist on this, that in the mouth the greatest length of the tube is indicated by the point of guttural contact, the smallest by the point of labial, and the intermediate by the point of guttural contact; and that it is by the simultaneous operation of the guttural and labial apertures that the vowels a, i, and u are formed. Whether there may not be at the same time in the human organ a cooperating difference of pitch in the chordæ vocales, is a question which can only be determined by anatomical experiments.

The Lingual and Dental Vowels.

Besides the three vowels struck at the guttural, palatal, and labial points of contact, the Sanskrit, in strict analogy, forms two peculiar vowels as modifications of the lingual and dental semi-vowels. *R* and *L*, subjected to the same process which changes 'or 'h into a, y into i, and w into u, become ri, li, or rĕ and lĕ. At least these sounds ri and li, approach as near to the original value of the Indian vowels as with our alphabet we can express it. According to their origin, they may be described as r and l opened and vocalised.

* See J. Müller, Elements of Physiology, p. 1047.

Unmodified Vowels.

If we attempt in singing to pronounce no particular vowel, we still hear for a time the vowel-sound of the Italian a. This vowel expresses the quality of the musical vibrations emitted from the human larynx and naturally modified by a reverberation of the palate. But if we arrest the vibrations before they pass the guttural point of contact — if, either in a whispered or a vocalised shape, we emit the voice without allowing it to strike against any part of the throat or mouth — we hear the unmodified and primitive sound as in but, bird, lull. It is the sound which, in Professor Willis's experiments, "seems to be the natural vowel of the reed," or, according to Mr. Ellis, "the voice in its least modified form." We hear it also if we take the larynx of a dead body, and blow through it while compressing the chordæ vocales.

In these experiments it is impossible to distinguish more than *one* sound; and most people admit but *one* unmodified vowel in English. According to Sir John Herschel, there is no difference in the vowels of the words spurt, assert, dirt, virtue, dove, double, blood. Mr. Ellis considers the u in cur as the corresponding long vowel. Other writers, however, as Sheridan and Smart, distinguish between the sounds of bird and work, of whirl'd and world; and in some languages this difference requires to be expressed. It is a very delicate difference, but may be accounted for by a slight palatal and labial pressure through which this obscure sound is affected after having escaped the guttural reverberation.

In English every vowel is liable to be absorbed by this obscure sound; as begg*a*r, off*e*r, b*i*rd, w*o*rk, b*u*t. It is sometimes pronounced between two consonants, though not expressed in writing; as in el-m, mar-sh, schis-m, ryth-m. Here it is really the breath inherent in all continuous consonants. In French it is the e muet, as in entendre, Londres. In German it is doubtful whether the same sound exists at all, though I think it may be heard occasionally in such words as leb*e*r, leb*e*n.

Quantity of Vowels.

All vowels may be short or long, with the exception of the unmodified breathing (Rapp's "Urlaut"), which, at least according to some authorities, is always short.

The sound of the long a we have in psalm, messa (It.); short, in Sam.
„ „ i „ neat, Italia; „ knit.
„ „ u „ fool, usarono (It.); „ full.*
The sound of ĕ we have in bird.
„ ŏ „ work.

Long vowels naturally terminate in their corresponding liquids. This is heard most distinctly in pronouncing the long i, where the liquid element of the y is almost unavoidable at the end. Arab grammarians therefore consider that a long *a* consists of the short a + the pectoral semi-vowel (ا); the *i* of the short i + the palatal liquid (ى); the *u* of the short u + the labial liquid (و). See Wallin, p. 2, 24.).

DIPHTHONGS.

From the organic local succession of the three simple vowels a, i, u, it follows that real compound vowels can only be formed with A, as the first and most independent vowel, for their basis. The a, on its onward passage from the throat to the aperture of the mouth, may be followed or modified by i or u. It may embrace the palatal and labial vowels, and carry them along with it without having to retrace its steps, or occasioning any stoppage, which of course would at once change the vowel into a semi-vowel. In Sanskrit, therefore, the palatal and labial vowels, if brought in immediate contact with a following a, relapse naturally into their correspon-

* The examples are mostly taken from Ellis, who distinguishes between the short a in messa and the stopped a in Sam; a distinction which, though essential in a theoretical analysis, does not require to be expressed in alphabetical notation.

ding liquids, y and w, and never form the base of diphthongs. The vowels i + a, or u + a, if pronounced in quick succession, become ya and wa, but they will never coalesce into one vocal sound, because the intonation of the a lies behind that of i and u; the vocal flatus has to be inverted, and this inversion amounts in fact to a consonantal stoppage sufficient to change the vowels i and u into the breathed liquids y and w.

The four Buses of Diphthongs.

According to our definition of diphthongs, their basis can only be guttural; but as the guttural a may be short or long, and as the two unmodified vowels (ĕ, ŏ) lie even behind the guttural point of contact, we get really a four-fold basis for diphthong sounds. Each of the four vowels (ă, â, ĕ, ŏ) being liable to a palatal or labial modification, we may on physiological grounds expect eight different compound vowels.

This will best be represented by a diagram:

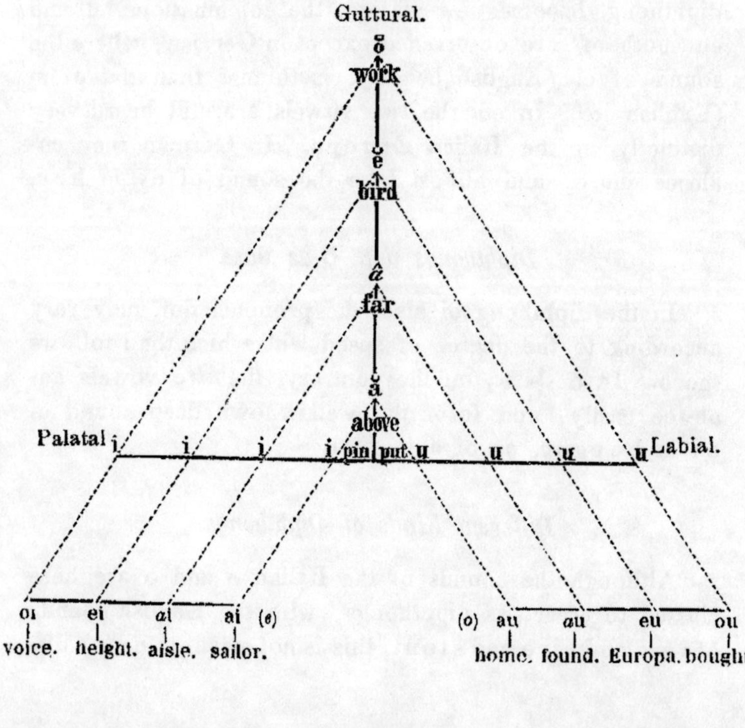

Diphthongs with Ă as base.

If the short a is quickly followed by i and u, so that, as the Hindus say, the guttural is mixed with the palatal and labial vowels like milk and water, we get the diphthongs ai and au, pronounced as in French. They correspond in sound to the Italian e and o, and to the English sounds in sailor and home.

Diphthongs with Ā as Base.

If the a, as the first element, retains more of its independent nature, or is long, then â + i pronounced together give the German diphthong ai, as in aisle and buy; a + u give the German diphthong au, as in found.

Diphthongs with Ĕ as Base.

If, instead of the short or long a, the base of the diphthong becomes ĕ, we get the combinations ei and eu, both of rare occurrence except in German, where the sound of ei (English height), is thinner than that of ai (English ire). In eu, the two vowels are still heard very distinctly in the Italian Europa. In German they coalesce more, and almost take the sound of oy in boy.

Diphthongs with ŏ as Base.

In the diphthong oi also, the pronunciation may vary according to the degree of speed with which the i follows the ŏ. In ŏ + u, on the contrary, the two vowels coalesce easily, and form the well-known deep sound of ou in bought, or of a in fall.

Different Kinds of Diphthongs.

Although the sounds of the Italian e and o are here classed together, as diphthongs, with the English sounds of i and ou in ire and stout, this is not meant to deny a difference in degree between the two. The former might be called monophthongs, because the ear receives but one impression, as when two notes are struck simultaneously. It is only by theoretical analysis that we can detect the two component parts of e and o — a fact well known to every Sanskrit scholar. The âi and âu, on the contrary, are real diphthongs; and an attentive ear will perceive ah + ee in the English "I," ah + oo in the English "out." Sir John Herschel compares these sounds to quick arpeggios, where two chords are struck almost, but not quite, simultaneously.

In African dialects, as, for instance, in Zulu, some Missionaries say that two vowels combine for the formation of one sound, as in h a i (no), U m c o p a i (a proper name); others, that there are no diphthongs, but that, whenever two vowels meet, the separate power of each is distinctly marked and preserved in pronunciation.* This may depend on a peculiar disposition in the organ of hearing as well as in the organ of speech.

Objections are likely to be raised against treating the vowel in "bought" and "fall" as a diphthong. There is, however, a diphthong sound which stands to au (proud) in the same relation as oi (voice) to ai (vice). I imagine I hear it in the English b r o a d, which has the same vowel as a l l, b a w l, P a u l, n o r, w a r; and we certainly have it in the Swedish å. The sound of the English "to call" is almost identical with the Arabic qaul (قَوْل), and here the derivation of the sound ou (as in bought or call), from an original diphthong cannot be doubted.** Perhaps the same sound was intended by the Old German ou in b o u m. The labial element, no doubt, is very slight; still, let anybody pronounce â and ou (far and bought), and a looking-glass will tell him that he adds a distinct labial pressure in order to change the â into ou.

* An Essay on the Phonology and Orthography of the Zulu and kindred Dialects in Southern Africa, by L. Grout, p. 441.

** See Wallin, On pronunciation of Arabic, in the Journal of the German Oriental Society, IX, p. 44.

Vowels broken by E *or* I.

In some languages we find that certain vowels are modified by an inherent ĕ, or, as some say, by i. The vowels most liable to this modification are a, o, u.

The a, with an inherent e, becomes German ä, as in väter, very nearly the same sound as in the English substantive bear. O, by the same influence, takes the German sound of ö in König, or that of the French eu in peu. U, in German, becomes ü, the French u in jurer.

To many organs these sounds are so troublesome that they are sometimes avoided altogether, as in English. Their pronunciation varies in different dialects; and the German ä sounds in some places like e, the ü like u.

If we remember how the simple vowel sounds were represented by Kempelen in a mathematical progression according to the amount of aperture of the throat and lips required for their formation, we shall see that what takes place, if an a is changed to ae, an o to oe, and an u to ue, is in each case a diminution of the guttural aperture. While the pure a is formed by 5 degrees of labial and 3 degrees of guttural aperture, the ae is produced by 5 degrees of labial, but only 1 degree of guttural aperture. Thus, in the pronunciation of oe, the labial aperture remains at 2 degrees, and in the pronunciation of ue at 1 degree; but in either case the guttural aperture is respectively reduced from 4 degrees and 5 degrees to 1 degree. We may, therefore, represent the broken vowels (Grimm's Umlaut) in the following manner: —

ae = V. 1; oe = II. 1; ue = I. 1.

There is one class of languages, the Tataric, where these broken sounds are of frequent occurrence, and of great importance. The "harmony of vowels" which pervades these dialects would be lost altogether (as it is, to a great extent, if Tataric languages are written with Arabic letters), unless to these broken vowels a distinct category were assigned. Besides the broken or softened a, o, and u, the Tataric languages have a fourth vowel, a softening of the i, which is said to be like the sound of i in will. Thus we have, in Yakut:

Hard vowels	a, o, i, u.	Heavy vowels	a, ä, o, ö,
Soft vowels	ä, õ, ĭ, ü.	Light vowels	i, ĭ, u, ü.

All the vowels in a Yakut word depend on the first. If the first is hard, all following vowels must be hard; if soft, all become soft. Again, if the vowel of one syllable is heavy, that of the next can only be the same heavy vowel, or its corresponding light vowel. If it is light, that of the next syllable must be the same light vowel, or its corresponding heavy vowel. For instance, if the first syllable of a word has a, the next can only have a or i; if ä, ä or ĭ; if o, o ur u; if ö, ö or ü.

The vowels would, therefore, come under the following physiological categories: —

Guttural	a,	short,	as in	*Sam*;	long, as in	*psalm*;
"	ŏ } O	"	"	*work* }	"	*cur (?)*
"	ĕ	"	"	*bird*		
Palatal	i	"	"	*knit*;	"	*neat.*
Labial	u	"	"	*full*;	"	*fool.*
Gutturo-palatal	ai (e)	"	"	*debt*;	"	*date.*
" "	*ai*	"	"		"	*aisle.*
" "	ei	"	"		"	*height.*
" "	oi	"	"		"	*voice.*
Gutturo-labial	au (o)	"	"	*not*;	"	*note.*
" "	*au*	"	"		"	*proud.*
" "	eu	"	"		Ital.	*Europa.*
" "	ou	"	"			*bought.*
Lingual	rĕ	"	"	*fiery*;	"	*reach.*
Dental	lĕ	"	"	*friendly*;	"	*leach.*

A broken, as in	*Väter.*	I broken, as in	*Diener.*
O "	*König.*	U "	*Güte.*

It has frequently been remarked that the short vowels in English (sam, debt, knit, not, full) differ from their corresponding long vowels, not merely in quantity, but in quality also. As they mostly occur in unaccented syllables, they have lost that vocal "timbre" which the short vowels in German and Italian have preserved. Yet it is not necessary to invent new signs for these surd vowels, because in origin they correspond exactly to the short vowels in other languages, only that they are uniformly modified by a peculiarity of pronunciation inherent in the English tongue. It is not by the eye, but by the ear only, that foreigners can learn this peculiar pronunciation of the short vowels in English.

II.

How can these principal Sounds, after proper Classification, be expressed by us in writing and printing, without obscuring their physiological Value, and without creating new typographical Difficulties?

The results at which we have arrived in the first part of our inquiry are those on which, with very slight and unimportant exceptions, all may be said to agree, who, whether in India or Europe, have attempted to analyse scientifically the elements of human speech. There are, no doubt, some refinements, and some more accurate subdivisions, as will be seen in the extracts from the Pr*a*tis*a*k*h*yas, which it will be necessary to attend to in exceptional cases, and particularly in philological researches. But, as far as the general physiological outlines of our phonetic system are concerned, we hardly expect any serious difference of opinion.

Widely different opinions, however, start up as soon as we approach the second and apparently less important question, how these sounds are to be expressed in writing. Omitting the different propositions to adopt an Oriental alphabet, such as Sanskrit or Arabic, or the Greek alphabet, or newly invented letters, whether shorthand or otherwise, we shall take it for granted that the

Latin alphabet, which, though of Semitic origin, has so long been thé armour of thought in the struggles and conquests of civilisation, has really the greatest and most natural claims on our consideration.

There are two principles regulating the application of the Latin alphabet to our physiological sounds on which there has been a general agreement since the days of Halhed and Wilkins:

1. *That the sound of every physiological category shall have but one representative letter, and that therefore each letter shall always express the same sound.*

2. *That simple sounds shall be expressed by simple letters, and compound sounds by compound letters.*

If with these two principles we try to write the forty-four consonants of our physiological alphabet by means of the twenty-four consonants of the Latin, it follows that we must raise their number by the addition of diacritical signs, in order to make them answer our purpose.

Now in the invention of new diacritical signs, two ways seem at first to be open. Every nation might express the sounds for which the Latin alphabet does not supply a simple letter, in the same manner in which these sounds are expressed in its own language, only that by this method the two principles of expressing the same sound by the same letter, and simple sounds by simple letters would at once be placed in jeopardy. The Latin has no letter for the diphthong ai in aisle. An English Missionary, hearing the sound of ai in the dialect of an African tribe, might therefore feel inclined, if he took it as a diphthong, to write it either ai, as in aisle, or ei as in height, or uy as in buy; or if he took it for a simple vowel, i as in ire. The confusion arising from this would be endless, for though in English we know what sound is meant by ai, ei, uy, and i, in certain words like aisle, height, buy, and ire, it would be impossible to guess what sounds they were meant to stand for in a foreign dialect. But suppose that English Missionaries fixed upon the i to express the sound of i in ire: the consequence would be that no Missionary belonging to any other country would be able to avail himself of their translations of the Bible, because no German, no Frenchman, no Italian, no Spaniard, would admit that i was the fittest sign to express the diphthong ai, as heard in ire. Again, an English Missionary might naturally write the palatal tenuis, as heard in church, by ch; but a French Missionary would write tch, a German tsch, an Italian cia. Uniformity, therefore, would be impossible, and a translation of the Bible for instance, into the Galla language, published in England, would have to be rewritten before a Missionary of any other country could avail himself of it. The practical inconveniences of such a system, if system it can be called, are so great and so glaring, that it would hardly find an advocate at present, though it has been, and is still, adopted to a great extent in geographical and historical works.

In order to avoid this uncertainty which must arise if every nation adopted its own system of spelling in writing foreign languages, it has been proposed by an opposite party, that no characters which have a different value in the principal European alphabets, should be admitted into a general alphabet. This extreme view, however, would deprive us of half of the alphabet, and like most general principles, it requires considerable qualification, before it can be made available for practical purposes.

If then we exclude all national and exclusive systems of spelling, and retain as much as possible the three general principles, of expressing

a simple sound by a simple letter,

a compound sound by a compound letter,

and the same sound by the same letter, —

if besides we bear in mind that none but Latin letters are to be admitted into the Universal alphabet, it will be seen that there remain only two ways in which our problem can be solved.

We must first of all find out certain physiological analogies which exist between those sounds for which the Latin alphabet supplies simple letters, and others for which it does not. Thus we should find that there is analogy between the Linguals and the Dentals, between the Palatals and the Gutturals, between different nasals, such as n, ng, ny, and between different sibilants, such as s in please and pleasure. If then we retained t and d, as we naturally should, for the usual dental sounds, expressed by these letters in Latin, we might use the same, with some diacritical marks, to express the lingual sound of t and d, wherever it occurs in a foreign tongue. Again, as we know that the palatal sound of ch and j, arises most frequently from an original guttural, we should naturally use k and g, with a diacritical mark, to express these modified sounds which in English are usually expressed by ch and j, in Italian by ci and gi, in German by tsch and dsch. In the same manner we should retain the general base of n, where we had to express the guttural n as in-cur, the palatal n as in inch, or the lingual n as in some Indian dialects.

After the analogies of certain classes of letters have been established, — and this has in fact been done by the physiological explanation of the alphabet, given in the first part — the only dilemma which has still to be solved is this: Shall we invent a peculiar diacritical mark for every modification? Shall we have one mark to express palatality, another to express linguality, a third to express cerebrality and so on — or shall we be content with indicating by one uniform process the fact of any letter being modified? The former plan would be more perfect in theory, but practically hopeless; the latter is practically more convenient, but not exempt from theoretical objections.

If every letter, which is used as a base was liable to but one modification, two sets of letters, say simple, and dotted, would be sufficient for our purpose. The simple letters would express the original, the dotted the modified sound of a letter, and our new alphabet would be perfect and unobjectionable. A guttural k can only become a palatal a dental t can only become a lingual. Hence if we fixed upon a dot as the general sign of modification, ḳ and ṭ, would be perfectly intelligible, and perhaps more than if we took the dot as the peculiar exponent of linguality, and a line as the peculiar exponent of palatality, writing ḵ and ṭ, instead of ḳ and ṭ.

It ought to be stated, however, that there are a few letters, h, n, and l, which are liable to more than one modification, and where therefore, more than one sign of modification would be required. Here the most natural plan seems to be that adopted by Professor Wilson. He marks the first modification of any letter by one dot, the second by two, the third by three. Thus he expresses the dental n by n; the lingual n by ṇ, the Tamil n by ṇ̈; the guttural n by ṇ̤, and the palatal n by ṇ. This is by far the most systematic plan that has as yet been proposed, because it is far easier to remember the different degrees of modification, the first, the second, the third &c., according to the number of dots, than to recall the hidden powers of accents, lines, hooks, crooks, and half-moons &c., which have no meaning in themselves, and which different people would adopt for different purposes. If Professor Wilson had carried out his plan consistently, his system might have become the standard of a universal alphabet. He deviates, however, in some most essential points from his own principles. He writes the simple palatal tenuis by a compound letter ch, instead of *k*, the corresponding media by j, instead of *g*, and he thus places himself in opposition with his own theory by giving up the principle of analogy and adopting the common system of English spelling against which no one has brought forward more powerful arguments than he himself. This has rendered his system of transcription more convenient perhaps for English readers, but has deprived it of that character of universality which it might otherwise have claimed.

What, however, is most essential to determine in every system is not so much how certain modifications of a Latin base should be expressed typographically, but rather that there should be a uniform arrangement of these modifications. If all scholars could be brought to agree on what is to be treated as the first, the second, or the third modification of a base-letter, it would be of less consequence which sign was fixed upon to indicate the first, the second, or third degree of modification. Professor Wilson's points would answer, and so would mathematical types n, n_1, n_2, n_3, as pointed out by Professor Newman;* so would Latin letters mixed with Greek types, to express modifications of the first, and with Russian types, to express modifications of the second degree.

Supposing our letters have been arranged in such a manner that those which can be expressed by Latin types form the first class; we should then have a second class consisting of modified letters which can be traced back physiologically to one of the letters of the first class,

* Mathematical types would be particularly useful for transliterating Inscriptions containing letters the power of which is not yet sufficiently determined to enable us to refer each sign to its proper physiological category, or where the same sound is expressed by different signs as in the Babylonian and Egyptian Inscriptions. The following remarks are taken from a letter of Professor Newman, to whom I am indebted for several useful remarks on the problem of transcribing and transliterating Oriental languages: "But beside these, he writes, we have the mathematical types. The objection to letters with double or triple accent, as $\overset{\prime}{c}$, $\overset{\prime\prime}{c}$, $\overset{\prime\prime\prime}{c}$ . . . is that it wastes room and looks ugly in printing; but this does not equally apply to k, k_2, k_3, k_4 . . . It seems to me that such types would be of great value as applied to the Cuneiform inscriptions, and I beg leave to call your attention to this. Colonel Rawlinson, some years back, told me that he had ascertained that certain letters in the Scythian inscriptions of Behistun were of the T class, but he did not know whether they were T, D, Th, Dh, etc. I tried to convince him that he would do a vast service to the knowledge of the language by printing transcriptions into a European type, by aid of arbitrary conventions. Let T, T_2, T_3, T_4, T_4, T_5, T_6 represent six characters, each of which he has good reason to believe to be some kind of dental, and so of all other characters. Thus we might have a line such as the following,

K_2 A T_3 L_2 I_2 R K_3 O_2 . . . . . which by means of the key would at pleasure be reconvertible into the original.

and which therefore would have to be expressed by modified types of the first degree. A few letters only would then remain requiring to be represented by modified types of the second degree.

Now if the first class was represented by simple types, the second might consist of types with one, the third of types with two dots. There is, however, a grave objection against this and any other plan which requires types, not supplied by a common English fount. It is useless for a Missionary who in a remote station has to print translations, or tracts and prayers, and has nothing but a small fount at his disposal. For him it is necessary that an alphabet should be devised, capable of expressing all the categories of the physiological scale of letters, and yet not requiring one single new or artificial type. This can be done in the following way:

Let the first class of letters be printed in Roman characters;

the second, comprising the modified letters of the first degree, in Italics;

the third, comprising the modified letters of the second degree, in Small Capitals. We shall now examine each class in particular.

Guttural, Dental, and Labial Tenuis.

The guttural, dental, and labial tenues are naturally expressed by k, t, p.

Guttural, Dental, and Labial Media.

The modification which changes these tenues into mediæ should consistently be expressed by a uniform diacritical sign attached to k, t, p. For more than one reason, however, we prefer the Latin letters, g, d, b.

It is understood that g, after once being chosen as the representative of the guttural media, like g in gun, whatever vowel may follow, can never be used promiscuously both for the guttural and the palatal media, as the English g in gun and gin.

How to express Aspirated Letters?

The aspirated tenues and mediæ in the guttural, dental, and labial series which, according to the description given above, are not compound, but simple though modified sounds, should be written by simple consonants with a diacritical mark of aspiration. This would give us:

kʻ, tʻ, pʻ, gʻ, dʻ, bʻ.

These types have been cut many times since Count Volney founded his prize at the French Academy for transcribing Oriental alphabets, and even before his time. They exist at Berlin, Paris, Leipzig, Darmstadt, Petersburg, and several other places. They have been cut in different sizes and on different bodies. Still the difficulty of having them at hand when required, making them range properly, and keeping always a sufficient stock, has been so great even in places like London, Paris, and Berlin, that their adoption would defeat the very object of our alphabet, which is to be used in Greenland as well as in Borneo, and is to be handled by inexperienced printers even in the most distant stations, where nothing but an ordinary English fount can be expected to exist. In our Missionary alphabet we must therefore have no dots, no hooks, no accents, no Greek letters, no new types, no diacritical appendages whatsoever. No doubt, Missionary Societies might have all these letters cut and cast on as many sizes and bodies as necessary. Punches or founts might be sent to the principal Missionary stations. But how long would this last? If a few psalms or catechisms had to be printed at Bangkok, and if there were no hooked letters to represent the aspirated palatal sound by a single type (kʻ), is it likely that they would send to Calcutta or London for this type, which, after it arrived, might perhaps be found not to range with the rest? It is much more likely that, in the absence of the type prescribed by the Missionary Societies at home, each missionary would find himself thrown on his own resources, and different alphabets would again spring up in different places. Besides, our alphabet is not only to be an alphabet of missionaries. In time it is to become the alphabet of the tribes and nations whose first acquaintance with writing will be through the Bible translated into their language and transcribed in a rational alphabet. Fifty or a hundred years hence, it may be the alphabet of civilised nations in Africa, Australia, and the greater part of Asia. Must all the printers of Australian advertisements, the editors of African newspapers, the publishers of Malay novels or Papua primers, write to Mr. Watts, Crown Court, Temple Bar, for new sorts of dotted and hooked letters? I do not say it is impossible; but many things are possible, and still not practical; and this is exactly what I fear with regard to these new hooked and dotted types. Surely, if the problem of a uniform Missionary Alphabet could have been solved by the trifling outlay of a few new punches, it would have been solved long ago.

In questions of this kind, no harm is done if principles are sacrificed to expediency; and I therefore propose to write the aspirate letters, as all English and most French and German scholars have written them hitherto, by

kh, th, ph, gh, dh, dh.

What do we lose by this? The spiritus asper (ʽ) is after all but a faintly disguised H, changed into ⊢ and ⊣, for asper and lenis, and then abbreviated into ʽ and ʼ.* Besides, the languages where these simple aspirates occur are not many; and in India, where they are of most frequent use, the phonetic system is so carefully arranged that no ambiguity can arise whether kh be meant for an aspirated guttural tenuis or for k followed by the semivowel h. If the liquid h comes in immediate contact with k, k + h is always changed into g + gh, or a stop (*virama*) has to be put after the k. This might be done where, as in discussing grammatical niceties, it is desirable to distinguish between kh and k-h. The missionary, except

* A different but fanciful explanation of these signs is given by Wallin, p. 63.

in India, will hardly ever suffer from this ambiguity; and if the scholar should insist on its being removed, we shall see immediately how even the most delicate scruples on this point could be satisfied.

There is still, if we examine the alphabets hitherto proposed or adopted, a whole array of dots and hooks, which must be eliminated, or at least be reduced, as far as possible; and though we might, after gaining our point with regard to the h, get through gutturals, dentals, and labials, we still have new and more formidable enemies to encounter in the palatals and linguals.

How to express Palatals?

Palatals are modifications of gutturals, and therefore the most natural course would be to express them by the guttural series, adding only a line or an accent or a dot, or any other uniform diacritical sign to indicate their modified value. So great, however, has been the disinclination to use diacritical signs, that in common usage, where the palatal tenuis had to be expressed, the most anomalous expedients have been resorted to in order to avoid hooks or dots. In English, to represent the Sanskrit palatal tenuis, ch has been used; and as the h seemed to be too much in the teeth of all analogy, the simple c even has been adopted, leaving ch for the aspirated palatal. On the same ground, the Germans write tsch for the palatal tenuis, and tschh for the aspirate. The French write tch and tchh. The Italians do not hesitate to use ci for the tenuis, though I do not see how they could express the corresponding aspirate. The Russians recommend their ч; and the Brahmans would probably recommend a Sanskrit type. Still all, even the German tsch, are meant to represent simple consonants, which, with the exception of the tenuis aspirata in Sanskrit, would not make a preceding short vowel long. That in English the ch, in Italian ci, and in German tsch, have a sound very like the palatal tenuis, is of course a mere accident. In English the ch is not always sounded alike;

and its pronunciation in the different dialects of Europe varies more than that of most letters. Besides, our alphabetic representative of the palatal sound is to be pronounced and comprehended, not by a few people in Germany or Italy, but by all the nations of Africa and Australia. Now to them the ch would prove deceptive; first, because we never use the simple c (by this we make up for the primary alphabetical divorce introduced by the libertus of Spurius Carvilius Ruga), and, secondly, because the h would seem to indicate the modification of the aspirate.

The natural way of writing the palatals, so as not to obscure their close relationship to the gutturals, would be, ḳ, ḳh, g̣, g̣h.

But here the same difficulty arises as before. If the dots or marks are printed separately, the lines where these dots occur become more distant than the rest. For one such dotted letter the compositor has to compose a whole line of blanks. These will shift, particularly when there are corrections, and the misprints are endless. In Turnour's edition of the Mahavansa, which is printed with dotted letters, we get thirty-five pages quarto of errata to about a hundred pages of text. But they might be cast on one body. True, they might be — perhaps they will be. At all events they have been; and Volney offered such types to anybody that would ask for them. Still, when I inquire at a press like the University press of Oxford, they are not forthcoming. We must not expect that what is impossible in the nineteenth century at Oxford, will be possible in the twentieth century at Timbuktu.

Now the difficulty, so far as I can see, was solved by a compositor to whom I sent some manuscript, where each palatal letter was marked by a line under it. The compositor, not knowing what these lines meant, took them for the usual marks of italics, and I was surprised to see that this answered the purpose, saved much trouble and much expense, and, on the whole, did not look badly. As every English fount includes italic letters, the usefulness of these modified types for our Missionary alphabet "springs to the eyes," as we say in German. They are sufficiently startling to remind the reader of their modified pronunciation, and at the same time they indicate, as in most cases they ought, their original guttural character to the reflecting philologist. As in an ordinary book italics are used to attract attention, so also in our alphabet. Even to those who have never heard the names of guttural and palatal letters, they will show that the *k* is not the usual k. Persons in the slightest degree acquainted with phonetics will be made aware that the *k* is, in shape and sound, a modification of the k. All who admit that palatals are modifications of gutturals would see that the modification intended by *k* could only be the palatal. And as to the proper pronunciation of the *k*, as palatal tenuis, in different dialects, people who read their own language expressed in this alphabet will never hesitate over its pronunciation. Others *must* learn it, as they now learn the pronunciation of Italian ci and chi, or rest satisfied to know that *k* stands for the palatal tenuis, and for nothing else. Sooner or later this expedient is certain to be adopted. Thus we get, as the representatives of the palatals,

k, kh, g, gh.

Now, also, it will appear how we can avoid the ambiguity before alluded to, whether the h of aspirated consonants expresses their aspirated nature or an independent guttural semi-vowel or flatus. Let the h, where it is not meant as a letter, but as a diacritical sign, be printed as an italic *h*, and the last ground for complaint will vanish. Still this is only needful for philological objects; for practical purposes the common h may remain.

In *writing*, the dots or lines under the palatals will have to be retained. This has been considered as a grievous inconsistency, because, it is said, people could never be taught that an italic letter in printing corresponded to a dotted letter in writing. I do not take so low a view of the human intellect, and I find that wherever the art of printing has been introduced, the current handwriting has always diverged, and sometimes very considerably, from the form of printed types. Hence I do not despair that a well educated Missionary will succeed in making his converts understand that, unless they can imitate italics in writing, they may indicate these modified letters by a uniform sign of modification, a line or a dot. At all events the natives will find less difficulty in learning this, than in piling up a quantity of mysterious signs at the top of every modified letter. Even the mere dots under these letters take too much time to allow us to suppose that the Africans will retain them for any length of time when they come to write for themselves. They will find some more current marks, as, for instance, by drawing the last stroke of the letter below the line. In writing, however, anybody may please himself, so long as the printer knows what is intended when he has to bring it before the public. As a hint to German missionaries, I beg to say that, for writing quickly in this new alphabet, they will find it useful in manuscript notes to employ German letters instead of italics.

An accidental, though by no means undesirable, advantage is gained by using italics to express the palatals. If we read that Sanskrit vâch (or vâtch, or vâtsch) is the same as Latin vox, but that sometimes vâch in Sanskrit is vâk or vâc, the eye imagines that it has three different words to deal with. By means of italics, vâk and vâ*k* are almost identical to the sight, as kirk and *k*ur*k* (church), would be if English were ever to be transcribed into the missionary alphabet. The same applies to the verb', where the phonetic distinction between va*k*mi, vakshi, vakti, can thus be expressed without in any way disguising the etymological identity of the root. It would be wrong if we allowed the physiological principles of our alphabet to be modified for the sake of Comparative Philology; but where the phonetic changes of physiological sounds and the historical changes of words happen to run parallel, an alphabet, if well arranged, should be capable of giving this fact clear expression.

If the pronunciation of the palatals is deteriorated, they sometimes take the sound of tch, ts, s, sh, or even th. Cœlum (κοῖλον) becomes Italian cielo; where the initial sound is the same as in church (kirk). In old Friesic we have tzaka instead of English check. In French, ciel is pronounced with an initial sharp dental s; chose, with an initial sharp palatal *s*. In Spanish, the pronunciation of c before e and i is that of the English th. In these cases when we have to deal with unwritten languages, the sounds, whether simple or double, should be traced to their proper phonetic category, and be written accordingly. It will be well, however, to bear in mind that pronunciation may change with time and vary in different places, and that the most general representation of these sounds by palatals or italicized gutturals will generally prove the best in the long run.

It must be clear that, with the principles followed hitherto, it would be impossible to make an exception in favour of the English j as representative of the palatal media. It would be a schism in the whole system, and would besides deprive us of those advantages which Comparative Philology derives from a consistent representation of modified sounds. That Sanskrit yuga (ζύγον) is derived from yu*g*, to join, would be intelligible to everybody; while neither the German, to whom j is y, nor the Frenchman nor the Spaniard would see the connexion between j and g.

How to express Linguals?

The linguals, as modifications of the dentals, have been hitherto written by common consent as dentals with dots or lines. In writing, this method must be retained, though no doubt a more current form will soon grow up if the alphabet is used by natives. They will probably draw the last stroke of the t and d below the line, and connect the body of the letter with the perpendicular line below. The linguals, therefore, will be, ṭ, ṭh, ḍ, ḍh;

only here also the printer will step in and convert the dotted or underlined letters into italics, *t*, *th*, *d*, *dh*.

I am at a loss how to mark that peculiar pronunciation of the dental aspirate, whether tenuis or media, which we write in English simply by th. It is not of frequent occurrence; still it occurs not only in European, but in Oriental languages, — for instance, in Burmese. If it occurs in a language where no trace of the pure dental aspirate remains, we might safely write th (and dh) or t*h* (and d*h*), as we do in English. The Anglo-Saxon letters Þ and ð would be very convenient; but how few founts, even in England, possess these forms. Again, *ʒh* and *zh*, and even ϑ‘ and ϑ’, have been proposed; but they are liable to still stronger objections. Where it is necessary to distinguish the aspirated th and dh from the assibilated, I propose for the latter a dot under the h (tḥ and dḥ). But I think th and dh will, on the whole, be found to answer all practical purposes, if we only look to people who have to write and read their own language. Philologists, whatever we attempt, cannot be informed of every nicety and shade in pronunciation by the eye. They must learn from grammars or from personal intercourse in what manner each tribe pronounces its dental aspirate; and Comparative Philology will find all its ends answered if th represents the organic dental aspirate, until its pronunciation deteriorates so far as to make it a mere flatus or a double consonant. In this case the Missionary also will have to write it ts, or ss, or whatever sound he may happen to hear.

Adopting therefore italics to express modifications of the first degree, we should have to write the five principal classes of physiological sounds, by the following typographic exponents: —

	Tenuis.	Tenuis asp.	Media.	Media asp.
Guttural	k	k*h*	g	g*h*
Palatal	*k*	*kh*	*g*	*gh*
Dental	t	t*h* (t*ḥ*)	d	d*h* (d*ḥ*).
Lingual	*t*	*th*	*d*	*dh*
Labial	p	p*h*	b	b*h*

How to express the Nasals?

In each of these five classes we have now to look for an exponent of the nasal.

Where the nasal is modified by the following consonant, it requires no modificatory sign, for reasons explained in the first part of our essay. The nasal in sink and sing is guttural; in inch and injure, palatal; in hint and bind, dental; in imp and dumb, labial.

But where these nasals occur at the beginning of words or at the end of syllables, each must have its own mark,, and we must therefore introduce here for the first time our second class of modified letters, the Small Capitals. They were suggested to me by Professor Newman and they are recommended also by Mr. Ellis. They are henceforth to mark all modifications of the second degree. Let then the dental nasal be n, the labial nasal m, the lingual nasal *n*. Where the guttural nasal is really so evanescent as not to bear expression by ng, we must write ɴ, instead of n· as originally proposed in the Missionary alphabet. What we call the palatal n is generally not a simple but a compound nasal, and should be written ny. For transliterating, however, we want a distinct sign, because the palatal nasal exists as a simple type in Sanskrit, and every single type must be transliterated by a single letter. Here I should propose the Spanish ñ, because it causes the least difficulty to the printer.

The lingual n occurs in Sanskrit only. Its character is generally determined by lingual letters either following or preceding. Still, where it must be marked in Sanskrit transliterations, let it be represented by the italic *n*.

How to express the liquid Semi-vowels?

The Latin letters which naturally offer themselves as the counterparts of the semi-vowels, are 'h, y, r, l, and w.

The delicate sound of the guttural liquid semi-vowel is in reality the same as the guttural flatus lenis, and both categories may therefore be represented by one sign. In Semitic dialects the ע 'hain, has usually been considered as the primitive guttural liquid semi-vowel, but the more pectoral and less modified א, has perhaps a better right to this place, where, at the beginning of words and syllables, it is used with the same intention as the Greek spiritus lenis. Where the Arabic ا, is used for this purpose, it is marked by the Hamzeh, أَ, أُ, إِ. If in these cases, we look upon the elif hamzatum as the spiritus lenis, we might indeed distinguish this, as spiritus lenis, from the Elif, as a liquid semi-vowel, heard at the end of a long a, as y and w are heard at the end of a long i and u. Thus Wallin says that أَ, if used as a long initial a, consists of the Hamzeh, or spiritus lenis, the vowel-motion of the throat, a, and the guttural liquid semi-vowel. The long initial i and u, would likewise consist of the Hamzeh, the palatal or labial vowel-motions, and the palatal and labial liquid semi-vowels, y and w. This is intelligible as a theory, but practically it seems impossible to make a distinction between the liquid semi-vowels and the spiritus lenis on any point of articulation, anterior to the palatal. Here there is for the first time a slightly perceptible distinction between the liquid, as heard in ja, and the flatus lenis, as heard in täglich, and the same applies to the dental and labial classes. It is therefore in these classes only that we require different representative types for the liquid and the flatus lenis, while in the guttural series, and in three series which precede it in the Semitic alphabet, the same type may be used to express liquid and flatus lenis; sounds, differing in definition, but identical in pronunciation.

The palatal liquid is transcribed in Germany by j, which, as far as archæological arguments go, would certainly be the most appropriate sign to represent the semi-vowel corresponding to the palatal vowel i. As, however, the j is one of the most variously pronounced letters in Europe, and as in England it has been usual to employ it as a palatal media, it is better to discard it altogether from our alphabet, and to write y.

The lingual liquid is r; if in some dialects the r is pronounced very near to the throat, this might be marked by an italic *ŕ*, or *rh*.

The dental liquid is written l. The *mouillé* sound of l may be expressed by an italic *l*.

Where the labial liquid is formed by the lips, let it be written w. More usually it is formed by the lower lip and the edge of the upper teeth. It then becomes what the Hindus call a labio-dental semi-vowel, but is hardly to be distinguished from the labial flatus lenis.

How to express the Flatus (Sibilants)?

As the unmodified flatus, or, as it should more properly be called, the spiritus asper and lenis, can only occur before a vowel, the printer would find no difficulty in representing these two sounds by the usual signs ʿ and ʾ placed before or over the vowel. At the beginning of words there could be no reasonable objection to this mode of representing the very slight and hardly consonantal sound of the spiritus asper and lenis. But it is objectionable in the middle of words. In such cases the Greeks did not mark it. They wrote ἅρμα, chariot, but εὐάρματος, with beautiful chariots; they wrote ἀνήρ, man; but εὐανδρία, manliness. As to the spiritus asper, which we have in vehement, vehicle, I fear that veʿment, veʿicle, will be objected to by the printer, and it will therefore be preferable to express the spiritus asper in every case by an h.

The guttural flatus asper, as heard in loch, must then be expressed by ʿh. The flatus lenis cannot be distinguished in pronunciation from the guttural liquid, and there can be no objection to marking both by the same sign, 'h.

The Semitic dialects which are very fond of guttural sounds, have divided the guttural flatus into two as for instance in Arabic, where we have ح (asper), ع (lenis), and خ (asper), غ (lenis). The most accurate description of these sounds is given by Wallin, and it is evident that the difference between ح and خ ع and غ, arises from the higher or lower position of the point of contact by which these consonants are produced in a Semitic throat. In transcribing Arabic we can distinguish the خ and غ by Italics, ʿ*h* and ʾ*h*, from their corresponding letters ح and ع, ʿh and ʾh. At all events ʿh and ʾh must remain as basis modified by a uniform diacritical mark.

The dental flatus sibilans, pronounced sharp as in sin or grass, has, of course, the best claims on the letter s as its representative. Its corresponding soft sound, as heard in please or zeal, is best expressed by z; only we must take care not to pronounce it like the German z. The more consistent way of expressing the sonant flatus would be to put a spiritus lenis over the s. This, however, would hardly be tolerated, and would be against the Third Resolution of our alphabetical conferences, where it was agreed that only *after* the Roman types, and the modifications of Roman types as supplied by common founts (capitals, italics &c.), had been exhausted, diacritical signs should be admitted into the standard alphabet.

As all palatals are represented by italics, the palatal sibilant will naturally be written with an italic *s*. This would represent the sharp sound as heard in sharp or chose. The soft palatal sibilant will have the same exponent as the soft dental sibilant, only changed into italics (*z*). This would be the proper sign for the French sound in je, genou, and for the African soft palatal sibilant, which, as Dr. Krapf, Dr. Tutschek, and Mr.

Boyce remark, will never be properly pronounced by an adult European.

Where it is necessary to express the original, not yet assibilated, palatal flatus, which is heard in könig and kön'ge, an Italic y, with the spiritus asper and lenis, would answer the purpose (ʽ*y* and ʼ*y*).

The labial flatus should be written by f. This is the sharp flatus, as heard in life and find. The soft labial flatus ought consistently to be written as f with a spiritus lenis. But here again I fear we must sacrifice consistency to expediency, and adopt that sign with which we are familiar, the Latin v. As we express the labial semivowel by w, the v is still at our disposal, and will probably be preferred to ʼf by the unanimous votes of missionaries and printers.

The lingual flatus is a sound peculiar to Sanskrit, and, owing to its hollow guttural pronunciation, it may be expressed there, as it has been hitherto, by s followed by the guttural h (sh). The Sanskrit knows of no soft sibilants; hence we require but one representative for the lingual sh.

Rask in his essay "De pleno systemate sibilantium in linguis montanis, item De methodo Ibericam et Armenicam linguam literis Europaeis exprimendi," Havniæ 1832, admits ten distinct sibilants. The old Scandinavian language and Danish, he says, have but one sibilant, the hard s; so has Latin, because the z is a Greek, not a Latin, sound. Bohemian and Russian have six, Servian and Italian seven, Polish eight. In order to express these numerous sounds Rasks adopts the Bohemian orthography, adding two new signs which Grimm had adopted for similar purposes in his German Grammar. Thus he establishes the following system:

	Non-aspirated.	Aspirated.
I.	c, like Ital. pezzi (M.A. z or ʒ).	č, like Ital. cibo (M.A. *k*).
II.	s, like Ital. cosa (M.A. s).	š, like Ital. scimia (M.A. *s*).
III.	z, like Ital. rosa (M.A. z).	z, like Engl. pleasure (M.A. *z*).
IV.	ʒ, like Ital. mezzi (M.A. ds).	ʒ, like Ital. magi (M.A. *g*).

To these he adds two more sibilants which occur in Lapponian and the pronunciation of which he describes by ďz and đzh, while he transcribes them by ʒ and ʒ̉.

Rask admits, however, that four only are simple sibilants, while the remaining six are mixtae or cryptocompositae:

	Purae.	Mixtae.
Nudae	s, z.	c, ʒ, ʒ.
Adspir.	ṡ, ż.	ċ, ʒ̉, ʒ̉.

The different categories of consonantal sounds which we represented at the end of the first chapter by means of English words may now be filled out by the following graphic exponents: —

	Mutae.				Semivocales.			
	a.	*b.*	*c.*	*d.*	*e.*	*f.*	*g.*	
	Tenuis.	Tenuis asp.	Media.	Media asp.	Nasalis.	Liquida.	Flatus sibilantes. asp.	len.
I. Guttur.	k	k*h*	g	g*h*	ɴ (ng)	ʼh	ʻh	ʼh
II. Pal.	*k*	*kh*	*g*	*gh*	ñ (ny)	y	*s*	*z*
III. Dent.	t	t*h*	d	d*h*	n	l (*l*)	s	z
IV. Ling.	*t*	*th*	*d*	*dh*	*n*	r (*r*)	sh	-
V. Labial.	p	p*h*	b	b*h*	m	w	f	v

Spiritus asper: ʻh.
Spiritus lenis: ʼ.

Although these exponents of the physiological categories of articulated sound have not been chosen because their present pronunciation in English, or French, or German is nearest to that physiological category which each has to represent, still, as we have avoided letters of which the pronunciation fluctuates very much (such as c, j, x, q), it will be found, on the whole, that little violence is done by this alphabet to the genius of any of these languages, and that neither an Englishman, nor a German, nor a Frenchman will ever feel much hesitation as to how any one of our letters should be pronounced.

Objections have been raised against Italics, because it is said they look ugly. Now this objection I must confess, fails to convince me. Letters are intended for a distinct purpose, and if they answer that purpose, we have no right to expect that they should at the same time produce an artistic effect upon our senses. Hieroglyphic letters might be called beautiful or ugly, but all other alphabets withdraw themselves from „aesthetic" criticism, and must be judged by their utility alone. If we allow ourselves to be influenced by similar considerations, we shall soon find that some critics will object to dots over the i, others to capitals, as is the case in some German publications, others to a t because it towers above, or to a p because it falls below the other letters, and thus disturbs the harmony of a line. How much can be done, however, to remove even this fanciful objection, will be seen by the new Italic types which have been devised for the Missionary Alphabet by Mr. Auer, the distinguished Director of the Imperial Press at Vienna.

But while I decline to listen to these aesthetic objections, I feel the weight of another argument brought forward by Mr. Ellis. "The common fount, he says, consists of large and small capitals, lower-case, numerals and points. Most founts are furnished with Italics, but as these are sloping letters and the others upright, the union of the two in one word is dazzling to the eye. As also the Roman and Italic founts are kept in cases laid side by side, the intermingling of letters from the two founts would become exceedingly laborious to the compositor. Accented letters are often not supplied at all to founts, especially to such as are found in country-places, colonies, and missionary stations, where a Latinic alphabet is a great desideratum. Even where found, they only exist in very small quantities. They are also dazzling to the eye, and very troublesome to the compositor. On the other hand, small capitals are so nearly of the same size and cut as lowercase letters, that they "work" very respectably side by side. They lie, too, in the "upper-case," just under the hand of the compositor, and are furnished in tolerably large quantities to all founts."

As to the dazzling effect of Italics, I have only to say that Italics are dazzling till the eye gets accustomed to them, and that all new and unusual types will at first be dazzling. What can be more dazzling than such letters as t, l; n, m, u; placed in juxta position? Yet every child masters them, and nobody complains. Now Italics have lately been used to a considerable extent in transcribing foreign languages, and the effect has been very satisfactory. Dr. Sprenger in his valuable and voluminous works on Arabic literature employs Italics for diacritical purposes; so does Dr. Weber in his Sanskrit publications. Even in political works, such as the Coorg Memoirs, published in 1855, Italics are used with very great effect. Mr. Ellis himself employs Italics, and their use is decidedly spreading.

But if the other objections which Mr. Ellis starts against Italics, are founded, there is no reason why Italics should not be replaced by more convenient types. All I insist on is this, that there should be one class of simple or base-letters; and that there should be a second and third class of modified letters, expressive of the first and second degrees of modification as explained in the physiological alphabet. If anybody prefers to use red letters for the first, and blue for the second class, I see no greater objection to this than if small Capitals, or even inverted types or mutilated types are used instead of Italics. Only the three classes of simple and modified letters must be kept distinct. An interesting illustration of this is given in the Tamil Grammar and Reading book, just published by Dr. Graul. In the first portion of this work he expresses the linguals by dots underneath, the palatals by accents above, the aspirated letters by a spiritus asper &c.; but in the second portion, in his Tamil grammar, he avoids dotted and accented letters, and uses instead, not Italics, but very broad or fat types. Thus he expresses the linguals no longer by ṭ, ṇ, ṛ, but by **t**, **n**, **r**. If anybody likes these types better, their substitution for Italics does not interfere at all with the universal character of the Missionary Alphabet, for it is easy to discover by the frequency of some and the scarcity of other modified types, which are meant to express the modifications of the first and of the second degree. As to myself, I retain Italics for the first, and I adopt Small Capitals for the second degree of modification, because I believe that on the whole these two classes of letters are more easily to be procured in any part of the world, than any other two classes of modified types.

Vowels.

The pronunciation of the vowels is more liable to change than that of the consonants. Hence we find that literary languages, which retain their orthography in spite of changes in pronunciation, have no scruple in expressing different sounds by the same sign. Again, where two originally different vowels have sunk down to one and the same intermediate sound, we see this same sound expressed often by two different vowels. In the selection, therefore, of letters to express the general vowel sounds of our physiological alphabet, we can pay less attention to the present value of each vowel sign in the spoken languages of Europe than we did with the consonants. And as there it was impossible, without creating an unwieldy mass of consonantal signs, to express all the slight shades of pronunciation by distinct letters, we shall have to make still greater allowance for dialectical varieties in the representation of vowels, where it would be hopeless should we attempt to depict in writing every minute degree in the sliding scale of native or foreign pronunciatiou.

The reason why, in most systems of phonetic transcription, the Italian pronunciation of vowels has been taken as normal, is, no doubt, that in Italian most vowel signs have but one sound, and the same sound is generally expressed by one and the same vowel. We propose, therefore, as in Italian, to represent the pure guttural vowel by a, the pure palatal vowel by i, and the pure labial vowel by u.

Besides the short a, we want one, or according to others, two graphic signs to represent the neutral sound of the vocal breathing, which may be modified by a slight and almost imperceptible palatal or labial pressure. This produces the sounds which we have in birch and work, and which, where they must be distinguished, we propose to write ĕ and ŏ. As we do not want the signs of ˘ and ¯ to mark the quantity of vowels, we may here be allowed to use this sign ˘ to indicate indistinctness rather than brevity.

In most languages, however, *one* sign will be sufficient to express this primitive vowel; and in this case the figure O has been recommended as a fit representative of this undetermined vowel.

Among the languages which have an alphabet of their own, some, as, for instance, Sanskrit, do not express these sounds by any peculiar sign, but use the short a instead. Other languages express both sounds by one sign; for instance, the Hebrew Shĕwa, the pronunciation of which would naturally be influenced, or, so to say, coloured either by the preceding or the following letter. Other idioms again, like Latin, seem to express this indistinct sound by e, i, or u. Thus besides the long e in res and the short e in celer, we have in Latin the indistinct ĕ in words like adversum and advorsum, septimus and septumus, where the Hindus write uniformly saptama, but pronounced it probably with vowels varying as in Greek and Latin. Besides the long o in odi, and the short o as in moneo, we have the instinct o or u in orbs or urbs, in bonom or bonum. In Wallachian, every vowel that has been reduced to this obscure, indefinite sound, is marked by an accent, ȁ, ȅ, ȉ, ȍ, ȕ; but if Wallachian is written with Cyrillic letters, the Yerr (Ъ) is used as the uniform representative of all these vowels. In living languages one sign, the figure 0, will be found sufficient, and in some cases it may be dispensed with altogether, as a slight Shĕwa sound is necessarily pronounced, whether written or not, in words such as mil-k, mar-sh, el-m, &c. The marks of quantity, and ¯, are superfluous in our alphabet; not that it is not always desirable to mark the quantity of vowels, but because here again, as with the dotted consonants, a long syllable can be marked by the vowel in Italics, while every other vowel is to be taken as short. Thus we should write in English b*a*th, b*a*r, but above, bank; rav*i*ne, and pin; b*u*t (i. e. boot), and butcher. We should know at once that *a* in b*a*th is long, while in above it is short, though I admit that a line over the vowel (ā, ī, ū) would not cause any serious inconvenience.

All compound vowel sounds should be written according to the process of their formation. Two only, which are of most frequent occurrence, the guttural short a, absorbed by either i or u, might perhaps be allowed to retain their usual signs, and be written e and o, instead of ai and au. The only reason, however, which can be given for writing e and o, instead of ai and au, is that we save a letter in writing; and this, considering how many millions of people may in the course of time have to use this alphabet, may be a saving of millions and millions of precious seconds. The more consistent way would be to express the gutturo-palatal sound of the Italian e by ai, the a being short. The French do the same in aimer, while in English this sound is expressed by ey in prey, by a in gate, and by ai in sailor. The gutturo-labial sound of the Italian o should consistently be written au, which the French pronounce o. For etymological purposes this plan would be preferable, as it frequently happens that an o (au), if followed by a vowel, has to be pronounced av. Thus in Sanskrit bh*u*, to be, becomes bhau (pronounced bho), and if followed by *a*mi, it becomes bhav-*a*mi, I am.

The diphthongs, where the full or long guttural *a* is followed by i and u, must be written *a*i and *a*u. To buy would have to be written b*a*i; to bow, b*a*u. Whether *a*u coalesce entirely, as in German, or less so, as in Italian, is a point which in each language must be learned by ear, not by eye.

Most people would not be able to distinguish between

*a*i and ei. Still some maintain that there is a difference; as, for instance, in German kaiser and eis. Even in English the sound of ie in he lies is said to be different from that of he lies. Where it is necessary to mark this distinction, our diagram readily supplies *a*i and ei.

The diphthong eu is generally pronounced so that the two vowels are heard in succession, as in Italian Europa. Pronounced more quickly, as, for instance, in German, it approaches to the English sound of oy in boy. According to our diagram, we should have to write ĕi and ĕu; but ei and eu will be preferable for practical purposes.

The same applies to the dipthong ŏi. Here, also, both vowels can still be heard more or less distinctly. This more or less cannot be expressed in writing, but must be learned by practice.

The last diphthong, on the contrary, is generally pronounced like one sound, and the deep guttural 0 seems to be followed, not by the vowel u, but only by an attempt to pronounce this vowel, which attempt ends, as it were, with the semi-vowel w, instead of the vowel. In English we have this sound in bought, aught, saw; and also in fall and all.

The proper representation of these diphthongs would be ŏi and ŏu; but oi and ou will be found to answer the purpose as well, except in philological works.

For representing the broken sounds of a, o, u, which we have in German väter, höhe, güte, in the French prêtre, peu, and une but which the English avoids as sounds requiring too great an effort, no better signs offer themselves than ä, ö, ü. They are objectionable because they are not found in every English fount. For the Tataric languages a fourth sound is required, a broken or soft i. This, too, we must write ï.

The Sanskrit vowels, commonly called lingual and dental, are best expressed by *r*i and *l*i, where, by writing the *r* and *l* as italics, no ambiguity can arise between the vowels *r*i and *l*i, and the semi-vowels r and l, followed by i. Instead of i, ĕ also or the figure 0 may be used.

Thus have all the principal consonantal and vowel sounds been classified physiologically and represented graphically. All the distinctions which it can ever be important to express have been expressed by means of the Roman alphabet without the introduction of foreign letters, and without using dots, hooks, lines, accents, or any other cumbersome signs. I do not deny that for more minute points, particularly in philological treatises, new sounds and new signs will be required. In Sanskrit we have Visarga and the Anusv*a*ra (the N*a*sikya), which will require distinct signs (*h, m*) in transliteration. In some African languages, clicks, unless they can be abolished in speaking, will have to be represented in writing. On points like these an agreement will be difficult, nor would it be possible to provide for all emergencies. It is an advantage, however, that we still have the c, j, and x at our disposal to express the dental, palatal, and lateral clicks. Further particulars on this and similar points I must reserve for a future occasion, and refer the reader, in the mean time, to the very able article of the Rev. L. Grout, alluded to before. But I cannot leave this subject without expressing at least a strong hope that, by the influence of the Missionaries, these brutal sounds will be in time abolished, at least among the Kaffirs, though it may be impossible to eradicate them in the degraded Hottentot dialects. It is clear that they are not essential in the Kaffir languages, for they never occur in Sechuana and other branches of the great Kaffir family.

If uniformity can be obtained with regard to the forty-four consonantal and the twenty-four vocal sounds, which are the principal modulations of the human voice fixed and sanctioned in the history of language, so far as it is known at present; if these sounds are accepted, as defined above, solely on physiological grounds, and henceforth expressed by those letters alone which have been allotted to them solely for practical reasons, a great step will have been made towards facilitating the intellectual intercourse of mankind and spreading the truths of Christianity.

But the realisation of this plan will mainly depend, not on ingenious arguments, but on good-will and candid co-operation.

III.

How can this Physiological Alphabet be applied to existing Languages?

a. *To unwritten Languages.*

After the explanations contained in the first and second parts, there is little more to be said on this point.

The missionary who attempts to write down for the first time a spoken language, should have a thorough knowledge of the physiological alphabet, and have practised it beforehand on his own language or on other dialects the pronunciation of which he knows.

He should put from recollection, as much as possible, the historical orthography of German, English, French, or whatever his own language may be, and accustom himself to write down every spoken sound under the nearest physiological category to which it seems to belong. He should first of all endeavour to recognise the principal sounds, guttural, dental, and labial, in the language he desires to dissect and to delineate; and where doubtful whether he hears a simple or a modified secondary sound, such as have been described in our alphabet, he should always incline to the simple as the more original and general.

He should never be guided by etymological impressions. This is a great temptation, but it should be resisted. If we had to write the French word for knee, we should feel inclined, knowing that it sounds *gi*nokyo in Italian and g*e*nu in Latin, to write it *gĕ*nu. But in French the initial palatal sound is no longer produced by contact, but by a sibilant flatus, and we should therefore have to write *zĕnu*. If we had to write down the English sound of k n e e, we should probably, for the same reason, be willing to persuade ourselves that we still perceived, in the pronunciation of the n the former presence of the initial k. Still no one but an etymologist could detect it, and its sound should be represented in the Missionary alphabet by *nī*.

Those who know the difficulty of determining the spelling of words according to their etymology, even in French or English, although we can follow the history of these languages for centuries, and although the most eminent grammarians have been engaged in analysing their structure, will feel how essential it is, in a first attempt to fix a spoken language, that the writer should not be swayed by any hasty etymological theories. The Missionary should give a true transcript of a spoken language, and leave it to others to decipher it. He who, instead of doing this, attempts, according to his own theories, to improve upon the irregular utterance of savages, would deprive us of authentic documents the loss of which is irreparable. He would act like a traveller who, after copying an inscription according to what he thought ought to have been its meaning, destroyed the original; nay, he may falsify unawares the ethnic history of the human race.

Several sentences having been once written down, the Missionary should put them by for a time, and then read them aloud to the natives. If they understand what he reads, and if they understand it even if read by somebody else, his work has been successful, and a translation of the Bible carried out on these principles among Papuas or Khyengs will assuredly one day become the basis for the literature of the future.

Although the basis of our Standard Alphabet is purely physiological, still no letter has been admitted into it, which does not actually occur in one of the well known languages of Asia or Europe. The number of letters might easily have been increased if we had attempted to represent all the slight shades of pronunciation, which affect certain letters in different languages, dialects, patois, or in the mouth of individuals. But to increase the number of letters is tantamount to diminishing the usefulness of an alphabet.

It may happen, indeed, as we become acquainted, through the persevering labours of Missionaries, with the numerous tongues of Africa, Polynesia, and Asia, that new sounds will have to be acknowledged, and will have an independent place allotted to them in our system. But here it should be a principle, as binding as any of the principles which have guided us in the composition of our alphabet, that

> "*No new sound should ever be acknowledged as such, until we are able to give a clear and scientific definition of it on physiological grounds.*"

We are too prone perhaps to imagine, particularly where we have to deal with languages gathered from the mouth of a single interpreter, or in the intercourse with a few travellers, that we hear sounds of an entirely new character, and apparently requiring a new sign. But if we heard the same language spoken for a number of years and by a thousand speakers, the natural variety of pronunciation would make our ears less sensitive, and more capable of appreciating the general rule, in spite of individual exceptions. We are not accustomed to pay attention to each consonant and vowel, as they are pronounced in our own language; but if we try for the first time to analyse each word as we hear it, and to write down every vowel and consonant in a language we do not understand, say Russian or Welsh, we shall be able to appreciate the difficulties which a Missionary has to overcome, if he tries to fix a language alphabetically, before he himself can converse in it freely. It has happened, that travellers collecting the dialects of tribes in the Caucasus or on the frontiers of India, have brought home and published lists of words gathered on the same spot and from the same people, and yet so different in their alphabetical appearances, that the same dialect has figured in ethnological works, under two different names. Much must be left to the discretion of Missionaries; for in most cases it is impossible to control the observations which they have made in countries hitherto unexplored, and in dialects known to themselves alone. But it will be found that Missionaries who know their language best, and have used it for the greatest number of years, familiar thus with all its sounds and accents, are least clamorous for new types, and most willing to indicate in a general manner, what they know can never be represented with perfect accuracy. Too much distinction leads to confusion, and it shows a spirit of wise economy in the Phenician, the Greek, the Roman, and Teutonic nations, that they have contrived to express the endless variety of their pronunciation by so small a number of letters, rather than invent new signs and establish new distinctions. Attempts have been made occasionally, at Rome and elsewhere, to introduce new letters; but they have failed; and though *we* may feel no scruple to introduce new signs, and marks and accents into the African alphabets; though *we,* with our resources, may succeed for a time in framing an alphabet of our own where each letter, besides its simple value, has two or three additional values expressed by one, two, or three accents piled one upon the other, — common sense, without appealing to history, should teach us, that Africa will never bear what Europe has found insupportable.

The following alphabet, taken out of the general system of sounds, defined physiologically and represented graphically in the preceding pages, will be found to supply all that is necessary for the ordinary purposes of the Missionary, in his relation with tribes whom he has to teach the writing and reading of their own spoken language, pronounced inevitably by them with shades of sound that no alphabet can render. In philological works intended for a European public, the case will be different. Here it will be necessary to represent the accents of words, the quantities of vowels, and other features essential for grammatical purposes. Here the larger alphabet will come in; and it will always prove a reserve-fund to the scholar and Missionary, from which they can draw, after their usual supply of letters has been exhausted.

It should be borne in mind, that although in this smaller alphabet it would be easy to suggest improvements, no partial alteration can be made with any single letter, without disturbing at once the whole system of which it is but a segment.

Missionary Alphabet.

1.	a, *a*	Sam, psalm.	21.	y	yet.
2.	b	bed.	22.	z	zeal.
3.	d	dock.	23.	*g*	join, gin.
4.	e, *e*	debt, date.	24.	*k*	church.
5.	f	fat.	25.	N (ng)	English.
6.	g	gate.	26.	ñ (ny)	España, new.
7.	h (')	hand.	27.	'h	loch.
8.	i, *i*	knit, neat.	28.	*s*	she.
9.	k	kite.	29.	*z*	pleasure.
10.	l	let.	30.	th	thin.
11.	m	man.	31.	dh	the.
12.	n	not.	32.	0 (ĕ, ŏ)	but, birch, work.
13.	o, *o*	not, note.	33.	ai	ire.
14.	p	pan.	34.	au	proud.
15.	r	run.	35.	oi	voice.
16.	s	sun.	36.	ou	bought.
17.	t	tan.	37.	ä	Väter.
18.	u, *u*	full, fool.	38.	ö	König.
19.	v	vail.	39.	ü	Güte.
20.	w	will.			

If we compare this list of letters with the Anglo-Hindustáni alphabet, so ably advocated by Sir Charles Trevelyan, the differences between the two are indeed but small; aud if we had only to agree upon a small alphabet sufficient to express the sounds of the spoken Hindustáni, there is no reason why the Anglo-Hindustáni alphabet should not be adopted. It expresses the general sounds which occur in Oriental dialects, and it employs but five dotted letters, for which new types would be required.

The defects of this system become apparent, however, as soon as we try to expand it; and we are obliged to do this even in order to write Hindustáni, unless we are ready to sacrifice the etymological distinction of words by expressing ه and ح by h, س, ث, and ص by s, ت and ط by t, and ز, ذ, ض, and ظ by z. As it is necessary that distinct types should be selected to distinguish these letters, the array of dotted letters will be considerably increased. Even in Hindustáni we should have to use different diacritical marks where we have to express two, three, or four modifications of the same type; and it would become extremely perplexing to remember the meaning of all these marks. Our difficulties would be considerably increased if we tried to adapt the same letters to more developed alphabets, like Sanskrit and Arabic; and if we went on adding hooks and crooks, crosses and half-moons, dots and accents, &c., we should in the end have more modified than simple types.

These modified types might, no doubt, be reduced to a certain system; and, after determining the possible modifications of guttural and dental consonants, each diacritical mark might be used as the exponent of but one modification. A glance at the comparative table* of the different systems of transliteration will show how this has been achieved by different scholars more or less successfully.

But it is only after this has been done, after all letters have been classified, after their possible modifications have been determined, after each modification has been provisionally marked by a certain exponent — such as the accent for expressing the palatal, dots for expressing the lingual modification, — it is *then* only that the real problem presents itself: "How can all these sounds be expressed by us in writing and printing, without sa-

* See Chevalier Bunsen's Outlines of the Philosophy of Universal History, vol. II, Appendix D.

crificing all chance of arriving in the end at one uniform and universal alphabet?" It is clear that every type that has to be compounded or cast afresh is an impediment in the progress of uniformity, because those who have once provided themselves with diacritical types will not change them for others, and those who have but a common English fount at their disposal will express the necessary modifications as best they can. The question, then, that must be solved, is not whether we should take dots or hooks, which in itself is perfectly indifferent, but whether it is possible to express all essential modifications in such a manner as to take away all excuse for individual crotchets, by proposing an expedient accessible to every one. This can be done if we avail ourselves of the resources of our founts, which invariably contain a supply of two classes of modified letters — Italics and Small Capitals. Many scholars, from Halhed down to Ellis, have seen the use to which these letters can be put in transliterating Oriental languages; but they have not hitherto been employed systematically. The principle by which we have been guided in making use of italics is this:

As in each language most letters are liable to but one modification, let that first modification, whatever it be, be expressed by italics.

In the few cases where a letter is liable to more than one modification, let the second modification, whatever it be, be expressed by Small Capitals, or by any other set of letters, sufficiently distinct from Roman and Italic types.

b. *To written Languages.*

Though this is a question which for the present hardly falls within the compass of Missionary labours, still it may be useful to show that, if required, our alphabet would also be found applicable to the transliteration of written languages. Besides, wherever Missionary influence is powerful enough, it should certainly be exerted towards breaking down those barriers which, in the shape of different alphabets, prevent the free intercourse of the nations of the East.

The philologist and the archæologist must, indeed, acquire a knowledge of these alphabets, as in the case when their study is a language extinct, and existing, perhaps, in the form of inscriptions alone. But where there is no important national literature clinging to a national alphabet, where there are but incipient traces of a reviving civilisation, the multiplicity of alphabets — the worthless remnant of a bygone civilisation bequeathed, for instance, to the natives of India — should be attacked as zealously by the Missionary as the multiplicity of castes and of divinities. In the Dekhan alone, with hardly any literature of either national or general importance, we have six different alphabets — the Telugu, Tamil, Canarese, Malabar, Tuluva, and Singhalese — all extremely difficult and inconvenient for practical purposes. Likewise, in the northern dialects of India almost every one has its own corruption of the Sanskrit alphabet, sufficiently distinct to make it impossible for a Bengalese to read Guzerati, and for a Mahratta to read Kashmirian letters. Why has no attempt been made to interfere, and recognise at least but one Sanskritic alphabet for all the northern, and one Tamulian alphabet for all the southern languages of India? In the present state of the country, it would be bold and wise to go even beyond this; for there is very little that deserves the name of a national literature in the modern dialects of the Hindus. The sacred, legal, and poetical literature of India is either Arabic, Persian, or Sanskrit. Little has grown up since, in the spoken languages of the day. Now it would be hopeless, should it ever be attempted, to eradicate the spoken dialects of India, snd to supplant them by Persian or English. In a country so little concentrated, so thinly governed, so slightly educated, we cannot even touch at present what we wish to eradicate. If India were laid open by highroads', reduced by railways, and colonised by officials, the attempt might be conceivable, though, as to anything like success, a trip through Wales, and a glance at the history of England, would be a sufficient answer. But what might be done in India, perhaps even now, is to supplant the various native alphabets by Roman letters. The people in India who can write are just the men most open to Government influence. If the Roman alphabet were taught in the village schools — of late much encouraged by the Government, particularly in the north-western provinces — if all official documents, in whatever language, had to be transcribed into Roman letters to obtain legal value; if the Government would issue all laws and proclamations transcribed in Roman characters, and Missionaries do the same with their translations of the Bible and other works published in any dialect of India, I think we might live to see one alphabet used from the "snows" to Ceylon.

Let us see, then, how our physiological Missionary alphabet could be applied to languages which have not only an alphabet of their own, but also an established system of orthography.

We have here to admit two leading principles: —

First, *that in transliterating written languages, every letter, however much its pronunciation may vary, should always be represented by the same Roman type, and that every Roman type should always represent the same foreign letter, whatever its phonetic value may be in different combinations.*

Secondly, *that every double letter, though in pronunciation it may be simple, should be transliterated by a double letter, and that a single letter, although its pronunciation be that of a double letter, should be transliterated by a single letter.*

If these two principles be strictly observed, everyone will be able to translate in his mind a Canarese book, written with Roman letters, back into Canarese letters, without losing a tittle of the peculiar orthography of Canarese. If we attempted to represent the sounds in transcribing literary languages, we should be unable to tell how, in the original, sounds admitting of several graphic representations were represented. In written languages, therefore, we must rest satisfied with transliterating letters, and not attempt to transcribe sounds.

This will cause certain difficulties, particularly in languages where pronunciation and spelling differ considerably. In Arabic we must write al ra'hman, though we pronounce arra'hman; and even in Greek, if we had to transliterate ἐγγύς, we should, no doubt, have to write 'eggus, though none but a Greek scholar would know how to pronounce this correctly ('engūs). In Armenian e and o are now pronounced ye, we, or ie, ue; but in transliterating Armenian texts we must write e and o, and leave the pronunciation to be learned from grammars.* If, instead of imitating the letters, we attempted to represent their proper pronunciation at a certain period of history, how should it be known, for instance, in transcribing the French of the nineteenth century, whether "su" stood for "sou," halfpenny, or "sous," under, or "soul," tipsy. In historical languages the system of orthography is too important a point to be lost in transcribing, though it is a mistake to imagine that in living languages all etymological understanding would be lost if phonetic reforms were introduced. The change in the pronunciation of words, though it may seem capricious, is more uniform and regular than we imagine; and if all words were written alike according to a certain system of phonetics, we should lose very little more of etymology than we have already lost. Nay, in some cases, the etymology would be re-established by a more consistent phonetic spelling. If we wrote foreign forĕn, and sovereign, soverĕn, we should not be led to imagine that either was derived from reign, regnum, and the analogy of such words as Africĕn would point out foranus or

* See Rask l. c. p. 43.

foraneus as the proper etymon of forĕn. But although every nation has the right to reform the orthography of its language, with all things else, where usage has too far receded from original intention, still, so long as a literary language maintains its historical spelling, the principle of transliteration must be to represent letter by letter, not sound by sound.

Which letter in our physiological alphabet should be fixed upon as the fittest representative of another letter in Arabic or Sanskrit, in Hindustáni or Canarese, must in each case depend on special agreement. If we found that ह in Sanskrit had in most words the nature of the guttural spiritus, we should have to write it ʻ or h, even though in some respects it may represent the guttural liquid. If ע in Hebrew can be proved to have been originally the simple guttural liquid, it will have to be written ʼh, even though it was pronounced as semi-vocalis fricata ʼ*h*, as guttural media aspirata (gh), or not pronounced at all. Likewise, if English were to be transliterated with our alphabet, we should not adopt any of the principles of the Fonetic Nus; but here also, if the letter h had once been fixed upon as on the whole the fittest representative of the English letter h, we should have to write it even where it was not pronounced, as in honest.

It will be the duty of Academies and scientific societies to settle, for the principal languages, which letters in the Missionary alphabet will best express their corresponding alphabetical signs.

The first question, taking a type, for instance, of the Sanskrit alphabet, would be, "What is its most usual and most original value?" If this be fixed, then, "Is there another type which has a better claim to this value?" If so, their claims must be weighed and adjusted. When this question is settled, and the physiological category is found under which the Sanskrit type has its proper place, we have then to look for the exponent of this physiological category in the Missionary alphabet, and henceforth always to transliterate the one by the other.

Physiological Definition. CONSONANTS.	Missionary Alphabet. Base-Letters.	Modifications of the first degree.	Modifications of the second degree.	Approximate pronunciation.	Sanskrit.	Arabic.	Persian.	Hindustani.	Nagari.	Hebrew.	Zend.	Tamil.
Linguales												
46 Liquida	r	....	....	correre, Italian	र	ر	ر	ر	र	ר	𐬭	ர
47 „ fricata	....	r	....	cur	..	..	....	....	..	..	..	..
48 „ diacritica	....	....	R	....	..	..	....	....	..	..	..	ழ
49 Flatus asper	sh	....	....	ष, Sanskrit	ष	..	....	ش	ष	..	𐬴	..
50 „ lenis	(zh)	....	....	....	..	..	....	....	..	..	..	..
Labiales												
51 Tenuis	p	....	....	pan	प	..	پ	پ	प	פ	𐬞	ப
52 „ aspirata	ph	....	....	top-heavy	फ	..	....	پھ	फ	פ	..	..
53 Media	b	....	....	bed	ब	ب	ب	ب	ब	ב	𐬠	..
54 „ aspirata	bh	....	....	club-house	भ	..	....	بھ	भ	ב	..	..
55 Tenuissima	....	p	....	pait, Ethiopic	..	..	....	....	..	..	..	..
56 Nasalis	m	....	....	mill	म	م	م	م	म	מ	𐬨	ம
57 Liquida	w	....	....	will	व	و	و	و	व	ו	𐬎	..
58 Flatus asper	f	....	....	life	..	ف	ف	ف	फ	..	𐬟	..
59 „ lenis	v	....	....	live	..	..	....	....	..	..	𐬬	வ
60 Anusvâra	....	m	....	Sanskrit	अं	..	....	....	अं	..	..	..
61 Visarga	....	h	....	Sanskrit	अः	..	....	....	अः	..	..	..
VOWELS.												
1 Neutralis	o	....	....	beggar, father, dirt, work, but, blood, double &c.	..	..	....	....	..	ְ	𐬆	..
2 Laryngo-palatalis	ĕ	....	....	dirt, whirl'd	..	..	....	....	..	..	..	..
3 „ labialis	ŏ	....	....	work, world	..	..	....	....	..	..	..	..
4 Gutturalis brevis	a	....	....	Sam	अ	َ	َ	ا	अ	ַ	𐬀	அ
5 „ longa	â	(a)	....	psalm	आ	ـَا	ـَا	آ	आ	ָ	𐬁	ஆ
6 Palatalis brevis	i	....	....	knit	इ	ِ	ِ	اِ	इ	ִ	𐬌	இ
7 „ longa	î	(i)	....	neat	ई	ـِی	ـِی	اِی	ई	ִי	𐬍	ஈ
8 Dentalis brevis	li	....	....	friendly	ऌ	..	....	....	..	..	..	..
9 „ longa	lî	...	....	....	ॡ	..	....	....	..	..	..	..
10 Lingualis brevis	ri	....	....	fiery	ऋ	..	....	رِ	ऋ	..	..	..
11 „ longa	rî	....	....	....	ॠ	..	....	رِی	ॠ	..	..	..
12 Labialis brevis	u	....	....	full	उ	ُ	ُ	اُ	उ	ֻ	𐬎	உ
13 „ longa	û	(u)	....	fool	ऊ	ـُو	ـُو	اُو	ऊ	וּ	𐬏	ஊ
14 Gutturo-palatalis brevis	e	....	....	debt	..	..	....	....	..	ֶ	𐬈	எ
15 „ longa	ê (ai)	(e)	....	date	ए	..	....	اے	ए	ֵ	𐬉	ஏ
16 Diphthongus gutturo-palatalis	âi	(ai)	....	aisle	ऐ	ـَی	ـَی	اَی	ऐ	..	𐬀𐬉	ஐ
17 „ laryngo-palatalis	ei (ĕi)	....	....	Eis, German	..	..	....	....	..	..	..	..
18 „ laryngo-palatalis	oi (ŏu)	....	....	voice	..	..	....	....	..	..	..	..
19 Gutturo-labialis brevis	o	....	....	not	..	..	....	....	..	ָ	𐬊	ஒ
20 „ longa	ô (au)	c	....	note	ओ	..	....	او	ओ	וֹ	𐬋	ஓ
21 Diphthongus gutturo-labialis	âu	(au)	....	proud	औ	ـَو	ـَو	اَو	औ	..	𐬀𐬊	ஔ
22 „ laryngo-labialis	eu (ĕu)	....	....	Freude, German	..	..	....	....	..	..	..	..
23 „ laryngo-labialis	ou (ŏu)	....	....	bought, all	..	..	....	....	..	..	..	..
24 Gutturalis fracta	ä	....	....	Väter, German	..	..	....	....	..	..	..	..
25 Palatalis fracta	ï	....	....	....	..	..	....	....	..	..	..	..
26 Labialis fracta	ü	....	....	Güte, German; une, French	..	..	....	....	..	..	..	..
27 Gutturo-labialis fracta	ö	....	....	König, German; peur, French	..	..	....	....	..	..	..	..

1 Physiological Definition. CONSONANTS.	MISSIONARY ALPHABET. Base-Letters.	Modifications of the first degree.	Modifications of the second degree.	Approximate pronunciation.	Sanskrit.	Arabic.	Persian.	Hindustani.	Nagari.	Hebrew.	Zend.	Tamil.
Gutturales												
1 Tenuis	k	....	....	kite	क	ك	ك	ك	क	כּ	[illegible]	க
2 „ aspirata	kh	....	....	inkhorn	ख	..	....	کھ	ख	כ	[illegible]	....
3 Media	g	....	....	gate	ग	ج	گ	گ	ग	גּ	[illegible]	....
4 „ aspirata	gh	....	....	springhead	घ	..	....	گھ	घ	ג	[illegible]	....
5 Tenuissima	q	....	or K	cur	..	ق	ق	ق	क़	ק	[illegible]	....
6 Nasalis	....	....	N (ng)	sing	ङ	..	....	ن	ङ	..	[illegible]	ங
7 Liquida	(ʼh)	....	....	ا, Arabic	..	(ا)	....	....	..	(א)	..	....
8 Spiritus asper	h	....	....	hear	ह	ه	ه	ه	ह	ה	[illegible]	....
9 „ lenis	ʼ	....	....	ear	..	أ	أ	أ	..	א	..	....
10 Flatus asper	ʼh	....	....	loch	..	ح	ح	ح	ह़	ח	..	....
11 „ lenis	ʼh	....	....	tage, German	..	ع	ع	ع	अ़	ע	..	....
12 „ asper fricatus	....	ʼh	....	خ, Arabic	..	خ	خ	خ	ख़	ח	..	....
13 „ lenis fricatus	....	ʼh	....	غ, Arabic	..	غ	غ	غ	ग़	ע	..	....
Palatales												
14 Tenuis	....	*k*	....	church	च	..	چ	چ	च	..	[illegible]	ச
15 „ aspirata	....	*kh*	....	church-history	छ	..	....	چھ	छ	..	..	....
16 Media	....	*g*	....	jolly	ज	..	ج	ج	ज	..	[illegible]	....
17 „ aspirata	....	*gh*	....	bridge-house	झ	..	....	جھ	झ	..	..	....
18 „ Nasalis	ñ	....	....	signe, French	ञ	..	....	ن	ञ	..	[illegible]	ஞ
19 Liquida	y	....	....	yet	य	ي	ي	ي	य	י	[illegible]	ய
20 Flatus asper	....	(*ẏ*)	....	ich, German	..	..	....	....	..	..	..	....
21 „ lenis	....	(*ẏ*)	....	täglich, Germ.	..	..	....	....	..	..	..	....
22 „ asper assibilatus	....	*s*	....	sharp	श	ش	ش	ش	श	..	[illegible]	....
23 „ lenis assibilatus	....	*z*	....	pleasure	..	..	ژ	ژ	ज़	..	[illegible]	....
Dentales												
24 Tenuis	t	....	....	tau	त	ت	ت	ت	त	תּ	[illegible]	த
25 „ aspirata	th	....	....	lanthorn	थ	..	....	تھ	थ	ת	[illegible]	....
26 „ assibilata	tḫ	....	or TH	thin	..	ث	ث	ث	स	..	[illegible]	....
27 Media	d	....	....	dock	द	د	د	د	द	דּ	[illegible]	....
28 „ aspirata	dh	....	....	landholder	ध	..	....	دھ	ध	ד	[illegible]	....
29 „ assibilata	dḫ	....	or DH	though	..	ذ	ذ	ذ	ज़	..	..	....
30 Tenuissima	....	....	T	ط, Arabic	..	ط	ط	ط	त़	ט	..	....
31 „ assibilata	....	....	T	ظ, Arabic	..	ظ	ظ	ظ	ज़	..	..	....
32 Nasalis	n	....	....	not	न	ن	ن	ن	न	נ	[illegible]	ந
33 Liquida	l	....	....	let	ल	ل	ل	ل	ल	ל	..	ல
34 „ mollis	....	*l*	....	moglie, Italian	ळ	..	....	....	..	..	..	ள
35 „ diacritica	....	....	L	Tamil, Welsh, &c.	..	..	....	....	..	..	..	ழ
36 Flatus asper 1	s	....	....	grass	स	س	س (ث)	س (ث)	स	שׂ	[illegible]	....
37 „ asper 2	....	....	S (ʃ)	Hebrew ס	..	..	....	....	..	ס	..	....
38 „ lenis	z	....	....	graze	..	ز	ز (ذ)	ز (ذ)	ज़	ז	[illegible]	....
39 „ asperrimus	....	....	Z (ʒ)	cats	..	ص	ص	ص (s)	स़	צ	..	....
40 „ diacriticus	....	....	Ẓ (ʒ)	Arabic ض	..	ض	ض	ض (z)	ज़	..	..	....
Linguales												
41 Tenuis	....	*t*	....	ट, Sanskrit	ट	..	....	ٹ	ट	..	..	ட
42 „ aspirata	....	*th*	....	ठ, „	ठ	..	....	ٹھ	ठ	..	..	....
43 Media	....	*d*	....	ड, „	ड	..	....	ڈ(ڑ)	ड	..	..	....
44 „ aspirata	....	*dh*	....	ढ, „	ढ	..	....	ڈھ	ढ	..	..	....
45 Nasalis	....	*n*	....	ण, „	ण	..	....	ن	ण	..	..	ண / ன N

The following lists will show how some of the Arian, Semitic, and Turanian languages can be transliterated; we have purposely selected those which have the most complete and difficult alphabets. Objections, I am aware, can hardly fail to be raised on several points, because the original character of several Hebrew, Arabic, and Sanskrit letters has been so frequently controverted. If the disputed value of these letters can be clearly settled by argument, be it so; and it will then never be difficult to find the exponent of that physiological category to which it has been referred. Failing this, the question should be decided by authority or agreement; for, of two views which are equally plausible, we must, for practical purposes, manifestly confine ourselves to one.

CONTENTS.

Collective names of branches and classes of languages have, as far as possible, been formed in *ic*, as Georgic, Teutonic. Adjectives in *ian* are mostly restricted to single languages and dialects, as Georgian, Ossetian, etc.

ON

THE LANGUAGES

OF THE

SEAT OF WAR IN THE EAST.

THE languages spoken in the countries which the English army may occupy in the course of the present war, are very numerous. Some, such as Wallachian, Bulgarian, Servian, Albanian, Circassian, and Georgian, are but little known; and as inducement has been hitherto wanting to study these semi-barbarous dialects, there are but few grammars and vocabularies from which an English officer might acquire a knowledge of them. Of others, as Russian, Modern Greek, and Turkish, grammars, written in English, may indeed be procured: but there are probably not many officers who will have, in matter of fact, studied even these more attainable languages before their departure for the Levant. The necessity, however, of being able to converse with the people in the East, will soon be felt; and although interpreters, ready to offer their services for any transactions, political or commercial, will not be wanting, yet it is hardly nenessary to say, with the experience of so many foreign campaigns before us, how much an officer's discharge of his duties will benefit by a knowledge of the languages of the people among whom he and his soldiers are, perhaps for years, to be quartered, and on whose good will and ready co-operation so much of the success of an expeditionary army must always depend. *Variety of languages spoken in the seat of war.*

The difficulty of acquiring a foreign tongue is generally much exaggerated. At school we spend indeed *Difficulty of acquiring foreign languages.*

many years in learning Greek and Latin, and even so simple a language as French is not acquired by children without many tedious lessons from governesses or French masters. But it should be borne in mind that in learning Greek and Latin as boys, we are learning more than a new language; we are acquiring an entirely novel system of thought. The mind has to receive a grammatical training, and to be broken, so to say, to modes of thought and speech unknown to us from our own language. At school we have to learn Grammar at large before we can learn Latin grammar, or rather we learn both together, and therefore have naturally to spend more time on the two classical languages than on those which we study later in life. If we once have learned that the cases which we express by means of articles and prepositions, "the man, of the man, to the man, the man," may be expressed by a change of terminations, "homo, hominis, homini, hominem;" that the persons of the verb which we express by pronouns, "we love, you love, they love," may be indicated by final syllables, such as "amamus, amatis, amant;" we have gained knowledge which will prove useful to us in acquiring other languages, as Greek, Sanskrit, Russian, or Persian; a kind of framework, in fact, serviceable for all languages we may have to learn hereafter. It does not take so much time to impress on our memory the mere terminations of the ablative, or the gerund, in Latin, as to learn first what is meant by an ablative or a gerund. Our slow progress in French, again, is owing, possibly, to the manner in which we are taught; generally by persons who possess no real knowledge of the language, though they may speak it fluently and correctly. What can be easier than to explain why the masculine possessive pronoun "his" in "his mother," should become a feminine in French, "sa mère." And yet the vast majority of governesses stumble on this point as much as a schoolmaster who tries to explain to his boys the construction of the accusative cum infinitivo in Latin, or the singular of the verb after a plural neuter in Greek. And, further, it is mostly in

French that we make our first practical attempt at expressing our thoughts in a foreign tongue. We have to learn to walk on stilts, and as in every thing else, "ce n'est que le premier pas qui coûte." But, while we study other languages, we acquire a general aptitude for casting our thoughts into foreign moulds of speech, and the task becomes easier at every step we make.

After having travelled long in foreign countries, we readily find our way wherever we go, and what Machiavelli says of a general who knows *one* country well, applies with equal force to a student of languages: "Mediante la cognizione e pratica di quelli siti con facilità comprende ogni altro sito, che di nuovo gli sia necessario di speculare; perchè i poggi, le valli, e' piani, e' fiumi, e' paduli che sono, verbigrazia, in Toscana, hanno con quelli delle altre provincie certa similitudine, tale che dalla cognizione del sito di una provincia, si può facilmente venire alla cognizione delle altre."

How soon do we find ourselves at home in Italian and Spanish if we know Latin and French! Dutch, again, hardly offers any difficulties to one who knows English and German. Very soon we discover that after all no grammar contains much more than paradigms of declension and conjugation; and that, these once mastered, it is possible to go on, with the help of a dictionary, and to spell out short sentences, and easy books. Everything else is matter of practice, and partly of talent; for it is true, that in spite of every effort, some people find it as impossible to master a language as to reproduce a melody.

Coincidences between different languages.

There is another fact which every one must have noticed in studying foreign languages. In some the grammatical forms which we have to learn by heart differ but slightly, and the words also frequently resemble those of other dialects. Compare for example the conjugation of the verb "to sing" in Latin, Spanish, Portuguese, Italian, Wallachian, and French: —

LATIN.	SPANISH.	PORTUGUESE.	ITALIAN.	WALLACHIAN	FRENCH.
Canto, I sing	canto	canto	canto	cantu	chante
Cantas, thou singest	cantas	cantas	canti	canti	chantes
Cantat, he sings	canta	canta	canta	canta	chante
Cantamus, we sing	cantámos	cantámos	cantiamo	cantamu	chantons
Cantatis, you sing	cantáis	cantáis	cantate	cantati	chantez
Cantant, they sing	cantan	cantão	cántano	canta	chantent

We find nearly the same coincidences if we compare English, German, and Dutch:

I hear,	Ich höre,	Ik hoor.
Thou hearest,	Du hörest,	Gy hoort.
He heareth,	Er hört,	Hy hoort.
We hear,	Wir hören,	Wy hooren.
You hear,	Ihr höret,	Gyl: hoort.
They hear,	Sie hören,	Zy hooren.

It is clear, therefore, that a knowledge of any one of these languages will materially assist us in learning the others. A German finds less difficulty in learning English or Dutch, than French or Italian, because many words in English and Dutch remind him at once of the corresponding forms in his own language; and, as we always remember most easily, if we are able to combine what we wish to know with what we know already, it follows that we shall advance more quickly in any given language if we are able, by comparison, to connect its forms and words with those of other idioms with which we are familiar. And any *special* study will be fitly preceded by an investigation of this relation between *all:* teaching us to take each language in natural sequence, in place of a confused pursuit of dialects that have little or nothing in common.

Comparative study of languages.

The coincidences between languages by which even the most indifferent linguist must be struck, have been made the subject of careful study, and a new science has sprung up under the name of Comparative Philology in which it has been found possible to arrange nearly all the languages of the world into classes or families, and to determine, by means of their coincidences, the more or less distant degree of their relationship. Analogies have been established between the most remote, and laws have been deduced which regulate the partial changes of words in their passage from one language into another. Now, if it is easier to remember words which are nearly alike, such as filius, son, Italian figlio, French fils, Wallachian fiul, it is of course a still greater aid if we know *what* changes a Latin word undergoes in passing into Italian or Wallachian. To take the same word filius; we should perhaps hardly recognise it at once in its Spanish garb, hijo. But Comparative Philologists prove it to be a law that every Latin f at the beginning of words is changed into h. Thus facies, face, is in Spanish haz; facere, to do, is hacer; folium, leaf, is hoja; forma, form, is horma; fabulari, to speak, hablar. Hence we know, once for all, that words beginning with h in Spanish may generally be referred to Latin or Italian words, if we substitute f for h.

Another general rule of practical use to remember, is, that Latin ct becomes in Italian tt, and in Wallachian pt or ft. We might, perhaps, guess ourselves that Italian fatto, petto, otto, cotto, are the Latin words factus, pectus, octo, and coctus. But Wallachian dóftor for doctor, copt for coctus, cooked; lapte for lac, milk; pept for pectus, breast; asteptare for expectare, to expect, will be more easily understood and remembered, if we know that, with very few exceptions, Latin ct becomes Wallachian pt.

That l may in the course of time be corrupted into r, we know in our own language, from the way in which we pronounce "colonel." But while with us this is the exception, it is a rule in Wallachian. In this language a Latin l, between two vowels, is changed either into r, or into i, pronounced like the semi-vowel y. This once known, we have no difficulty in recognizing, poporu (populus), people; mórȧ (mola), a mill; firu (filum), thread; ceriu (coelum), heaven; scarȧ (scala) steps. Or again, fiiu, for filius, son; muiiere, for mulier, woman; gaiina, for gallina, hen.

Another useful rule is the change of qu into p, if followed by a. This tells us at once the meaning of apà, water; épà, a mare; patru, four, and so forth.

Such examples may suffice for the present to show what kind of practical assistance we are likely to derive from a comparative study of languages.

Degrees of relationship between different languages.

The relationship between languages may be either direct or lateral, *i. e.*, languages may either stand to one another in the relation of mother and daughter, or of sister and sister. Italian is the daughter of Latin and sister to Spanish. The relationship becomes more complicated if two languages which descend from one common parent give rise each to new dialects. Latin, for instance, and Sanskrit, are sister-languages: Italian, therefore, we might call niece of Sanskrit, and first cousin to Hindustàni.

Means of determining the relationship of languages.

Now, in order to determine the exact relationship of languages we may compare either their dictionaries or their grammars. Let us consider each method by itself. If we had to determine the relationship of English with any other dialect of Europe or Asia, and if we trusted entirely to a similarity of words, we should find that English shares some words in common with Welsh, others with German, others with French and Latin. The history of England gives a sufficient explanation of this, for we know that the ancient Britons were Celts, that they were driven back by the Saxons, a Teutonic race; and that these again were conquered by the Normans, who, although originally Northmen, and therefore speaking a Teutonic dialect, had adopted the French language before they invaded England.

It is perfectly intelligible, therefore, that the language now spoken on British soil should be composed, so far as the dictionary goes, of these different elements, Celtic, Teutonic, and French; but if we were asked whether the present English is a Celtic, Teutonic, or Romance language, or whether it be a language mixed up of these three elements, on the evidence of the dictionary alone, we should find it impossible to give a decisive answer.

Grammar, the only decisive evidence of relationship between languages.

The life and soul of a language, that which constitutes its substantial individuality, and distinguishes it from all others, is its grammar. Every language is at liberty to admit into its dictionary large numbers of foreign words, to such an extent that they may even acquire a numerical majority. There is, in fact, no language on earth which has not adopted some words from neighbouring tribes or foreign nations. But few nations have admitted into their grammar the terminations of other dialects. In English we may form whole sentences consisting entirely of either Saxon or Latin words. If we say, "Avarice produces misery," every word is taken from Latin, yet the one letter *s*, in „produces," suffices to stamp the language in which it forms the exponent of the third person singular, as Teutonic, and not Romance. Again, the Turkish language is so entirely overgrown with Persian and Arabic words, that a real Turk from the country understands but little of the idiom of Constantinople, the so-called Osmanli; still all its grammatical elements are purely Tataric. „In a Turkish newspaper," to quote Professor Schott, in his *Essay on the Tataric Languages,* „the host of alien words is far superior in number to the genuine Turks. And yet how peculiar and truly Tataric this wonderful concatenation of sentences and intertwining of words! A sentence runs on in long periods through several folio columns, like a majestic stream — a true image of the Turkish Empire itself: the governing nation in a minority as compared with the conquered inhabitants, but still, through a long period of time, vindicating its rights with equal terror everywhere. The Turkish terminations and suffixes are like the small vassals, depending on the powerful and high-sounding gerunds; and these again govern and hold together the larger members of a period, like so many Pashas." Turkish, therefore, is a Tataric language, altogether distinct in grammatical character from Persian and Arabic, as English is a German dialect, and neither Celtic nor French.

The Anglo-Saxon was planted on the British soil where Celtic had been rooted out or crushed; it grew up (if, for clearness' sake, we may be allowed the comparison) like a wild fruit-tree, and the sprigs of the more refined Norman and Latin were grafted on it. But the original sap remained: — the grammar, giving life and vigour to all its words, native or foreign, is still pure Saxon, and through it alone we are able to determine, and that with certainty, the relationship between English and any other language in Europe or Asia.

When we have to deal with ancient languages, this fact is of great importance. In settling the original relationship of modern languages, we may generally avail ourselves of the records of history, and we should be able to prove, even without consulting dictionary or grammar, that the English could not have derived its original stock of words, still less its grammatical forms, from Latin or Hebrew. But in the ancient world we have no such assistance. Neither Greek nor Latin authors can tell us anything about the relationship between these two languages, because the time when they formed themselves into separate dialects lies many centuries before Homer and before the foundation of Rome. What Latin writers assert on their own language and on its descent from Greek is more apt to mislead than to guide us. They only knew the existence of a great similarity between Greek and Latin; and as in their literature, in their arts, laws, and traditions, they were conscious of having borrowed from the ancient treasures of Greece, they inclined to trace their language also to the same source. And if a language flows necessarily from the same source whence a nation received the first elements of civilization, we should be compelled to derive German from Latin, and Russian from German. Facts, howewer, disprove this principle. So far from being derived from Greek, Latin has been demonstrated by Comparative Philology to be more primitive and original than Greek in many points of its grammar, in its phonetic system, and in the derivation of words. Latin therefore could not have been derived from Greek, nor, on the other hand, can Greek be considered as the daughter of Latin. Each stands to the other in the relation of sisters, like French and Italian, like German and English.

If in the case of Greek and Latin, history gives no aid in settling their relationship, it does not oppose the verdict of Comparative Philology, according to which these two languages are to be treated as sister dialects. But nothing could be more in the teeth of historical tradition than the relationship between the languages of India and that of Italy, now established as firmly as that between French and Italian. Here, as elsewhere, the evidence of languages is indeed irrefragable; but here, as elsewhere, we must call on the assistance of *grammatical* comparisons to make the proof complete, and to silence objections. If Sanskrit agreed with Greek and Latin in words only, we might suppose that *these* had found their way into Sanskrit through Alexander's expedition, or through still earlier migrations, or commercial transactions between the Greeks of Asia-Minor, the Persians, and Indians. It would be difficult to understand how words of daily occurrence, names expressing the simplest relations of a primitive society, should have been imported ready-made from Greece into India: yet we could not deny the physical possibility of the supposition: and there have been, nay there still are, men who believe that the Hindus took such words as mâtar, mother, pitar, father, duhitar, daughter, from the Greek μήτηρ, πατήρ, θυγάτηρ. But no sceptic in linguistic matters could go so far as to deny a natural and ante-historical relationship between languages which agree in their *grammatical* terminations to so great an extent as Greek and Sanskrit. If we say in Sanskrit,

pitá(r) dadâti mâtré duhitáram,

and in Greek,

πατὴρ δίδωτι μητρὶ θυγατέρα(ν),

a sentence where not only the roots, but the derivative suffixes, the terminations of noun and verb, the construction, nay even the accent, agree, we find adequate proof, to any one who is capable of appreciating philological arguments, that Greek and Sanskrit are cognate languages, sprung from one common source, like Greek and Latin, or Italian and Spanish.

It has, therefore, been a rule in Comparative Philology, to determine the connection of languages, principally, if not entirely, by means of grammatical comparisons, and to use verbal coincidences merely as indications which should be tested and confirmed by arguments derived from grammar.

Resemblance of the grammatical outlines of cognate languages.

Few people are aware how closely the grammars of cognate languages resemble one another, when the peculiar element that made each, in the course of time, an individual language, is abstracted. It has been found possible, simply on grammatical evidence, to determine the relationship of nearly all the languages of the world, ancient and modern; and if we exclude, for the present, the dialects of America and Africa, and the Chinese which is distinguished by the absence of all we are accustomed to call grammar, we shall find that in the whole kingdom of speech there are but three grammatical families to which every known dialect can be referred. These have been named the Semitic, Arian, and Turanian. The general principles of these three systems of grammar once mastered, we may comprehend the grammatical forms and devices of all the languages of the civilized world.

Three systems of grammar, Semitic, Arian, Turanian.

These three systems, however, are perfectly distinct, and it is impossible to derive the grammatical forms of the one from those of the other, though we cannot deny that in their radical elements the three families of human speech may have had a common source. If we are surprised at the minuteness with which languages of the same family, though separated by centuries and by continents intervening, have preserved their grammatical features, our surprise is yet increased when we find other languages, perhaps less distant geographically or historically, but belonging to different families, differing completely in the application of their grammatical means.

Two languages can hardly be more distant than the

ancient Sanskrit, spoken in India about 1000 B. C., and the Lithuanian spoken in Prussia at the present day. But a Lithuanian peasant, even at the present day, could almost understand a Sanskrit verb, and *that* one in both languages of the utmost frequency. He says: —

esmi, I am,	esmi, we are,
essi, thou art,	esti, you are,
esti, he is,	(esti, they are.)

If we compare this with the corresponding forms in Sanskrit, Greek, and Old Slavonic, we shall be surprised at the strength displayed by the grammatical memory of nations.

Sanskrit.	Greek.	Old Slavonic.
asmi,	ἐσμί,	yesmě,
asi,	ἐσσί,	yesi,
asti,	ἐστί,	yestě,
'smas,	ἐσμέν,	yesmŏ,
'stha,	ἐστέ,	yeste,
santi,	ἐντί,	sŏmtě.

But on other points also we find that these four languages, Sanskrit, Greek, Lithuanian, and old Slavonic, do not differ more among themselves than Spanish, French, and Italian, and like these, therefore, they must be considered as standing to one another in the relation of sisters. It is extraordinary that neither Greeks nor Romans should ever have been struck by the similarity of their own language with that of the barbarians. Learned Greeks of Constantinople must have had frequent intercourse with the Goths, particularly at the time when the latter adopted Christianity: — yet neither seems ever to have been struck by coincidences, frequent as the following: —

Gothic.	Greek.
steiga, I mount,	στείχω, I mount,
steigis, thou mountest,	στείχεις, thou mountest,
steigiþ, he mounts,	στείχει, he mounts,
steigos, we two mount,	
steigats, you two mount,	στείχετον, you two mount,
steigam, we mount,	στείχομεν, we mount,
steigiþ, you mount,	στείχετε, you mount,
steigand, they mount,	στείχουσι (στείχοντι), they mount.

The Romans again, who since the time of Tacitus regarded the Teutonic tribes evidently with a feeling of fear and respect, never seem to have thought it possible that their own language and that of Herman could have anything in common. And yet, words of such constant occurrence as auxiliary verbs were identical in Latin and in Gothic.

LATIN.	GOTHIC.
habeo, I have,	haba,
habes, thou hast,	habais,
habet, he has,	habaiþ,
habemus, we have,	habam,
habetis, you have,	habaiþ,
habent, they have,	habant.

Pronouns, numerals, and particles, as means of determining the relationship of languages.

There are some classes of words which civilized languages retain with almost the same tenacity as their grammatical forms. These are the pronouns, the numerals, and some of the particles. We can accustom ourselves to foreign words for most things. We may speak of our "fusil," our "sabretash," our "chapeau"; but the very last words which we should think of borrowing from a foreign nation are pronouns, particles, and numerals. Thus, after the Norman conquest, the English language admitted French words largely among its substantives, adjectives, and verbs; but no single pronoun or numeral. "Trespass" was used instead of "sin," "country" instead of "land," "count" instead of "earl." But no one ever went so far as to speak of the "Dix Commandments," or "deux pieces de veal." The numerals remained the same, and the Normans had to learn them from their Saxon subjects and pronounce them as best they might. Again, no Saxon could ever be induced to speak of himself as "je," or of himself, his wife, and children, as "nous." He might be brought to say I pay and we pay, (from the French "payer," and this again from the Latin "pacare," to pacify or satisfy one's creditors); but he would not stoop to "Je pay" and "nous pay," as little as he would use the terminations of French nouns and verbs. Hence the numerals are generally a very safe criterion of an original relationship between languages, and the subjoined list will show that the difference between the numerals in Sanskrit, Persian, Greek, Latin, and Old Slavonic, is not much greater than between the numerals of French, Italian, Spanish, and Wallachian, though we know that these modern Romance dialects have not been separated from their common parent, Latin, for more than a thousand years, while, long before Romulus and Homer, the languages of Greece and Italy were distinct dialects, cut off not less completely from the languages of India and Persia than they are at present.

NUMERALS.

LATIN.	SPANISH.	PORTUGUESE.	ITALIAN.	WALLACHIAN.	FRENCH.
1 Unus	uno	hum	uno	unu	un
2 Duo	dos	dois	due	doi	deux
3 Tres	tres	tres	tré	trei	trois
4 Quatuor	quatro	quatro	quattro	patru	quatre
5 Quinque	cinco	cinco	cinque	quinqué	cinq
6 Sex	seis	seis	sei	şése	six
7 Septem	siete	sete	sette	şépte	sept
8 Octo	ocho	oito	otto	optu	huit
9 Novem	nueve	nove	nove	nové	neuf
10 Decem	diez	dez	dieci	dece	dix

LATIN.	SANSKRIT.	PERSIAN.	OLD SLAVONIC.	ANGLO-SAXON.	WELSH.
1 Unus	eka	yek	yedinŏ	ân	un
2 Duo	dvau	du	dŏva	tva	dau
3 Tres	tri	sih	tri	þri	tri
4 Quatuor	*k*atvar	*k*ehâr	*k*etŏiriye	feover	pedwar
5 Quinque	pan*k*an	pen*g*	pa*m*tĕ	fif	pump
6 Sex	shash	*s*es	*s*estĕ	six	chwech
7 Septem	saptan	heft	sedmĕ	seofon	saith
8 Octo	ash*t*an	hest	osmĕ	eahta	wyth
9 Novem	navan	nuh	deva*m*tĕ	nigon	naw
10 Decem	dasan	deh	desa*m*te	tyn	deg

Practical results on the study of cognate languages.

By a comparison of these lists we learn two things: first, that the Spanish, Portuguese, Italian, Wallachian, and French numerals are all derived direct from Latin, and not one from the other. No single set of numerals, except the Latin itself, would account for the various corruptions which the numerals of each of the modern dialects exhibit. It would be impossible to derive Wallachian "optu" from Portuguese "oito," or French "huit" from Italian "otto," and Spanish "ocho"; but each of these forms can be explained if we take the Latin „octo" as the original type which, in the progress of phonetic corruption, was modified according to general and well-established rules in each of the modern Latin dialects. Hence, even if we had no knowledge that there ever was such a language as Latin, and that, after the downfal of the Roman Empire, it was broken up into many modern provincial dialects, we should be able to say, upon the evidence of the modern Romance idioms alone, that there had existed a language towards which all these dialects point and converge, and from which they must, in common, have descended. The certainty with which Owen, from a few individual bones, re-creates a lost species, furnishes here a parallel to the results of Comparative Philology, so exact as to be worthy of notice. And many similar might be traced: for, reversing the historical course of language, unity is the progressive lesson and discovery of science.

Secondly, from this comparison we learn that in the *ancient* languages also, as Greek, Latin, Sanskrit, Slavonic, Anglo-Saxon, and Welsh, it is impossible to derive the numerals of the one from those of the other. Even the Sanskrit numerals are not preserved in a state sufficiently primitive to allow us the supposition that from them those of the other ancient languages were derived, as the Romance from Latin, or the English from Anglo-Saxon. We are forced, on the contrary, to admit the prior existence of a language from which these ancient dialects branched off, as in later times the Romance dialects from Latin; although history has not preserved even the name of this primitive form of speech, still less its source or its original abode. We cannot derive Latin from Greek, nor Greek from Sanskrit, for this simple reason, that on several points Latin is more primitive than Greek, and Greek more primitive than Sanskrit. The Latin "sex," for instance, has preserved the original s, which in Greek has been reduced to a spiritus asper, it would be impossible, therefore, to take the Latin *sex* as a corruption of ἕξ. In other cases, however, Greek has preserved a more original form than even Sanskrit. For if the original form of ten was dak, the κ has been preserved in Greek δέκα, while in Sanskrit it has been softened down to the sibilant *s* in dasan.

It is by indications of this kind that the exact relations of cognate lauguages must be determined, and a distinction established between lineal and collateral descent. We can draw from this some practical conclusions. Though we may compare languages which stand to one another in the relation of sisters, such as Greek and Latin, French and Italian, Russian and Bulgarian, we should never try to explain the forms and words on the one by derivation from the other. We must not explain otto as a corruption of huit, or vice versâ, but derive each, according to rules affecting the peculiar phonetic systems of French and Italian, from their common source, the Latin "octo." If we attempted to deduce rules respecting the change of words between secondary languages, such as French and Italian, we could do so only on the supposition that both dialects proceeded pari passu in their phonetic alteration, which may happen in isolated cases, but never as a rule.

It follows again, from what has been stated before, that all grammatical forms, in secondary or derivative languages, can be explained and understood in their most original power and meaning, if we know the primary language by which these forms were first created. As grammatical forms are not imported, like words, ready made, from a foreign tongue, no terminations for noun or verb can exist in Italian and Wallachian, which, after a careful analysis, are not reducible to Latin elements, so that in Latin we have the key to Spanish, Portuguese, French, Italian, and Wallachian; as in Sanskrit we have the key to Hindustani, Bengali, Mahratti, Guzerati, Asamese, Kashmirian, Khasîya, and all dialects descended from Sanskrit. An officer who goes out to India with a knowledge of Sanskrit knows more of Hindustani than a cadet who has learned Hindustani in this country, but is ignorant of Sanskrit. Many rules in Hindustani grammar which seem irrational, and are therefore difficult to remember, become clear and intelligible if we know what gave rise to them in Sanskrit. In the same manner any one who desires to learn the modern Romance languages, Italian, Spanish, and French, will find that he actually has to spend less time if he learns Latin first, than if he had studied each of these modern dialects separately, and without this pre-knowledge of their common parent.

Meaning of words restored by Comparative Philology.

Besides these practical advantages, consequent on a comparative study of languages, few men, perhaps, will be insensible to the pleasure we derive from being able to watch, in the course of our studies, the gradual growth of any form of human speech. The history of words is the reflection of the history of the human mind, and many expressions which we use in a merely conventional sense are full of historical recollections if we can but trace them back to their original form and meaning. When we speak of pagans, we hardly remember that paganus was originally the same as peasant, and that it took the sense of heathen during times when the great cities of the Roman Empire adopted Christianity, while the villagers, poor and uninstructed, clung fast to their ancient faith and customs. Still less do we feel that, speaking of companions, we call them, in fact, co-pagans; yet companion (the French compagnon), is a corruption of com-paganus, one who belongs to the same pagus or village, — a neighbour where neighbours are scanty. Savage again is a name originally applied to people who could not be brought to live in towns or villages, but roamed in forests: hence called silvatics, Wallachian silbatic, Italian selvaggio and salvaggio, French sauvage. Villain, originally the name of a villager (villaneus), received its present meaning under the influence of medieval prejudices. Infantry is derived from infans, a child not yet able to speak. Infans afterwards took the sense of boy or servant; and, as during the middle ages servants went a-foot, while the knights proceeded to battle on horseback, infanteria became the name of foot soldiers. Whether these foot soldiers marched before or behind their lieges is not clear. Still it would seem that those who had to clear the way, and to look out for the enemy, were men on foot, for they were called pioneers, which is again derived from the French pion, the Italian pedone: — our footpad in the days of highway insecurity.

Cavalry again is a name which has risen in dignity, for though caballus was probably applied rather to a cart-horse than to a charger, caballarius soon became in the Middle Ages the title not only of a horseman, but of a chevalier. Artillery did not derive its name from its art: ars, like machina, the Greek μηχανή, was used in the sense of an engine or engines of war; and hence the name of artillery. Nor are the French Ingenieurs called so from their ingenuity, but because ingenium also was employed in the sense of an engine; and hence ingenarius, an engineer. Sappers and miners derive their names from the work they have to do. In French sappe occurs as the name of an ancient weapon, a kind of spear. In the Medieval-Latin Dictionary of Ducange zapa is translated by hoyau, a pick axe, and it is frequently used in the sense of spade. The usual weapon carried by the sapper is the axe, but the "navvies" lately sent to the Crimea will have an equal right to the name of sapper, if not in the military, at least in the etymological sense of the word particularly if, as Diez supposes, zappa and zappare are derived from the Greek σκάπτειν, to dig. Cannon would seem the most harmless instrument if we took its own word for it. It is derived from canna, a cane, a hollow tube; but all that a thin cane and a twenty-pounder have now in common is that both answer the purpose of inflicting deserved chastisement. That soldier and the French sou, a halfpenny, should be derived from the same word may appear startling; still every step can be traced by which these two words came to their present meaning. Solidus (sc. nummus) was originally at Rome the name of a standard gold coin, but it afterwards took the sense of coin in general, and soldo was used in Italian instead of pay. Hence soldare, to pay, and soldato, a soldier, a man who receives pay—a name which might well have been formed in Italy during the Middle Ages, where war was carried on entirely by means of mercenary troops. The same word soldo, coin and pay, was again abbreviated into sol in Provençal; and as the French frequently change ol into ou (as le col, Lat. collum, and le cou, neck or collar), sol was degraded to sou, no longer a solid gold coin as at Rome, but the smallest copper coin at Paris.

Musket, French mousquet, Italian moschetto, was a word used long before the invention of fire-arms. It was the name of a sparrow-hawk, a bird serving the same purpose then which muskets did in later times. This hawk was probably called muscatus from its sprinkled plumage, moucheté meaning spotted, from mouche, musca, a fly, a spot. Another species of hawk being called tertiolus, another kind of fire-arm, a small pistol, was called in Italian terceruolo, in German terzerol.

The corporal, unconnected with corporal punishment, should be called caporal or caporale, as in French and Italian. The Italian caporale is derived from capo (caput), the chef or chief of the regiment. From the same source comes captain, Italian capitano; and we have it under two forms, captain and chieftain being the same word.

A general was so called from being the general commander, and having the general or highest orders to give in battle. A colonel had to command one column of soldiers. A lieutenant was the locum tenens of a superior officer, and in Italian he is simply called il tenente. Sergeant is probably a corruption of servant, the v being interchangeable with g, as in William and Guillaume.

It is known that the French language, though derived exclusively from Latin in its grammar, has a dictionary mixed considerably with German words. The Franks, who learned to speak a Romance language, retained many of their former Frankish expressions, as the Normans retained not a few Norman words in England after they had adopted the Saxon speech. Many of these originally German, but afterwards Frenchified words, were re-imported into England by means of the Norman Conquest; and as English was originally a German dialect, it happened frequently that the same word which the English language possessed in a pure German form, was again introduced under a Norman disguise. Thus *brevet* is the English *brief*; the former coming through a Norman, the latter through a German channel, both derived from the Latin *breve*, an abstract, a short note. *Guardian* is *warden*; the *guards* are *wards*; *forage* is derived from *fodder*, the Gothic *fodr*; from which Italian *fodero*, French *feurre* and *fourrage*, and then again the English *forage*. *Marshal*, now the highest officer in an army, was no doubt taken from the French *maréchal*. But the French took this word from German, where in the old dialect *marah-scalc* meant a farrier, from *marah* (a mare) and *scalc* (servant).

Every one of these words has a long tale to tell, if we had time here to listen to it. How they wandered from one country to another; how they changed in form and meaning, according to the times in which they lived and grew up; how they withered and were forgotten, and then sprang again into existence; how they were misunderstood and harshly treated; how sometimes they rose to high honours, because no one knew their humble birth, and sometimes were degraded in spite of noble descent — all this they are willing to tell, but we must leave their revelations and confessions for more peaceful times.

The meaning of grammatical forms restored by Comparative Philology.

Less interesting at first sight, but more important for determining the exact degree of relationship between languages, and for comprehending their gradual growth and ramifications, is the comparison of grammatical forms. We shall only take one well-known instance. The Italian Future canteró, I shall sing, is evidently not taken from Latin: nor could the French je chanterai, the Spanish cantaré, the Portuguese cantarei, be derived from the Latin cantabo. There is, however, an old Italian form canter-aggio, I shall sing; the termination of which (aggio) is known as a vulgar form of the verb Io ho, I have. That the auxiliary verb could be used for the formation of the Future, we learn from the Sardinian, where appu, I have, is put before the verb to form the same tense; appu essi, has essi, hat essi, I shall, thou wilt, he will be. It becomes, therefore, probable that canteró also was originally cantar ho, I have to sing, I shall sing; and that the Spanish cantaré, the Portuguese cantaréi, as well as the French je chanterai, were meant to express the same as j'ai à chanter, I have to sing. The original Latin Future was lost probably because, with the corrupt pronunciation of the later Latin, it was not easy to distinguish between the Imperfect cantabam and the Future cantabo, and hence a new periphrastic form took its place. The decisive proof of the correctness of this view we receive from the Provençal language, which, as the eldest sister of the Romance family, throws frequently considerable light on the early history of the other dialects. In Provençal the auxiliary verb "to have" is at times separated from the infinitive. We find dir vos ai instead of je vous dir-ai; dir vos em instead of nous vous dir-ons, expressions which leave no doubt as to the origin of all the Romance Futures.

Practical advantage of grammatical comparisons.

That these linguistic discoveries can be turned to practical use is clear. When we know, for instance, that the last portion of the Future is an abbreviation of the verb "to have;" we know also that the terminations of the Future in all Romance dialects must be and are exactly the same as those of the Present of the auxiliary verb "habere."

FRENCH.

j'ai,	je chanter-ai	nous avons	nous chanter-ons.
tu as,	tu chanter-as	vous avez	vous chanter-ez.
il a,	il chanter-a	ils ont	ils chanter-ont.

ITALIAN.

Io ho,	Io canter-ó	noi abbiamo	noi canter-emo.
tu hai,	tu canter-ai	voi avete	voi canter-ete.
egli ha,	egli canter-a	eglino hanno	eglino canter-anno.

SPANISH.

Yo he,	Yo cantar-é	nosotros hemos	nosotros cantar-emos.
tu has,	tu cantar-as	vosotros habeis	vosotros cantar-eis.
él ha,	el cantar-a	ellos han	ellos cantar-an.

As Wallachian was separated from Latin before the time when this new formation of the Future became fixed, we find that it has indeed, like its sisters, been unable to preserve the Latin Future in bo, but has replaced it in a different manner by using the auxiliary verb I will, instead of I have to, or I shall. The Wallachian Future is, Jo voiu cantá, tu vei cantá, el va cantá, noi vomu, voi veti, eli voru cantá.

Words generally the most difficult to understand in their grammatical formation are particles, conjunctions, and adverbs. As they are used in almost every sentence they have generally suffered most from phonetic corruption. They are difficult to remember in a new language, because they seem to have no meaning in themselves, but resemble mere sounds, with a conventional sense attached to them. Here, again, Comparative Philology offers practical aid, disclosing the ingenious, but frequently strange and startling, manner in which these words have been formed. We thus learn to take an interest in them, and remember them with greater facility. This applies both to ancient and modern languages; only that the ancient particles are more difficult to decipher, because they are remnants of a state of language which we know only by means of induction. It could be shown that the Latin tunc is an old case of a demonstrative pronoun, and originally the same as the English then, taken in a temporal sense. But granting this, we find that only in Wallachian has this ancient adverb been preserved, and Particles.

even there a preposition has been added, to make its meaning more apparent. The Wallachian atunci would be adtuncce in Latin, while the old Spanish estonze points to Latin extuncce. But in French and Italian an entirely new word has been introduced, to express with greater significance the meaning of then. This is the Italian allora, the French alors, both of which presuppose the Latin ad illam horam, at that hour. The same word hora may be recognized in the Spanish es ora, ipsà horà, at that very hour, and in the French and Italian encore and encora, *i. e.*, hanc horam, at this hour. The French désormais, henceforth, took this meaning, because it is really the Latin de ipsá horá magis, from this hour, while the corresponding Spanish, de hoy mas is an abbreviation and corruption of dè hodie magis, from to-day. In this manner words, the most formal, and as it were, immaterial, take again body and soul, and impress themselves more firmly on our memory. They re-assume the character of such particles as nothwithstanding, however, because, in English, or conciossiacosache (because), nondimeno (nevertheless), in Italian, where the original meaning is not yet obscured, while the component parts are still visible.

A comparison of these words is useful again for determining the genealogy of dialects, because they disclose the resources from which modern dialects recruited their dictionary. Words of this compound nature are seldom transferred from one language into another: they may be used, therefore, with almost as great advantage as pronouns and numerals, to determine the historical genealogy of the different families of speech.

Classification of languages.

After having as rapidly as possible explained the chief means by which the original relationship of languages may be determined, and even the points fixed at which certain dialects branched off from their common stem, we shall now proceed to give the general results that have been obtained by these philological researches; and in setting forth the outlines of a classification for the principal languages of Asia and Europe, we shall endeavour to show what place each of the dialects, now scattered along the Danube, the Black and Caspian Seas, and the Caucasus, ought to occupy in this general scheme.

Languages in general may be divided into three families which have been called the Semitic, the Arian, and the Turanian.

The Semitic nations appear first on the stage of history, and their languages may be examined first: though, being of less importance for our more immediate purposes, they need not be described with the same completeness as the Arian and Turanian dialects. Semitic family.

The Semitic family has hitherto been divided into three branches, the Aramaic, the Hebrew, and the Arabic. The Arabic, exhibiting the most developed, and at the same time, the most primitive type of the Semitic system of grammar, was taken as the basis, from which one branch of dialects spread towards the north, occupying the countries between the Mediterranean, Asia Minor, Armenia, and Persia, while a second branch took a southerly direction, and, as Ethiopic, struck roots on African soil. Aramaic Hebrew. Arabic.

But besides the Ethiopians, the Hebrews, the Phœnicians, Carthaginians, Syrians, and Arabs, it will be necessary to comprehend within the same family, the Babylonians and Assyrians on one side, and the Egyptians, together with several African tribes, on the other. The discoveries of Rawlinson and Hincks in Babylonia and Assyria leave no doubt as to the Semitic characters of the idiom engraved on the bricks of the palaces of Nebuchadnezzar; and Champollion's and Bunsen's researches have fairly etablished the Semitic origin of the language of the hieroglyphics. Yet it will be possible to retain the tripartite division of the language of Shem, as stated above, because Egyptian, and Babylonian though clearly marked with a Semitic stamp, represent two scions of the Semitic stem which branched off at a period of history so early, or rather so long before the beginning of all history, that they may be considered as independent colonies rather than as constituent parts of the Kingdom of Shem. The same applies to Semitic tribes in the north of Africa, the number and extent of which is almost daily increased by the researches of African travellers and missionaries.

Egyptian. The language of Egypt, as far as it has been deciphered from Hieroglyphical, Hieratic, and Demotic inscriptions, and as it is known to us again by its later representative, the Coptic, leans in its grammatical system towards the Semitic, but differs from it far more than Babylonian. Nay it may be doubted whether it is not sufficiently distinct, historically and grammatically, to constitute a separate branch of speech, the Chamitic. After the 17th century, the Coptic became a dead language. At present the Copts in Egypt are reckoned only as a sixteenth part of the population in the valley of the Nile, the rest being made up of Arabs established there since the conquest of Omar. Coptic colonies are mentioned near the frontiers of Tunis and Tripoli, on the mountains Mathmathah and Nawayl, and in the interior of Africa, in the province of Ghúber, in the midst of the area now occupied by the Tuarik dialects.

Berber dialects. A second lateral branch of the Semitic stem, though more closely connected with it than the former, are the Berber dialects, spoken in many varieties all over the northern coast of Africa from Egypt to the Atlantic Ocean; in fact, the speech of the people in Marocco, Algiers, Tunis, Tripoli and Fez, wherever it has not been supplanted by the language of the conquering Arabs. The Semitic character of these widely-scattered dialects was first proved by Francis Newman; and the Haussa also is now considered as Semitic. Much light on the ramification of this Semitic family in the north-west of Africa may be expected from Richardson's expedition, or rather from Dr. Barth, its only survivor, now on his way to Europe. How far the original area of this half-Semitic stratum of language in Africa may have to be extended, it is impossible to say: but traces of Semitic grammar have already been discovered in the Galla language on the north-eastern coast of Africa.

Babylonian and Assyrian. The Babylonian and Assyrian inscriptions are likely to throw much light on the early history of languages, because an ancient literature entombed for many centuries, is there rising again in all its fulness, and must disclose, if properly deciphered, the exact image of their ancient dialects, fixed by contemporaneous evidence. There are not only names of kings and dates of battles, but, according to Rawlinson, the "debris" of a royal library. "On the clay tablets," he writes in April 1853, "which we have found at Nineveh, and which are now to be counted by thousands, there are explanatory treatises on almost every subject under the sun; the art of writing, grammars and dictionaries, notation, weights and measures, divisions of time, chronology, astronomy, geography, history, mythology, geology, botany, &c. In fact, we have now at our disposal a perfect cyclopædia of Assyrian science, and shall probably be able to trace all Greek knowledge to its source." This promises, indeed, a rich harvest for the linguist and the historian, but as yet all that can be said with confidence is that the language of the ancient Babylonian, and the later Assyrian kingdoms, bears a greater resemblance in some of its words and in most of its grammatical forms to the Semitic than to the Arian or Turanian types. The Assyrian Conjugations and Pronouns have been traced back most convincingly to an original Semitic source by Dr. Hincks.

If we treat these three branches, the Egyptian, Berber, and Babylonian, as cognate descendants of Shem, we may still distinguish them from his three agnate descendants: the Aramaic, Hebrew, and Arabic.

Aramaic.

The Aramaic occupies the north, including Syria, Mesopotamia, and part of Babylonia. It is divided into two dialects, the Syrian and Chaldean. It was reduced by Macedonian and Greek conquests, and after a revival in the 4th and 6th centuries, nearly absorbed by the language of the Islam. It still lives among some tribes near Damascus, and in Kurdistan among the Nestorians or so-called Chaldeans.

Hebrew.

The Hebrew is the language of Palestine, where it was spoken from the days of Moses to the times of Nehemiah and the Maccabees. The language of the Phœnicians and Carthaginians belongs to the same branch. In the progress of history, the Hebrew was first encroached upon by Aramaic dialects, and at last swept away by Arabic, which since the conquest of Palestine and Syria in the year 636, has monopolised nearly the whole area formerly occupied by Aramaic and Hebrew dialects.

Arabic. The original seat of this last and most powerful branch of the Semitic family, the Arabic, was the Arabian peninsula. Here it is still spoken by a compact mass of aboriginal inhabitants, and the ancient inscriptions (Himyaritic) attest there its early presence. In ancient times it sent one colony into Africa, where, south of Egypt and Nubia, on the coast opposite Yemen, an ancient Semitic dialect has maintained itself up to the present day. This is the Ethiopic or Abissinian, or, as it is called by the people themselves, the Gees language. No longer spoken in its purity by the people of Habesh, it is still preserved in their sacred writings, translations of the Bible and similar works. The modern language of Habesh is Amharic, in which the purity of the Semitic idiom has suffered from mixture with African elements.

The great conquests of the Arabic language over Asia, Africa, and Europe, as the language of the Khalifs and the Koran, are matters of historical notoriety, and need not be entered into at present. Nor is it necessary for our purpose to give a detailed account of the grammatical characteristics of the Semitic family. The English army will hardly come in contact with Semitic dialects, except on its outward passage at Malta, where a corrupt Arabic dialect is spoken, greatly mixed with Italian. It will not have to fight in countries where the inhabitants speak Semitic idioms, though it may possibly have to charge side by side with Egyptians who speak Arabic. As to the 10,000 Zouaves whom the French promised to send to the seat of war, they will probably turn out Frenchmen under an Oriental disguise. The real Zouaves belong to the Berber branch, for in Algiers the Berbers are called Shawi, a word which means Nomads, and has been corrupted in Tunis into Suav, French Zouave.

There is one characteristic feature which may be mentioned, as it suffices to distinguish a properly Semitic from an Arian or Turanian language. Every root in Aramaic, Hebrew, and Arabic, must comprise three letters, while the Arian and Turanian roots consist of one or two, seldom of three. Numerous words are derived from the roots simply by changing the vowels, and leaving the consonantal skeleton as much as possible intact. Semitic languages enjoy great liberty in the formation of new words, but they are confined within narrow limits with regard to their position, and a free syntactical arrangement of sentences is hardly known even to the most advanced members of this family. Characteristic Features of the Semitic Family.

The close connection and common descent of the Semitic languages is further confirmed by the radical or material elements shared by all in common, and differing sufficiently from the roots and words of the other families to justify the philologist and historian in treating the Semitic as a distinct variety of the language of mankind. Although comparisons have been instituted between the roots of Semitic and Arian languages, still these are of far too general a character to allow us to suppose that the Arian were derived from the Semitic, or the Semitic from the Arian languages. Even the most distant members of the Arian family are in reality but modifications of the same mother-speech, while, after all attempts to draw the roots of Arian and Semitic languages more closely together, we cannot say more than that in their roots both have preserved faint traces which point towards a common centre, but which it is impossible to follow much further in their converging direction by historical evidence, or even by inductive reasoning.

The second family of languages is the Arian, or, as it used to be called, the Indo-European. The latter name indicates the geographical extent of this family from India to Europe, the former recalls its historical recollections, Arya being the most ancient name by which the ancestors of this family called themselves.* That the Sanskrit, the ancient language of India, the very existence of which was unknown to Greeks and Romans before Arian family

* In the later Sanskrit literature, ârya means "of a good family,"

Alexander, and the sound of which had never reached a European ear till the close of the last century, that this

"venerable," "a Lord;" but it is no longer used as a national name, except as applied to the holy land of the Brahmans, which is still called Ârya-âvarta, the abode of the Âryas. In the Veda, however Ârya occurs very frequently as a name of honour reserved to the higher classes, in opposition to the Dasyus, their enemies. For instance, Rigveda 1, 54, 8: "Know thou the Âryas, O Indra, and they who are Dasyus; punish the lawless and deliver them unto thy servant! Be thou the mighty helper of the worshipper, and I shall praise all these thy deeds at the festivals." And again, 1, 103, 3: "Bearing the thunderbolt and trusting in his strength, he strode about rending in pieces the cities of the slaves. Thunderer, thou art wise; hurl thy shaft against the Dasyu; let the power of the Âryas grow into glory."

In the later dogmatical literature of the Vedic age, the name of Ârya is distinctly appropriated to the three first castes of the Brahmanic society. Thus we read in the *S*atapatha-brâhma*n*a: „Âryas are only the Brahmans, Kshatriyas, and Vai*s*yas, for they are admitted to the sacrifices. They shall not speak with everybody, for the Gods did not speak with everybody, but only with the Brahman, the Kshatriya, and the Vai*s*ya. If they should fall into a conversation with a *S*ûdra, let them say to another man, «tell this *S*ûdra so.» This is the law for an initiated man." Again in the so-called Atharva-veda, we read, "be it an Ârya or a *S*ûdra."

But while this old name, "Ârya," fell into oblivion amongst the Hindus, it was faithfully preserved by the Medians and Persians. In the Zendavesta, the first-created and holy land is called Airyanem vae*g*o, "the seed of the Arians," and this name was in later times transferred to Media, a country too far west to be mentioned in the Zendavesta. Herodotus was told in his Oriental travels, that the Medians originally called themselves Ἄριοι, and Hellanicus gives Aria as a synonyme of Persia. And now that we can read, thanks to the wonderful discoveries of Rawlinson, Burnouf, and Lassen, the same records from which Herodotus derived his information, we find Darius calling himself, in the Cuneiform inscriptions, "a Persian, the son of a Persian, an Arian, and of Arian descent." About the same time Eudemus, the pupil of Aristoteles, as quoted by Nicolaus Damascenus speaks of "the Magi and the whole Arian race"; (Μάγοι δὲ καὶ πᾶν τὸ Ἀρεῖον γένος.) And when, after centuries of foreign invasions and occupation, the Persian Empire rose again to historical importance under the Sassanian sway, we find their kings also calling themselves in the Inscriptions deciphered by De Sacy, "Kings of the Arian and un-Arian races." This is the origin of the modern name of Iran. The name of the Armenians, Aghavan, is derived by Boré from Agho which is Alo which is Arya, and means language should be a scion of the same stem, whose branches overshadow the civilized world of Europe, no one would have ventured to affirm before the rise of Comparative Philology. It was the generally received opinion that if Greek, Latin, and German came from the East, they must be derived from Hebrew — an opinion for which at the present day not a single advocate could be found, while formerly, to disbelieve it would have been tantamount to heresy. No authority could have been strong enough to persuade the Grecian army that their gods and their hero-ancestors were the same as those of King Porus, or to convince the English soldier that the same blood was running in his veins, as in the veins of the dark Bengalese. And yet there is not an English jury now a-days, which, after examining the hoary documents of language, would reject the claim of a common descent and a legitimate relationship between Hindu, Greek, and Teuton. Many words still live in India and in England that witnessed the first separation of the northern and southern Arians, and these are witnesses not to be shaken by any cross-examiuation. The terms for God, for house, for father, mother, son, daughter, for dog and cow, for heart and tears, for axe and tree, identical in all the Indo-European idioms, are like the watch-words of an army. We challenge the seeming stranger, and whether he answer with the lips of a Greek, a German, or an Indian, we recognize him as one of ourselves. Though the historian may shake his head, though the physiologist may doubt, and the poet scorn the idea, all must yield before the facts furnished by language.

descendants of the Aryas. Again, in the Mountains of the Caucasus, we find, an Arian race, the Os, calling themselves Iron; Stephanus gives Ἀρία as a synonyme of Thrace, and Ario-vistus, the enemy of Caesar, and a tribe of Arii known to Tacitus, attest the presence of the same title in the forests of Germany. Thus we hear everywhere the faint echoes of a name which once sounded through the valleys of the Himâlaya; and it seems but natural that Comparative Philology, which first succeeded in tracing the common origin of all the nations enumerated before, should have selected this old and venerable title, for their common appellation. — *Edinburgh Review*, October, 1851.

There was a time when the ancestors of the Celts, the Germans, the Slaves, the Greeks and Italians, the Persians and Hindus, were living together beneath the same roof, separate from the ancestors of the Semitic and Turanian races.

Sanskrit in India.

The first branch of this family belongs to India. It is represented in ancient times by the Sanskrit, the language of the Vedas, or the sacred writings of the Brahmans. Although this language presents the most primitive type of the Arian family, still it is impossible to consider the Greek, Latin, and German as derived from Sanskrit in the same manner as the Romance dialects are from Latin. All we can say is, that Sanskrit is the eldest sister, and that therefore it can, on some points of grammar, reveal to us, as it were, the earliest impressions of the childhood of the Arian family. It stands to the other languages as Provençal to French and Italian: — a relation which does not exclude the possibility that occasionally the younger sisters may have preserved their original features more distinctly than Sanskrit or Provençal.

Besides the ancient Sanskrit of the Veda we can trace the Indian language through several later eras of its growth. In the Vaidik literature itself we can distinguish at least three periods, distinct in thought and style; and we may safely place the time when the Sanskrit of the hymns of the Veda was the spoken, and not as yet the sacred idiom of India, about 1,500 B.C. In the sixth century B.C., at the first rise of Buddhism, the Protestantism of ancient India, the spoken dialects were no longer Sanskrit, but languages standing to it in the same relation as the vulgar to the classical Latin.

Prâkrit, Páli, and Hindustani.

The later dialects of India are called by a general name, Prâkrit. If Pâli, which has since become in Ceylon the sacred language of the Buddhists, was the popular idiom in which Buddha preached to the people, it must be referred to this class of languages. But, if we judge from the Gâthâs of the Buddhistic literature, the dialect in which Buddha's doctrines were first embodied, was far less corrupt than the Pali of Ceylon, the origin of which has therefore been referred to a much later period by Professor Wilson. The public inscriptions of the time of Asoka, *i. e.*, of the third century B. C., exhibit the the first traces of a secondary formation in the spoken language of India, if compared with the more primitive Sanskrit. Yet Sanskrit continued for a long time after, the literary and sacred language of India; and in the present day the Brahmans are able to write and to speak it with the same facility as monks in the middle ages wrote and spoke Latin. We have the most elaborate Sanskrit grammars of the fourth century B. C., and the two great epic poems, the Mahâbhârata and Râmâya*n*a, and the so-called Laws of Manu, date probably though not in their present form, from the same time. Another period of Sanskrit literature is generally considered as contemporaneous with the Augustan age of Rome, but the language in which the poems of Kalidâsa, the chief poet of that time, are written, is of so artificial a structure, that it is impossible to believe this to have been at any time the spoken language of India. We find, in fact, that the same Kalidâs, when he represents scenes from real life, as in his plays, is obliged to let his heroines and inferior characters speak in the soft and melodious Prakrit idioms, while he reserves the more dignified and learned Sanskrit for Kings and Brahmans. A similar mixture of Latin and modern dialects is found in some of the plays of the middle ages. After Kalidâsa there have been several revivals of Sanskrit literature at the courts of different princes, and up to our own times Sanskrit is read and written by the learned. But, since the days of Pâ*n*ini, in the fourth century, B. C., the classical Sanskrit shows no longer signs of either growth or decay. It has ceased to live, and though it exists still like a mummy dressed in its own ceremonial robes, its vital powers are gone. Sanskrit now lives only in its offspring; the numerous spoken dialects of India, Hindustani, Mahratti, Bengali, Guzerati, Singhalese, &c., all preserving, in the system of their grammar, the living traces of their common parent.

Siah-posh and Gipsy language

Whether the Siah-posh dialect, spoken by the Kafirs in the north-eastern parts of the Hindukush, has preserved a closer similarity to Sanskrit than Bengali and Hindustani, is difficult to determine, till we gain more ample information on this language, first discovered by Sir A. Burnes.

We should not omit, however, in this place, the language of the Gipsies, which, though most degraded in its grammar and with a dictionary stolen from all the dialects of Asia and Europe, is clearly an exile from Hindostán.

Languages of Media and Persia. The second branch of the Arian family is the Persian, which may equally be followed in its historical growth and decay through different periods of literature. The language of the Zendavesta, the sacred remnants of the Zoroastrian religion; the inscriptions of Cyrus, Darius, and Xerxes; the Pehlevi of the Sassanian dynasty (226 A.D.), mixed with Semitic elements, but purely Arian in its grammar, proscribed by edict in the fifth century of our era; the Pâzend, or Parsi, the national Persian, freed of its foreign admixtures, the language of the grand epic poem of Firdusi (1000 A.D.), and the motley idiom now spoken in Persia, exhibit a complete biography of the Iranian language, the half-brother of Sanskrit.

There are some scions of the Arian stock which struck root in the soil of Asia, before the Arians reached the shores of Europe; but they are of far less interest for Comparative Philology, because they do not exhibit by their literature, what is most instructive, the gradual progress of a growing language. These are:

Afghan language. 1. The Afghan, or language of the Patans, the inhabitants of Kabul. It belongs by its grammar to the Persian branch. The Afghans call themselves Pushtun, in the plural Pushtâneh, which according to Klaproth was pronounced Puʿhtaneh, and corrupted into Patan. The Beluk also, the conquerors of Sind, the southern neighbours of the Afghans, speak a dialect closely allied to the Persian.

In the Tazkirât-ul-mulûk, Push or Pash is said to have been the name of the country where the Afghans, (according to their traditions, descendants of Saul, David and Salomon,) settled; and hence Pushtu, the name of the language of the country, which they adopted instead of Hebrew. Patân is there explained as an Arabic word, meaning the mast of a vessel, a title of honor, given to the first Afghan ruler who adopted Islam, by the prophet himself.

The Pushtu language is spoken with considerable variation in orthography and pronunciation from the valley of Pishín south of Kandahar to Kafiristan on the north; and from the banks of the Helmand on the west, to the Attok, Sindhu, or Indus on the east — throughout the Sama or plain of the Yusufzo's, the mountainous districts of Ba*g*awer, Pan*g*kora, Suwat, and Bunir, to Astor on the borders of little Tibet — a tract of country equal in extent to the Spanish peninsula. *

Language of Bokhara.

2. The language of the people of **Bokhâra**, a modern Persian dialect, spoken originally by the Ta*g*iks, north of Balkh, but to be met with in many parts of Asia, owing to the migratory habits of the people, well known as the travelling merchants of Central Asia.

Language of the Kurds.

3. The language of the **Kurds**, likewise of Iranian character, though strongly mixed with Semitic words, and without any literary cultivation. The relation between Persian and Kurdian has been compared with that between the literary language of Italy, the Toscan, and the popular dialect of Milan. There are many dialects of the Kurdian language, and Garzoni's grammar refers to the Northwestern idiom of Kurdistan. This country is surrounded on the North by Armenia, on the East by Aserbei*g*an and the Persian Irak, on the South by Khusistan and the district of Bagdad, on the West by the Tigris. The nomadic habits of the Kurds account for their presence in neighbouring countries, particularly during winter. Even in more distant regions, in Loristan as far as the Persian Gulf, in the Pashaliks of Haleb and Damascus, in Asia-Minor, Khorasan and elsewhere, Kurdish tribes are to be met with. The Zagros-mountains divide the whole of Kurdistan into two unequal parts. The country West of this line, a part of the ancient Assyria, between the Zagros and the Tigris, belongs to the Turkish empire. The other part, east of the Zagros mountains, and forming part of the ancient Media, is under Persian sway. The number of Kurds is vaguely estimated at two to three millions. Their name has frequently

* See Raverty in the Journal of the As. Soc. of Bengal No. 244.

been derived from the ancient Kasdim, the Chaldeans of Assyria. Strabo speaks of the Kurds as Κάρδακες and Κύρτιοι, Xenophon as Καρδοῦχοι. They call themselves Kurdmanġi, according to Klaproth, or Kurmanġi. Both names mean Kurd-men. They are divided into two classes, the Assireta, or Sipah (soldiers), and the Guran or Rayah (subjects); the latter cultivate the soil and are of lower rank, the former are the nobility and live on chase and pillage. The Yezídís near Mossul are Kurds. With this exception, the race is mostly Mohammedan.

Language of Armenia.

4. The Armenian language, decidedly Arian in its grammar, but differing both from the Indian and Iranian type. The ancient Armenian is now a dead language, and the spoken dialect has suffered greatly from Turkish influences. It has a rich literature, but only dating from the fourth century A.D. The Armenians are known as merchants in Asia and Europe, and have establishments at St. Petersburg, Vienna, Venice, Constantinople, Kairo, Bombay, Calcutta, Madras, Singapore, and elsewhere.

Ossetian, or language of the Iron.

5. Another Arian language, the Ossetian, barren altogether of native literature, has been collected from the mouths of the people on account of its linguistic importance. It is called Ossetian, from Osethi, which in Georgian means the country of the Os; Os being the name by which these people, who call themselves Iron, are known to their neighbours. The Ossetes occupy the country west of the great military road which crosses the Caucasus from north to south. They extend to the sources of the Rion, and are found principally in the valley of the Terek. West of the fortress of Vladikaukas, they inhabit a vast plain which in the north is divided from the Kabardah by a line of mountains, called Pshe'besh. More northern seats, which they occupied in earlier times, were taken from them by the Mongolians. While in the North they are called Os, their more usual name in the South is Dwal or Dwaleth. The Digores and Tagaures belong to them. Russian supremacy is acknowledged in Osethi, but little enforced.

This language spoken in the centre of Mount Caucasus,

and surrounded on all sides by tongues of different origin, stands out, like a block of granite errant in the midst of sandstone strata, a strayed landmark of the migrations of the Arian tribes. Whether, however, the Ossetian language has been fixed there, since the first movements of the Arians from Asia into Europe, that is before the beginning of all political history, is a point difficult to settle. According to their own traditions, and the accounts of Georgian historians, the ancestors of the Ossetes extended formerly from the Caucasus to the Don, and were driven back into the mountains, in the middle of the 13th century, by Batukhan, the grandson of *K*ingis-khán. Their former presence near the Don (Tanais), however, rests on very doubtful evidence: the name of the Ossilians, a people whom Ptolemy mentions near the mouth of that river, being the chief argument in favour of this view. Klaproth supposes that the first ancestors of this Arian colony on the Don were the Medians, transplanted, according to Diodorus Siculus, by the Scythians into Sarmatia in the 7th century B.C. There is little doubt that the Sarmatians were a Median colony of the 7th century before Christ, and that the Alanes, Yaxamates, Roxolanes, and Yazyges came all from the same source. After *S*afarik's investigations, no critical historian can for the future treat these Sarmatians as the ancestors of the Slavonic nations. The question is only whether the present Ossetes in the Caucasus, the Ossilians of Ptolemy, and the Alanes or Sarmatians are one and the same people. Klaproth endeavours to prove that the Median colonists of Sarmatia and the modern Ossetes meet in the Alanes of the Middle Ages, and that, at the time of Constantinus Porphyrogeneta (948 A.D.), they lived on the northern side of the Caucasus and north of Kasachia. The Alanes, according to an Italian traveller of the 15th century (Josafa Barbaro), still called themselves As, and a people called As or Yas is frequently mentioned in Russian chronicles together with the Kasoq, i.e. the *K*erkessians, who were then known by the name of Kasach, a name now monopolized by the Cossacks, the bastard descendants of Slavonic, Tataric, and Caucasian tribes. But whatever the time may have been when these As or Os settled in the central regions of the Caucasus, whether in the 7th century B.C. or at a still more remote period, in either case their language is a welcome link between the Arian dialects of Asia and Europe.

European Arians.

In Europe the Arian family has sent out five great branches, the Celtic, Teutonic, Italic, Hellenic and Slavonic or Windic.

Language of the Celts.

The Celts seem to have been the first to arrive in Europe, where the pressure of subsequent emigration, particularly of Teutonic tribes, has driven them toward the westernmost parts, and latterly, across the Atlantic. At present the only remaining Celtic dialects are the Cymric and Gadhelic. The Cymric comprises the Welsh, the Cornish (now extinct), and the Armorican of Brittany. The Gadhelic comprises the Irish, the Galic of the west coast of Scotland, and the dialect of the Isle of Man. Although these Celtic dialects are still spoken, the Celts themselves can no longer be considered an independent nation, like the Germans or Slaves. In former times however they not only possessed political autonomy, but asserted it successfully against Germans and Romans. Gaul, Belgium, and Britain, were Celtic dominions, and the North of Italy was chiefly inhabited by them. At the time of Herodotus, we find Celts in Spain; and Switzerland, the Tyrol, and the country south of the Danube, have been the seats of Celtic tribes. But after repeated inroads into the regions of civilization, familiarizing Latin and Greek writers with the names of their kings, they disappear from the east of Europe. Brennus is supposed to mean king, the Welsh brennin. A Brennus conquered Rome (390), another Brennus threatened Delphi (280). And about the same time a Celtic colony settled in Asia, founding Galatia, where the language spoken at the time of St. Jerome was still that of the Gauls. Celtic words may be found in German, Slavonic, and even in Latin, but only as foreign terms, and their amount much smaller than commonly supposed. A far larger number of Latin and German words have since found their way into the modern Celtic dialects, and these have frequently been mistaken by Celtic enthusiasts for original words, from which German and Latin might, in their turn, be derived.

Much more instructive for an analytical study of the Arian languages is Greek. We have here the advantage that various co-existent dialects, Aeolic and Ionic, Doric and Attic, have happily been preserved in their undying literature, affording thus a complete insight into the original individuality of the Greek tongue. We know which forms are ancient and genuine, and which of more modern growth; and when one dialect is deficient or corrupt, another frequently supplies the deficiency. A language without dialects is like a stem without branches: it gives us no idea of its full powers, and allows us no insight into the secret working of its organism. Helleni languag

In Italy again more than one dialect was spoken before the rise of Rome; but scanty fragments only have been preserved in inscriptions of the Umbrian in the north, and of the Oscan to the south of Rome. The Oscan language, spoken by the Samnitae, now rendered intelligible by the labours of Mommsen, had produced a literature before the Romans knew even the art of writing; and the tables of Iguvio, so successfully deciphered by Dr. Aufrecht, bear witness to a priestly literature among the Umbrians at a very early period. But all was destroyed and absorbed by the power of Rome; and though Oscan was still spoken under the Roman emperors, the only dialect of Italy which has preserved life, and rules even now over the greater part of Europe, was the language of Latium or Rome. Italic language

The Romance languages are amongst the most interesting subjects of Comparative Philology, because we can watch here the gradual decay of the mother-stock, and the formation of the new national dialects under six different phases, the Provençal and French, the Italian and Wallachian, the Spanish and Portuguese, not to mention the numerous patois of each. We can see the old forms of the Latin grammar gradually losing their ex- Romanc language pressive power, and auxiliary words, such as prepositions and articles, coming in to form the new declensions, while the decaying structure of the conjugations is propped up by auxiliary verbs. Some of the old forms linger on for a time, and the new periphrastic expressions are at first used with a certain reserve, but at last the whole structure of modern languages is overgrown by them. The old conjunctions and adverbs give way to more distinct expressions and circumlocutions, and these, by a rapid change, coalesce again into new words. It is this period of the decay of Latin and the growth of the Romance dialects, that alone gives an opportunity of gaining an insight into the regenerative process of a language; teaching us by analogy what process it was that in times beyond the reach of history broke up the common Arian type into various dialects, such as Greek, Latin, Sanskrit, Gothic, Celtic and Slavonic. We regret that we can afford only so brief an allusion to this interesting subject.

Wallachian. It will be necessary to give some detail on the Wallachian—a language known to few before the beginning of the war, but latety brought into notoriety by the fate of the unfortunate Wallachians, who have had to bear the first shock of the war, between their protectors on either side.

The people whom we call Wallachians, call themselves Romàni, and their language Romània.

This Romance language is spoken in Wallachia and Moldavia, and in parts of Hungary, Transylvania, and Bessarabia; while on the right bank of the Danube it occupies some parts of the old Thracia, Macedonia, and even Thessaly.

It is divided by the Danube into two branches; the Northern or Daco-romanic, and the Southern or Macedo-romanic. The former is less mixed, and has received a certain literary culture; the latter has borrowed a larger number of Albanian and Greek words, and has never been fixed grammatically.

The modern Wallachian is the daughter of the language spoken in the Roman province of Dacia.

The original inhabitants of Dacia were called Thracians, and their language Illyrian. We have hardly any remains of the ancient Illyrian dialect, and are unable to form an opinion as to its relationship with Greek or any other family of speech.

The frontiers of Dacia (according to Ptolemy) were the Theiss, the Upper Dniester, the Pruth, and the Danube; so that it then comprised part of Gallicia, the Bukovina, Moldavia, Wallachia, Transylvania, the Banat, and about one third of Hungary. It hence appears that the Wallachian, as spoken at the present day, has gained ground on the east, where it now stretches into Bessarabia as far as the Dniester; but lost it on the west, partly by the Hungarians, who occupy the country on the left side of the Theiss, partly by the Slaves, not to mention considerable Hungarian and German settlements in the interior of Wallachia. Of the 2,056,000 inhabitants of Wallachia, 900,000 are Wallachians, 700,000 Hungarians, 250,000 Germans, about 100,000 Slaves, the rest Greeks, Armenians, Jews, and Gipsies.

219 B.C., the Romans conquered Illyria; 30 B.C. they took Moesia; and 107 A.D., the Emperor Trajan made Dacia a Roman province. At that time the Thracian population had been displaced by the advance of Sarmatian tribes, particularly the Yazyges. Roman colonists introduced the Latin language; and Dacia was maintained as a colony to 272, when the Emperor Aurelian had to cede it to the Goths. Part of the Roman inhabitants then emigrated and settled south of the Danube.

In the year 489, Slavonic tribes began their advance into Moesia and Thracia. They were settled in Moesia by 678, and eighty years later a province was founded in Macedonia, under the name of Slavinia.

Northern Wallachians

At present the Wallachian language is surrounded on all sides by Slavonic dialects, except in the West, where it borders on the Hungarian. According to Safarik the Wallachian begins in the south near Golubatch, and follows the Danube downwards to its conflux with the Pruth. It then ascends with the Pruth, and after reaching the

Wallachian Faltchi, takes a north-eastern direction, crosssing the rivers Jalpuch and Kogalnik, in the neighbourhood of which several German colonies are found. Afterwards the frontier line of the Wallachian language recedes once more southward and westward, crosses the Kogalnik again, and meets the Bulgarian near the Jalpuch. Thence the frontier proceeds in a straight line towards Kilia, follows the northern branch of the Danube, Ismail remaining excluded, and reaches the Black Sea, following the southern arm of the Danube, but separated by it from the Tataric dialects, spoken in that part of the Dobrudsha. The Black Sea now forms its frontier as far as the mouth of the Dniester, Akerman being Wallachian, while Ovidiopol on the opposite side is Slavonic. Here also several German colonies are found, as Manheim, Freudenthal, Lustdorf, and Liebenthal. The Dniester may afterwards be taken as the frontier of the Wallachian, although it is spoken in some places on its left bank, such as Malajest, Dubosari, and Kamenka, while Tiraspol has a Slavonic population. Between Kamenka and Jampol, the frontier leaves the Dniester, turns north-west, enters Gallicia near Tchernowitz, and reaches the Theiss near Hussth in Hungary: hence directly south to Golubatch on the Danube. The chief places which it touches here, are Hussth (Hungarian), Halmi (Slavonic), Szathmar (Hungarian), Maiteny and Beltek (German), Bihar and Gross-Wardein (Hungarian), Lippa, Greifenthal, Brückenau (German), Arad and Temesvar (Wallachian), Denta (Slavonic), Weisskirchen and New Moldava (German). It is not always easy to determine which language is spoken in each of these places, particularly as it seems to be the policy of the Greek church to supplant, so far as lies in its power, the non-Slavonic dialects. In some Wallachian villages, as Murgu says, the presence of a few Servians is a sufficient pretext for using the Slavonic language in Wallachian churches. "Nay, I know several Wallachian villages," he writes in 1830, "where the Slavonic language is used in church, though not a single Raitz (i.e., Servian,) lives there; for instance in the Wallachian frontier-district,

No. 13, at Bosovics, Lapusnic, Budaria, and Banya. In other places, where a few Turkish Servians have settled, the Wallachian language has at once been banished, not only from the church, but from the schools. In the village of Old Moldova, two-thirds of the inhabitants are Wallachian, and but few Raitz, yet service is performed in Slovenian. In Wallacho-Pozseszena, where the inhabitants are Wallachian, there is no national school, and the people are compelled to pay for the Raitz schoolmaster at Raitz-Pozseszena."

Within the limits of the Wallachian, as described above, there are large districts in which different languages are spoken. In Transylvania there are three settlements, commonly called "the Sachsenland" (Saxon-country). The language spoken there is Low German. It is divided into three districts: 1, Sachsenland Proper, with the towns of Hermanstadt, Broos, and Schäsburg; 2, Burzenland, with its capital Kronstadt; 3, Nösnerland, with Bistritz for its capital. High German is spoken in Lugos, Krasova, and Oravitza. Again there is a large tract of country where the language is Hungarian. This comprises the towns of Neumark or Maros, Vasarhely, Karlsburg, and Klausenburg. Besides this, small Hungarian settlements are scattered near Bucharest and Jassy. Hungarian is spoken in the town of Radautz in Gallicia, and as far as Seret, in Kapnik, Gross-Banya (half-German); in Tasnad on the Krasna, in Krasna and Zilah on the same river, in Margitta (half-Slavonic); in Elesd, Ujlak, and Körös Banya, in Shoborshin, Deva on the Maros, and in Hatzeg in the south-west of Transylvania.

This northern or Daco-Romanic branch of the Wallachian is again divided into dialects, the one spoken in Wallachia, the other in Moldavia. Moldavia is called Kara-Iflak (Black or Little Wallachia) by the Turks, and the Moldavians sometimes go by the name of Kara-Wallachians.

When in 272 the Emperor Aurelian ceded Dacia to the Goths, large numbers of the Roman colonists crossed Southern Wallachian the Danube, and settled in Moesia and in the Haemus-mountains. These new colonies were named "Dacia Aureliana." These southern Wallachian are now called Makedo-Wallachians or Kutzo Wallachians (Lame Wallachians), or by another nickname "Zinzars," because they pronounce five "tzintz" instead of "chinch." They are also known as Moeso-Dacians (Μοισιόδακες).

But although in former times Wallachian was spoken in the country between the Danube and the Haemus—*i.e.*, within the limits of Thracia — Bulgarian alone is found there at present, and, except in the valleys of the Haemus, no traces seem to have remained of the old Wallachian idiom. The pressure of the Turks drove the Wallachians further South and Westward; and it is in Albania, Macedonia, and Thessaly that we now meet with clusters of Wallachian colonists. Our information, however, is not exact as to their number, and while some give half of the inhabitants of Thracia, and two-thirds of the inhabitants of Macedonia as Wallachian, Pouqueville states the total number of Wallachians in those parts of Greece at 74,470. A census is difficult, because of the migratory habits of the people, part travelling with merchandise, part with their flocks, throughout the country.

Massarets or Dassarets.

Pouqueville divides the southern Wallachians into three classes. The northernmost live in the mountains which separate Macedonia from Albania, principally however on the Macedonian side. They are called Massarets or Dassarets, but claim themselves the name of Romounis. They inhabit San Marina, Avdela, Perivoli, Voschopolis and Vlacho-Kleisura, and their number is given as 18,500.

Great Wallachians.

The second class live in the Pindus-mountains which separate Thessaly from Albania, and the country there is called Great or Upper Wallachia (Μεγάλη Βλαχία, or Ἄνω Βλαχία), as opposed to Little Wallachia, a name given sometimes to the ancient Aetolia and Akarnania. Their chief seats are East and South-east of Janina, the towns and villages of Mezzovo, Malakassi, Lesinitza, Kalarites, Kalaki, Klinovo, Zagori. Many of them understand and speak Greek, but the women speak Wallachian only. Their number is given by Pouqueville as 45,000. They call themselves Armeng, and not Rum.

The third class are the so-called Bovians or Bomaei, who live near the sources of the Evenus or Feidaris, and the Kephissos, near Zeitun. They are mixed with Albanians and Greeks. Their chief places are Nea-Patra, Karpenitza, Zeitun and Cossina, but they travel with their flocks into Aetolia, the villages of Amphissa, and Boeotia. Bovians.

The grammar of Wallachian is very easy, and any one acquainted with Italian and French could master it in a fortnight. As in the other Romance languages, the Latin terminations of the cases are lost and prepositions used instead. It will be seen, however, that the Wallachian, by preserving one oblique case of the article, was able to dispense with prepositions in cases where the other Romance languages have to employ them. We may render in Wallachian, I have sold the garden to my neighbour, by "Jo am vèndut vecinului miéu gràdina." In French we should have to employ a preposition, and say, à mon voisin, while in Wallachian the oblique case of the article (being always put after the substantive, as in Danish, and not before, as in English), suffices by its form lui to indicate the dative of the noun to which it is attached. If there should be an ambiguity, we may employ a preposition, but in this case the article is no longer in an oblique case, but in the nominative; for instance, Jo am vèndut la vecinul miéu gràdina, I have sold the garden to (la) my neighbour. Wallachian

Another peculiarity which Wallachian shares in common with the other Romance languages as compared with Latin, is the use of the articles; though here again Wallachian differs from her sisters by placing the article (ille) after and not before the noun. In Latin it was optional to say homo ille or ille homo; and while Italian, and the other Romance dialects, fixed upon the latter, the Wallachian preferred the former. It is likely that Albanian and Bulgarian, both near neighbours of Wallachian, have adopted this mode of expressing the article from Wallachian. We have no authority for ascribing this grammatical peculiarity to the ancient Illyrian language, but we know that Wallachian, as a modern Latin dialect, was at liberty, as noticed before, to say either ille homo, "the man," or homo ille, "man the."

Like the other Romance dialects the Wallachian has lost the neuter; and in the conjugation, auxiliary verbs have been used to replace several of the ancient Latin tenses, such as the perfect, the future, and the whole of the passive. The construction of sentences has been simplified, and inverted phrases are used with great caution. The pronunciation has been softened, and many derivative words have been added to the stores of the Latin vocabulary.

Hence the most difficult part of Wallachian is the dictionary, which, though originally derived from Latin, is now so full of Slavonic terms that the labour of acquiring a full knowledge of Wallachian is considerably greater than with Italian or Spanish. Another difficulty arises from the scantiness of books to assist foreigners desirous to study this dialect. There is indeed a very meritorious grammar by Alexi, but it is written in Latin, and rather cumbersome. Another grammar by Blasewics is written in German, but the use of the Cyrillic alphabet to express Wallachian makes it still more inconvenient for English students and travellers. A Wallachian dictionary published at Ofen is rather unwieldy; and there is hardly anything deserving of the name of literature. The only thing to be done is to learn the grammar, and then endeavour to pick up the most necessary phrases by ear. There are some vocabularies which may be used with advantage. Italian words will frequently be understood, although Slavonic synonymes may be more usual. According to a computation by Diez, the letter B in the Ofen dictionary contains only 42 Latin words; the rest, about 105, are foreign, Servian, Russian, Albanian, Hungarian, and German.

Wallachian Alphabet.

The alphabet which was used at first in reducing Wallachian to writing was the Cyrillic. The Wallachians took it from the Servians, and after adding some more signs, raised the number of their letters to 44. This alphabet was used in printing, in the year 1580. In 1677 the first attempt was made to write Wallachian with Roman letters; and after many experiments to settle a uniform alphabet, not less than 13 different systems of orthography are now employed among the Wallachians.

The most rational system is that used by **Alexi**, in his Grammatica Daco-Romana. It is principally founded on etymological considerations, and retains as far as possible the Latin spelling. Where the pronunciation has changed; where, for instance, an original c is pronounced as ch, a d as z, a t as ts, accents and hooks are used to indicate this alteration in order not to sacrifice etymology. The greatest inconvenience is the introduction of these new types—an inconvenience which can easily be removed, however, by adopting the "Missionary Alphabet." This would preserve the etymology, without the difficulty of accented letters.

	Alexi's Alphabet.	Pronunciation.	Missionary Alphabet.
1	A a	a *in* far	a
2	Ả ả	a *in* America	0 or ă
3	B b	b *in* bed	b
4	C c	c *in* car	k
		ch *in* church	*k*
5	Ç ç	ts *in* benefits	ʒ
6	D d	d *in* down	d
7	D̦ d̦	z *in* zeal	z
8	E e	a *in* date	e
9	Ẻ ẻ	e *in* mother	0 or ĕ
10	É é	ea *in* yearn (?)	ea
11	È è	e *in* scene	i
12	F f	f *in* find	f
13	G g	g *in* go	g
		j *in* join	*g*
14	H h	ch *in* loch	ʽh
15	I i	i *in* ravine	i

Alexi's Alphabet.	Pronunciation.	Missionary Alphabet.
16 Ỉ ỉ	i *in* bird	0 or ĭ
17 i	y *in* yea	*y*
18 J j	s *in* pleasure	ʒ
19 L l	l *in* low	l
20 M m	m *in* mind	m
21 N n	n *in* no	n
22 O o	o *in* no	o
23 Ȯ ỏ	o *in* work	0 or ŏ
24 Ó ó	a *in* fall	ou
25 P p	p *in* pay	p
26 Qu qu	c *in* car	k
	ch *in* church	*k*
27 R r	r *in* run	r
28 S s	s *in* sin	s
29 Ş ş	sh *in* she	*s*
30 T t	t *in* town	t
31 Ţ ţ	ts *in* benefits	ŧ
32 U u	u *in* full	u
33 Ù ù	oo *in* fool	u
34 V v	v *in* veil	v

Although the Roman alphabet is decidedly superior to any other for writing languages derived from Latin, yet the influence of the Slavonic tribes, by whom the Wallachians are surrounded, has been so great as to induce the Wallachians to prefer the Cyrillic alphabet. It will be necessary, therefore, to give a short account of this, and to show, by means of a comparative table, how the sounds of Wallachian may be and have been rendered in this foreign alphabet. Besides, in order to understand the system of any Slavonic alphabet now in use, it is necessary to have a clear idea of the Cyrillic, because they all depend on, or are at least influenced by it.

The Cyrillic Alphabet.

This alphabet was invented by Cyrillus, a Greek monk, who, together with Methodius, was sent from Constantinople to preach the Gospel to the Slaves, in 862.

It is chiefly taken from the Greek, but some signs are added to represent sounds peculiar to the Slavonic dialects, and foreign to Greek. New signs not taken from Greek are—

Ж for the sound of s in pleasure, or j in French jamais.
Ш „ „ sh in she.
Щ „ „ sht, abbreviation of Ш + Т.
Ц „ „ ts in benefits.
Ч „ „ ch in church.
Ъ „ „ ŏ in work.
Ь „ „ ĭ in bird.
Ѫ „ „ ŏn in the French balcon.
Ѣ „ „ ea in yea.

Others are modifications of Greek letters, as—

Б for b, to distinguish it from B, which represented the sound of v.

Ѧ to express the nasal sound of in, as in the French enfin.

What produced, however, the greatest inconvenience in this new alphabet was the introduction of a whole class of vowels with the inherent initial y. These are—

Ꙗ for the sound of ya in Yarmouth.
Ю „ „ yu in yule.
Ѥ „ „ yea.
Ѩ „ „ ien in French bien.
Ѭ „ „ ion in French nation.

These compound letters were invented because the Greek alphabet offered no consonant for the simple sound of y. It would have been far better, however, to have added one simple new sign instead of introducing a number of compound vowels. As it is, not every vowel has received its own type to represent it when preceded by y. The sound of yi (yee) has no sign of its own, and the simple H must stand for both i and yi, even in Old-Slavonic. To the Ѣ (ê) also the double power of ê and yê (ay and yea) was assigned. Still greater confusion arose where, as in Russian, the pronounciation of these liquid, or as they are called pre-iotized, vowels, changed in the course of time, and became simple again, while the original orthography remained, so that Я in Russian is now pronounced not only as ya (in yard), but also like a simple e (in bed). Besides the Я, the Е, Ѣ, and И also vary in Russian between the sounds ye, ye, yi and e, e, i (the vowels pronounced as in Italian).

The letters Ъ and Ь were intended by Cyrillus to express the shortest sounds of u and i. In modern Bulgarian Ъ has still preserved the sound of u, and it is used for the same purpose in Wallachian. In Russian, however, these two final letters are no longer pronounced as vowels; yet the letters have been retained in order to indicate the peculiar pronunciation of the preceding, and now final, consonant. Where the final Ъ ceases to be pronounced, the preceding consonant, becoming final, takes a harsh and strong sound as though the letter was double, and a soft or sonant consonant becomes hard or mute. For instance, the masculine termination of the nominative singular was originally in all Arian languages an s, preceded by a short vowel, as, os, us. This final s was frequently dropped in modern languages. Thus bonus became in Italian bono; sunus, son, which still exists in Lithuanian, became sunu. Now this short vowel at the end would in Slavonic be written by Ъ; and originally this was intended for pronunciation. But as we find that, for instance, in French, bonus and bono became bon, so in Russian also the final vowel was suppressed in speaking. Yet the sign was retained in writing in order to indicate that the last consonant was to be pronounced harshly or, in some cases, like a double consonant. Syn, son, therefore, with Ъ at the end, was no longer to be sounded sunu but sunn; gladu, hunger, where *u* is written by Ъ, is pronounced glatt. The Ь, on the contrary, was originally a short i, and as the i exercises in Slavonic a mollifying influence on a preceding consonant, the letter Ь, where it is no longer pronounced as a vowel, causes the preceding, and now final, consonant to take a mouillé or slender sound.

Cyrillic Alphabet.	Numerical Value.	Corresponding letters of the Mission. Alphab.	Pronunciation in English.	Safarik's transcription.	Schleicher's transcription.	Russian.	Russian Pronunciation.	Bulgarian. Cankof.	Illyrian or Servian. Vuk.	Illyrian or Servian. Gaj & Berlic.	Polish.	Bohemian.	Hungarian.	Wallachian. Old.	Wallachian. New.	Wallachian. Alex.
35 Т	300	t	tan	t	t	Т *Т*	t or d	t	Т	t	t	t	t	Т	Т	t
36 Ѣ	..	ty	tune	t'	deest	....	....	...	Ђ	tj, or ć (like ci in Italian)	......	t'	ty like ti in metier	......	..	......
37 ОУ	..	u	full	u	u	У *У*	u in full	u	У	u	u	u, ů	u	Оу	Ү	u
38 Ȣ	..	u	full	u	u	....	....	...	......	......	......	......		Ȣ	..	......
39 Ф	500	f	fat	f, ph	ph	Ф *Ф*	f in fat, or ph	f	Ф	f (hv)	f	f	f	Ф	Ф	f
40 Х	600	'h	loch	ch	ch	Х *Х*	ch in loch	h (ch)	......	......	ch	ch	......	Х	Х	h
41	..	h	hand	...	.....	....	....	...	X, (if final, not pronounced)	h	h	h	h	......	..	......
42 Ѡ	..	o	note	ó	o	....	....	...	......	......	......	......	......	Ѡ	..	......
43 Ѿ	800	...	not	ot	deest	....	....	...	......	......	......	......	......	......	..	......
44 Ц	900	z	its	c	z, ts, c	Ц *Ц*	ts	c	Ц	c	c	c	cz	Ц	Ц	ţ, ç
45 Ч	..	*k*	church	č	tsch, č	Ч *Ч*	ch in church, or sh	č	Ч	č, like tch	cz	č	cs	Ч	Ч	ci, qui
46	..	.....	.....	...	.....	....	....	...	Ћ	ć, or tj, like Ital. c in cio	ć	......	......	......	..	......
47 Ш	..	*s*	she	š	sch, š	Ш *Ш*	sh in she	š	Ш	š	sz	ss, š	s	Ш	Ш	ş
48 Щ	..	*sk, st*	shch, sht	št, šč	scht	Щ *Щ*	sh, tsh, or sh	...	......	......	......	......	......	Щ	..	şt
49 Ъ	..	ŏ	favor	...	(ŭ)	Ъ *Ъ*	not pronounced: hardens the preceding letter	ă	......	......	......	......	......	Ъ	Ъ	ǎ, ě, ǐ, ǒ, ǔ
50 Ъl	..	ŏ (ŏi)	....	y	ui, y	....	....	...	......	......	......	......	......	......	..	......
51 Ы	..	ĕ (ei)	....	y	deest	Ы *Ы*	e in we	...	......	......	y like ü or e	y	......	......	..	......
52 Ь	..	ĕ	mother	...	ĭ	Ь *Ь*	not pronounced: softens the preceding letter	...	......	......	......	......	......	......	..	......
53 Ѣ	..	ie, ye	....	ě	je	Ѣ *Ѣ*	yea; or a in date, or e in bed, or yo	ĕ (ea)	e, Ѥ, je	je (ĕ, ie)	ė, like yeast	ě, like ie in niego	......	Ѣ ea	..	ia, ė
54	..	e	....	.....	.....	Э *Э*	e in end	e	Е	e (e, ė ä). as e in end, or e in father	e	e	......	......	..	......
55 Ю	..	yu	yule	ju	ju	Ю *Ю*	yu in yule, or ü	...	......	......	......	......	......	Ю	..	iu
56 Ꙗ	90	ya	yard	ja	ja	Я *Я*	ya in yard, or ye in yet, or e	...	......	......	......	......	......	Ꙗ	..	ia
57 Ѥ	..	ye	yea	je	je	....	....	...	......	......	......	......	......	......	..	......
58 Ѧ	..	*en*	elin	ę	ę	....	....	...	......	......	ę	......	......	Ѧ (ïa) ya	..	......
59 Ѫ	..	*ŏn*	on	ą	ą	....	....	...	......	......	ą	......	......	Ѫ (ä, ui), yu	..	......
60 Ѩ	..	*yĕn*	rien	ję	ję	....	....	...	......	......	......	......	......	......	..	......
61 Ѭ	..	*yŏn*	nation	ją	ją	....	....	...	......	......	......	......	......	......	..	......
62 Ѯ	60	ks, x	ks	x	x	....	....	...	......	......	x	x	......	Ѯ	..	......
63 Ѱ	700	ps	ps	ps	ps	....	....	...	......	......	......	......	......	Ѱ	..	......
64 Ѳ	9	th	th	th	th	Ѳ *Ѳ*	f	...	......	......	......	......	......	Ѳ, ft	..	......
65 Ѵ	400	i	ravine?	y	y	Ѵ *Ѵ*	i in ravine, or i in knit	...	......	......	......	......	......	Ѵ, i or v	..	......
66	..	....	.....	...	.....	....	....	...	......	......	......	......	......	Ⱥ like ŭng	î	......
67	..	ŭ	.....	...	.....	....	....	ě	......	......	......	......	......	......	..	......

(To page 49.)

Cyrillic Alphabet.		Numerical Value.	Corresponding letters of the Mission. Alphab.	Pronunciation in English.	Safarik's transcription.	Schleicher's transcription.	Russian.	Russian Pronunciation	Bulgarian. Cankof.	Illyrian or Servian. Vuk.	Illyrian or Servian. Gaj & Berlic.	Polish.	Bohemian.	Hungarian.	Wallachian. Old.	Wallachian. New.	Wallachian. Alexi.
1	А	1	a	psalm	a	a	А *А*	a in psalm; or e in debt, or o in note	a	А	a	a	a	a	Ꙗ	A	a
2	Б	..	b	bring	b	b	Б *Б*	b or p	b	Б	b	b	b	b	Б	Б	b
3		..	by	....	....	....	....	....	...	...	...	b́	...	...	...	..	...
4	В	2	v	veil	v	w	В *В*	v or f	v (w)	В	v	w	w (v)	v	В	В	v
5		..	vy	....	....	....	....	....	...	...	...	ẃ	...	...	...	..	...
6	Г	3	g	go	g	g	Г *Г*	g; or k, h, v	g	Г	g	g	ǧ (g)	g	Г	Г	g
7	Д	4	d	do	d	d	Д *Д*	d or t	d	Д	d	d	d	d	Д	D	d
8		..	g	gin	....	....	....	....	dž	Ђ	ǵ (dj) like gi in Italian	dź	...	...	Џ	Џ	gi
9		..	dz	....	....	....	....	....	...	Џ	dž (cž) only in Turkish words; like dsh	dz (dż)	...	...	...	..	...
10			dy	....	....	....			...	...	...	...	d', like dy	gy, like di in dieu	...	..	...
11	Є	5	e, ye	....	e	e	Е *Е*	yea; & a in date; or yo, & o in note	...	...	...	...	...	e	Ѥ, like yen, or è	E	e
12	Ж	..	ž	pleasure	ž	j, ż	Ж *Ж*	s in pleasure	ž	Ж	ž	ż like з	ž	zs	Ж	Ɉ	j
13			zy	....	....	....	....	....	...	...	...	ż like zy	...	...	...	..	...
14	Ѕ	6	z	zeal	z	z	....	....	...	...	...	...	...	...	Ѕ	..	...
15	Ꙁ	7	z	zeal	z	z	З *З*	z in zeal	z	З	z	z	z	z	З	Z	ḑ
16	И	8	i	ravine	i	i	И *И*	i in ravine & i in knit, or yea in year	i	И	i	i	í (j)	i	И	..	...
17	Ї	10	i	ravine	i	i	І *І*	i in ravine & i in knit									
18		..	i	....	....	....	Й *Й*	short final i	...	...		...	...	...	і	I	ì, è
19	І	..	y	yet	i, j	deest	....	....	j	Ј	j	j	g (j)	j	...	..	...
20	К	20	k	kite	k	k	К *К*	k	k	К	k	k	k	...	К	K	c, ch, qu
21	Л	30	l	let	l	l	Л *Л*	l or ll	l	Л	l	l, & ł hard	l	l	Л	L	l
22		..	ly	....	....	....	....	....	...	Љ	lj, like Ital. gl.		l'	ly, like il in email	...	..	...
23	М	40	m	man	m	m	М *М*	m	m	М	m	m	m	m	М	М	m
24		..	my	....	....	....	....	....	...	...	...	ḿ	...	...	...	..	...
25	N	50	n	not	n	n	Н *Н*	n	n	Н	n	n	n	n	Н	N	n
26		..	ny	....	....	....	....	....	...	Њ	nj, like Ital. gn.	ń	ň	ny	...	..	...
27	О	70	o	note	o	o	О *О*	o, in note, or a in psalm	o	О	o	o	o	o	О	O	o, ó
28		..	ou	....	....	....	....	....	...	...	...	ó like ou	...	...	...	..	...
29	П	80	p	pan	p	p	П *П*	p	p	П	p	p	p	p	П	П	p
30		..	py	....	....	....	....	....	...	...	...	ṕ	...	...	...	..	...
31	Р	100	r	run	r	r	Р *Р*	r	r	Р	r	r	r	r	Р	P	r
32		..	....	....	....	....	....	....	...	...	...	rz, like rsh	ř	...	...	..	...
33	С	200	s	sun	s	ſs	С *С*	s in sin, or z in zeal	ś (ss)	С	s	s	s	sz	С	S	s
34		..	sy	....	....	....	....	....	...	...	...	ś, like sy	...	...	...	..	...

Thus the old form esmi, which is still used in Sanskrit and Lithuanian, became in Russian yesmi, where the final is written by ь, but no longer felt as a vowel, except so far as it imparts an expiring vibration to the preceding consonant m.

The Russians used the Cyrillic alphabet to the time of Peter the Great. This great reformer struck off nine letters of the ancient alphabet as useless, gave the rest a more rounded form, had his new types cast in Holland, and printed the first Russian periodical with them at Moscow in 1704.

It has been the policy of Russia to support the introduction of her alphabet among the nations which in the course of time she expects to absorb. Still it is a curious fact that the whole Western branch of the Slavonic family, and some even of the Eastern Slaves (Bulgarians and Illyrians) have preferred the Roman or German alphabet, and have introduced it even where the Cyrillic letters had formerly been used.

Modern Greek.

While Latin, in its ancient history standing almost alone as the language of Italy, bursts out in this vast growth of dialects, Wallachian and Italian, Provençal and French, Spanish and Portuguese, the Hellenic languages, on the contrary, so rich in dialectic formations in ancient times, have come down to us only in one narrow stream, as the modern Greek. In Provençal, French, Italian, Wallachian, Spanish, and Portuguese we have as it were the diaries of several travellers, who all set out on the same journey, but, according to their individual tastes and characters, received different impressions, and noted down the various events in their passage from place to place in a different style and spirit. But in attempting to account for the new grammatical forms of the Greek language, we look in vain for that kind of collateral evidence which the six parallel dialects of the language of Rome offer in such abundance; so that if we cannot explain the new modes of expression by reference to the old common stock (ἡ Κοινή), we are left without further help. Happily, the changes which the language of Athens suffered in its transition from the ancient to the modern Greek, are less considerable by far than those experienced by the Latin during the vicissitudes of its historical and national development. Most of the new grammatical forms can still be recognised by a classical scholar. The declension of the ancient grammar has been almost entirely preserved. The conjugation, also, hardly contains any new elements. Some forms have gone out of use, as, for instance, the Dative in the declensions, the Dual in declension and conjugation, the Optative, and also to a great extent the old Infinitive. There are also some few periphrastic tenses which have found their way into the modern Greek; but they are by no means so perplexing as similar forms in the Romance dialects. Any one acquainted with the character of secondary formations in language, will understand at once the process by which compound tenses, such as ϑέλω γράψει, I shall write, ἤϑελα γράψει I should write, ἔχω γράψει I have written, εἶχα γράψει, I had written, have been formed. Θέλω in ancient Greek means I will, and though it is incorrect to say I will, instead of I shall, write, yet a foreigner is understood if he uses will, instead of shall. As to ἔχω, I have, and εἶχα, I had, these are the same auxiliaries which we find in our own and in most modern languages.

Albanian. The Albanian language, spoken within the limits of the ancient Illyricum in the north, and of Epirus in the South, offers one of the most difficult problems with regard to its origin and its relationship with other languages.

Xylander gives an account of the various opinions that have been proposed on this point, and their contradictory character will at least show the difficulty of the problem that has still to be solved.

Leibnitz supposed that the Albanians were of Celtic origin, and that their language was connected with that of Germany and Gaul.

Thunmann after remarking that the Albanians had been

derived by others from the Caucasus, from the Caspian Sea, and from Calabria; that they had been taken for Slaves, whether Chorwatians, Serbians, or Bulgarians, or for descendants of the ancient Illyrians and Macedonians, expresses his belief that the Albanians are the remnants of the ancient Illyrians, so long the neighbours of the Greeks, and the subjects of Rome. In the same manner he recognises in the Wallachians the descendants of the Thracians and Macedonians, and he ventures an opinion that these two languages, the Albanian and Wallachian, are mutually related.

Herder takes a similar view in declaring both the Albanians and Wallachians the remnants of one of the chief nations of ancient Europe.

The Illyrian origin of the Albanians is likewise supported by Ange Masci in his Essay "Sur l'origine de la nation albanaise", in Malte-Brun's Annales des Voyages. Malte-Brun himself remarks that Greek and Teutonic elements preponderate in Albanian, and that the traces of a Slavonic influence are small. He states it as his opinion that Albanian cannot be derived from any other known language, and that it must be considered as an independent idiom, the origin of which goes back to that antehistorical period in which the Greek, the Celtic, the Slavonic, and Teutonic branched off as independent national languages.

Adelung on the contrary imagines that, after separating the German, Slavonic, Roman, Greek, and Turkish ingredients, the remaining portion of Albanian is Tataric, and he derives the Albanians either from the Bulgarians, an originally Tataric race, or from a tribe, settled East of the Black-Sea, between the Caucasus and the river Cyrus, a tribe that had been identified with the Alanes of Southern Russia (see page 35), particularly because these Alanes had made inroads into Bulgaria and Thracia as late as 1308. In other places, however, he hints at a Thracian or Illyrian origin for the Albanians. Pouqueville admits the immigration of the Albanians from the country East of the Black Sea.

Vater again seems inclined to take Albanian as the modern form of a language as ancient as Latin, and connected with it by community of origin.

The following remarks are taken from Leake's Researches in Greece, London 1814.

"The Albanian", he says in his preface, "must be considered as holding a distinct character in the midst of the languages by which it is surrounded, being in all probability the ancient Illyric, with some alterations of the same kind as Latin and Greek have undergone from the Teutonic and Slavonian conquerors of Southern Europe."

In his Chapter on the Albanian Language, he writes, "Through the whole course of Grecian History, from its earliest records to the fall of the Constantinopolitan Empire, we find a people, distinct from the Greeks in race and language, inhabiting the North-Western side of the country, and extending along the ridges which border the sea-coast, or run parallel to it. They appear to have reached as far South as the Bay of Ambracia, for Scylax deems this gulf the northern boundary of Greece upon the West-side, and Thucydides calls the Amphilochi, who inhabited the hills at the head of it, barbarians; by this word implying that they spoke a language different from the Greek. The same historian also applies the word Barbarians to the people on the coast of Epirus, opposite to the island of Sybota, and Strabo informs us, that the Epirotic tribes were mixed with the Illyrian, and spoke two languages: meaning either that, like the greater part of the present Albanians, they used both the Greek and their own vernacular language, or that the Epirotic was distinct from the Illyrian tongue, and perhaps another dialect of the language, which was spoken throughout Macedonia and the neighbouring countries, before the letters and civilization of Greece had spread over these provinces. It would appear, that in Epirus, and that part of Illyricum, afterwards called New-Epirus, this change never took effect to so great a degree as it did in Thessaly and Macedonia; and that the lofty mountains and extreme ruggedness of this part of the country, have in all ages afforded to the remains of the Aborigines a security against intruders. This supposition is in a great measure confirmed by those remnants of a distinct language, which forms the basis of the modern Albanian dialect: and it is observable, that all the words, which resemble those of the same import in other modern languages, may be accounted for by the revolutions which brought so many foreign nations into Albania, or its vicinity; and that these extraneous words will be found to exist in the same proportion as the impression made upon the country by the several races of foreigners."

"Of the Greek words which occur in Albanian, a few have internal marks of having been adopted before the corruption of the language; a larger proportion afford the same evidence of having been taken from the Romaic Greek; and there are many also, whose forms, being the same both in the ancient and modern Greek dialect, are of uncertain date."

"Latin words are two or three times as numerous as Greek, but still much below the proportion in which they are found in the other modern languages of Europe. This may partly be accounted for by the secluded position and warlike habits of the mountaineers of Albania, which, defending them from being ever completely subjugated by the Romans, preserved their language like that of the Pyrinean and Cantabrian mountains, from ever receiving so large an admixture of Latin; and partly by the study of the Latin language, which has prevailed to so great an extent in civilized Europe since the revival of letters."

"The few words of Gothic origin, which exist in Albanian, must have come into use in the fifth century, when the Goths of Alaric became complete masters of the greater part of the two Epirus provinces, especially the Northern, where we afterwards find some of their descendants settled in quiet possession of a part of the country. One of these, named Sidismund, was in alliance with Theodoric the Great, when in his compaign against the Romans of the Eastern Empire, he entered Macedonia, and they procured for him, by stratagem, the city of Dyrrhachium. It also appears that the Goths were in great force in Dalmatia at the time when the Emperor Justinian the First made war upon them, and reannexed that province to the empire."

"About the same period, another tribe of strangers, who proved to be the most numerous, and the most formidable of any to the Greek emperors, began to make their appearance in the same part of the country. The Sclavonians, chiefly under the name of Bulgarians, continued their irruptions into the European provinces of the Empire during the seventh, eighth, and ninth centuries; and about the year 870, Achris, the ancient Lychnidus, was the residence of a King of Bulgaria, and the see of an Archbishop, whose spiritual authority extended to Kanina and Ierikhó, the ancient Orichus. In the tenth century the same race was settled at Nicopolis, the chief place of a Theme, which comprehended all old Epirus; and it appears, that about this time all the more accessible parts of Epirus, were occupied by strangers of Sclavonian origin. Until the last periods of the Greek empire, the Kings of Bulgaria and Servia continued to make occasional conquests and settlements in Greece, and even in the Morea: and they have, to this day, left traces of their long residence, by the numerous names of places of Sclavonian derivation to be found in every part of the country. It was in these ages of Bulgarian prowess, that the remains of the Illyrian and Epirotic nations became finally included within the boundaries, which they have ever since held. Many Sclavonian words then found their way into the Albanian language, and have been increased in number by the intercourse between Albania and the extensive regions of Servia and Bulgaria, which surround it on the North and East, and throughout which the Bulgarian dialect of Sclavonic is spoken. It may be thought surprising, perhaps, that under these circumstances, the proportion of the Sclavonian words is not larger, and it may be considered as a proof, that the strength of the Epirotic and Illyrian mountains, and the spirit of their inhabitants, were still equal, as in the time of the Romans, to protect them from being completely subdued."

"In 1079 the army of Nicephorus Basilaees, who was defeated by Alexius Comnenus, consisted of Franks, Bulgarians, Greeks (Ῥωμαῖοι) and Albanians (Ἀρβανῖται), all distinguished by their languages."

"The Franks had been invited from Italy by the Bishop of Deabolis. These were the first swarm of those Normans, who soon afterwards gave so much trouble to the Greek emperors. About the year 1185 the Norman Kings of Sicily occupied with their troops Thessaly, and a great part of Macedonia, and these monarchs obtained permanent possessions on the Western coast of Greece. In these operations, as well as throughout the whole course of the crusades, during 150 years, the coast of the present Albania was the frequent resort of the Franks, and Durazzo was very often their depot and place of retreat and safety. It is not surprising, therefore, that many words of French origin should have become indigenous in the Albanian language."

"The words derived from Italian, Turkish and the Romaic, will be sufficiently accounted for by the vicinity and the intercourse between the Albanians and these nations."

Arndt in his work on "the Origin of the European Languages", gives it as his opinion that Albanian might properly be considered as the aboriginal language of the country, because there is no evidence of an earlier language, except perhaps the Iberian. If Iberian was spoken there at a very early period, he thinks we might account for the similarity of many Albanian words with the Bask language. Again he finds coincidences between Albanian and Celtic, and he accounts for Greek, Roman, Slavonian and German admixtures either by later contact or by a community of origin between the Celtic and Indo-european languages.

Xylander himself begins by pointing out coincidences between Albanian words and Greek, ancient and modern, Latin, ancient and modern, German, Swedish, Danish,

English, the Slavonic dialects, Turkish, Bask, Celtic, Wallachian and Bulgarian, and Sanskrit. He states that Slavonic words form $^1/_{60}$, the Turkish $^1/_{18}$, the Greek $^1/_8$, the Teutonic $^1/_7$, the Latin $^1/_5$, of the Albanian dictionary which he was able to analyse. This would make more than one half of the Albanian dictionary of foreign origin, and there would still be subtracted other words which Arndt considers to be Celtic, Bask, and Tchudic. By an examination of the grammatical forms of Albanian, Xylander arrives at the following conclusions,

1) that the Albanian is not a mere jargon compounded of elements derived from the Romance languages;
2) that the Albanian is not a branch of the Tataric or Turanian family;
3) that the Albanian language does not contain a residuum of words of unknown origin, but that the greater portion of its words is Indo-Germanic or Arian.

He, therefore, inclines to a belief, first expressed by Thunmann, that the modern Albanian is the representative of the ancient Illyrian (or Thracian) language, and he places the Illyrian in the same category as Greek, Latin, Slavonic, and Celtic, as an independent branch of the great Indo-European family.

Territorial limits of Albanian and Modern Greek.

The Albanians call themselves Skipetars (from σκίπε mountain), while the Turks know them by the name of Arnauts, which is a corruption of Arbanites instead of Albanites. The province of Albania is surrounded on the North by Montenegro, Bosnia, and Servia; on the East by Macedonia and Thessaly; on the South by the Kingdom of Greece; on the West by the Ionic and Adriatic Seas. The limits of these dialects, the Modern Greek, the Albanian, the Turkish, Bulgarian and Wallachian, may be stated here according to Safarik and Griesebach, though subject to correction, from further researches.

West of Saloniki the Greek language is no longer heard; and Bulgarians inhabit the country thence to the frontier mountains of Albania. Greek is spoken very nearly in the same regions where it lived in ancient times, in the peninsula of Epirus and Macedonia, and in the Archipelago, whether on European or Asiatic soil. South of Janina, Greek is spoken in Albania, and its northern frontier proceeds thence across the chain of mountains between Thessalonia and Macedonia. Pouqueville heard Greek spoken along the Pindus. In Anasetitza, he says, they speak Greek; near Kastoria, Bulgarian. From the Olympus range the frontier line of Greek takes in a small portion of the coast as far as Saloniki, then turns towards Seres, and follows the southern branch of Rhodope till it reaches the meridian of Adrianople. All the country south and south-east of Adrianople as far as Marmora and the Straits, is Greek. The same line which reaches the Ægæan Sea near Saloniki, forms, with the exception of the Albanian, the southern frontier of the Slavonic languages, which extend northward towards the Danube — the Bulgarian in the east, the Servian in the west.

The Albanian extends from Janina, or rather, as in the town itself the principal language is Greek, and this very pure, from Conidsha in the valley of the Upper Viosa to the White Drin, somewhat beyond 42°. Its eastern frontier is the Pindus, extending in an almost uninterrupted line to 42°. Albanian villages, however, are found on the eastern declivity of the Pindus, and particularly in the north. Albanian here oversteps its natural frontier and encroaches on Bulgarian ground. Emigration has brought some Albanian colonies to the coast of Calabria and Sicily, where they fled from the persecutions of the Turks.

Besides the Albanian, Bulgarian, and Servian, which are the chief languages of Rumelia, Turkish is understood to a certain extent in almost all the towns and villages north of 40°; but it cannot be called the language of the country. Where, as in Rumelia, different dialects are mingled together, a necessity is felt for some means of communication intelligible to all. In Rumelia this is naturally the language of the conqueror, Turkish.

But the knowledge which an Albanian or Bulgarian acquires of this language, seldom goes beyond the number of words and phrases indispensable for commercial transactions and the carrying on of a scanty social intercourse. Villages purely Turkish are scarce in Epirus and Macedonia; and in many cases the people have adopted the Mahommedan religion, but maintained their national speech. The great towns are generally divided into quarters, according to language and religion. In Saloniki there is a considerable Jewish population, and Spanish is spoken there as much as Turkish. In the higher ranks of Greek society, Italian is learnt more usually than French. Some Greek merchants who have connections at Vienna, speak German; English is hardly ever studied, and natives conversing in it are more scarce in Greece than in any other part of Europe.

Professor Pott's opinion on Albanian.

The following remarks on the Albanian Language have been sent to me by Professor Pott, the celebrated author of the "Etymological Researches". Although the Albanian language occupies here perhaps more space than its practical or literary importance might seem to warrant, yet I believe that the opinion of one of the founders and highest authorities in Comparative Philology on the quaestio vexata of the origin of the Albanian, will be read with interest by many to whom his article on Dr. Hahn's work in the "Blätter für literarische Unterhaltung" is less accessible.

The language of the Albanians, the Arnauts, or, as they call themselves, the Shkipetars, is divided into two principal dialects, the Northern or Geghian, spoken in the ancient Illyria, and the Southern or Toskian, in Epirus. After the time of Skanderberg's heroic exploits, Albanian colonies took refuge in Southern Italy and Sicily, where Albanian is still spoken by their descendants. These Albanians in Italy possess even something like a literature, as may be seen in a work by Vicenzo Dorsa, Su gli Albanesi, Ricerche e Pensiere; and in an article by G. Stier in the "Kieler Monatsschrift", 1854. Girolamo di Rada, himself a poet, is likely to become the M'pherson of his nation, and has published several poems in Albanian. The New-Testament, published at Corfu, in 1827, is a translation in the Toskian dialect, while several works, printed by the Propaganda in the interest of the Roman-Catholic Albanians (see Leake, p. 268), are written in the Northern or Geghian idiom. The chief authority at present is Joh. George von Hahn, "Albanesische Studien", Vienna, 1853, 4°.

With regard to the Albanians the two principal questions that can be asked, are

1) Are they ancient aboriginal inhabitants of Europe, or do they belong to those numerous tribes who penetrated at a later period into the Byzantine Empire?
2) Is their language Arian (Indo-germanic) or not?

The second question is at present generally answered in the affirmative, for instance by G. Stier in the "Kieler Monatsschrift", 1854, p. 860—872, chiefly on account of the Numerals, the auxiliary verb, and the personal pronouns. The language, however, shows much that is foreign and strange, particularly in its dictionary, and in words which it cannot be suspected of having borrowed from other nations. Hence its right to be counted one of the Indo-germanic languages cannot be admitted without limitation and condition.

With regard to the first question, no doubt can remain at present, that the Albanian, together with the Moldavian and Wallachian, descends in a straight line from the ancient Illyrian. In the Wallachian language, the Illyrian element breaks through now and then, although it is smothered by the weight of the Latin language. The name, Illyrian, is no longer borne by these nations who have a right to it, while the Southern Slaves, the Kroatians, and Slavonians have assumed it with a kind of learned conceit, having no claim to it, by nationality or language, but only, perhaps, by their geographical position.

The old Illyrian is one of the most comprehensive and most ancient stocks of Europe, though at present it exists only as a ruin. In this respect it is like the

Iberian, represented by the small remnant of the Basks, and the Rhaetian, probably closely allied with the Etruscan.* The interest of this Illyrian stock is greatly increased because, from the most ancient times, it occupied the same seats as the Hellenic nations. Nay it probably preceded the Hellenes in its occupation of the Greek peninsula, and was afterwards broken by the Hellenic tribes pressing onward from the North, and partly displaced. If the famous name of Pelasgoi had really an ethnic meaning, and were not an unsubstantial and merely chronological designation of early Aborigines in general, the Illyrians would best answer to this name. The Dacians and Getae (wrongly identified by J. Grimm, in his history of the German Language with the Goths); the Thracians, perhaps even the Macedonians, with their decidedly non-Hellenic speech; the Panonians, and even the Veneti and other Illyrian settlers in Italy, belonged to the Illyrian stock, and with all of these the Albanians must be considered as more or less related. This gives a vast importance to this small remnant of an ancient European nationality.

They were recognised as Illyrians by Thunmann and others; by Kopitar in his well-known article on the Albanian, Wallachian and Bulgarian (Wiener Jahrbücher, 1829, p. 59—106); by Xylander, by Hahn, and lastly by myself. Little is known of the ancient Illyrian language; but Dioscorides, for instance (IV, 37) mentions μαντεία as the Dacian name of the bramble. In Albanian bramble is μάνε φέρρε (Hahn, p. 140) from man (morus), and ferra (sentis), given by Bianchi. Mandë, mulbery-tree, a cognate word, approaches still more closely to the name given by Dioscorides. Again the

* See on this subject the important work of L. Steub, "On Rhaetian Ethnology", Stuttgardt, 1854, 8vo. The author has thrown considerable light on names of places in the Tyrol, Vorarlberg and the neighbouring Alpine countries. Besides the German and the strangely disfigured Romance names, he separates a third class of names, inexplicable in themselves, but showing a startling similarity with Etruscan forms.

uniform post-position of the article in Albanian, Wallachian, and Bulgarian is rightly pointed out by Kopitar as a proof of a most energetic and primitive use of the article in the Danubian countries. If in your work on the Classification of the Turanian Languages, p. 5, you explain domnul in Wallachian as Latin dominus ille, this is right in itself, but we must still ask, how came the Wallachians, alone among all the Romance languages, to place the article in so peculiar a manner, and we may best answer this by supposing that like the Slavonic idiom of the Bulgarians, it followed the example of the Illyrian or Albanian syntax with which it came in contact. A good parallel to this is found in Jutland, where against the genius of the Danish language, a prepositive article is used, evidently through the influence of the German. Thus à Mand, the man, à Barn, the child, instead of Danish mand*en*, barn*et*. I have summed up this linguistic problem elsewhere in the following manner.

I. Wallachians, Moldavians, Transylvanians, on one side, and Albanians on the other, form a common national stock, as far as their blood, not as far as their language is concerned, "the Old Illyrian." Whether this stock belonged originally to the Indo-germanic family or not, it was certainly unconnected with the Greek, or any other Indo-germanic stock, and claims an independent origin.

II. All these nations are neither Gothic nor Slavonic, nor, like the Magyars, of Finnic origin, nor Turks * (as for instances the Kumani were, if we may judge by a vocabulary, originally in the possession of Petrarca, and published by Klaproth in his Mem. Asiat.), nor Barbarians, pushed forward by the Great Migrations of the fifth Century A.D., nor anything in fact, but Autochthones, in the same sense in which the Greek inhabitants of

* What Mr. Latham, according to the "Athenaeum", 1854, Jan. p. 122, brings forward with regard to an identity of Dacians and Turks, does not hold good. Turkish tribes in those parts of Europe are of later date, as may be seen from Klaproth's Asia Polyglotta.

that Eastern peninsula of Europe may be called so, although of course mixed to a greater extent.

III. The Wallachian, as we know it, is decidedly a Romanic language, like Italian, and the other more Western daughters of Latin. It owes its origin chiefly to Roman colonies, sent into Dacia by Trajan, though there were earlier Roman conquests which may not have been without effect on the language of Dacia. The Provinciales of Gaul (Celtic by origin, or, as Holzmann endeavours to prove, Germanic) and of Spain (originally Iberian), were deprived of their ancient languages, while their bodies, with the exception of a small infusion of Roman blood remained Celtic and Iberian, haunted, as it were, by a Roman ghost. The Wallachians and Albanians offer an exact parallel to the French together with the Bas Bretons, or to the Romanising Spaniard together with the Basks. In the French and Spanish Languages the ancient Celtic and Iberian words have melted away almost entirely, while the Bask is still Iberian, and the Bas-Breton Celtic. The same applies to the romanised Wallachian side by-side with the more primitive Albanian. Yet both the Wallachians and Albanians are in blood descendants of the ancient Illyrians.

IV. Albanian and Wallachian contain, besides some few syntactic coincidences, nearly the same elements in their dictionaries, only in different proportions. In Albanian the original Illyrian element preponderates, in Wallachian it is represented by a very small percentage. The Latin preponderates in Wallachian, but it exercised the same influence on the Albanian, different only in degree, but not in kind. Whether the Latin influenced the Albanian directly, or indirectly through the Wallachian, is still uncertain. Of the Turkish the Albanian contains much, the Wallachian little; the latter has instead a small ingredient of Magyar words. Greek is found in both: in Wallachian, chiefly through ecclesiastical influences, in Albanian through commercial and political intercourse, and then generally Modern or Romaic. Some medieval and Byzantine terms will find their explanation by a reference to Du Cange. Whether the ancient Illyrian borrowed from the ancient Greek and vice versâ, is doubtful, but of great importance in settling the question of the origin and ethnological position of the Albanians. Finally the Wallachian has admitted many, the Albanian a few Slavonic words."

Besides the Celtic, and the two classial languages, Greek and Latin (sometimes comprised under the common title of Pelasgic), we have in Europe two other mighty branches, the Teutonic and Slavonic, both belonging to the Arian stem. Teutonic languages.

The Teutonic is divided into three dialects, the Low-German, the High-German, and Scandinavian.

The oldest documents of the Low-German exist in Gothic. The Gothic translation of the New Testament by Ulphilas belongs to the 4th century. The Saxon, which equally belongs to the Low-German class, is represented on the continent by the Old Saxon, formerly spoken in the north of Germany, the only important document of which is the Heljand, a poem of the 9th century. After the 5th century, Saxon was transplanted to the British Isles, and produced a literature of which the earliest documents are referred to the 7th century. Low-German Branch

Other dialects belonging to the Low-German class are Friesic, rapidly dying out, but once spoken on the Elbe and along the northern coast of Germany; Dutch, the language of Holland, and Flemish, now nearly absorbed by French in Belgium. Several Low-German dialects (Platt-deutsch) are still spoken in different parts of Germany, but since Luther, Low-German has gradually ceased to be used as a literary language, and it is only in the lower ranks that it maintains its existence. Most of the sailors along the coast of the Baltic Sea speak Low-German, which is more intelligible to an Englishman than the literary language of Germany. At Hamburg, Lübeck, on the island of Rügen, and along the Pommeranian coast, at Dantzig, and as far as Königsberg, the whole class with which the English sailors are likely to mix, speaks a language which a German educated at Berlin or Vienna would hardly find easier to understand than an Englishman.

High-German Branch. The High-German class comprises the Old High-German from the 7th to the 11th century; the Middle High-German from the 12th century to Luther, and the New High-German, since Luther, the literary language of Germany.

The Scandinavian branch is represented in ancient times by the Old Norse, the language of Norway, and (by colonization in the ninth century) of Iceland. In that island the old language has suffered less from alterations than in its original locality, and is spoken to the present day. On the Continent the Old Norse expanded into three different dialects, Norwegian, Swedish, and Danish, of which the first has now become a mere patois, leaving Danish and Swedish the two literary representatives of the Scandinavian tongue.

No language has sent so many colonies throughout the world as Teutonic. Germans are to be met with in Algiers, on the coast of Guinea, and on the Cape of Good Hope; German colonies are settled in Australia and New Zealand, in Java and Sumatra, in the interior of Russia, in the Crimea, in the Valleys of the Caucasus, in North and South America. But the mightiest branch of the Teutonic stem has been the Anglo-Saxon. It has stretched its boughs from England across the Atlantic to overshadow the new Continent of America. It is the language of civilisation in India, it preaches the gospel on all the coasts of Africa, and Australia is receiving in it her first laws. On all the five Continents it is the language that grows and conquers, the language of the future, the language of the world. Grimm speaks thus:—"None of the modern languages has through the very loss and decay of all phonetic laws, and through the dropping of nearly all inflections, acquired greater force and vigour than English, and from the fulness of those vague and indefinite sounds, which may be learned, but can never be taught, it has derived a power of expression such as has never been at the command of any human tongue. Begotten by a surprising union of the two noblest languages of Europe, the one Teutonic, the other Romanic, it received that wonderfully happy temper and thorough breeding, where the Teutonic supplied the material strength, the Romanic the suppleness and freedom of expression. Nay the English language, which has borne, not as it were by mere chance, the greatest Poet of modern times, great in his very contrast with ancient classical poetry, — I speak of course of Shakespeare—this English language may truly be called a world-language, and seems, like England herself, but in a still higher degree, destined to rule over all the corners of the earth. In wealth, wisdom, and strict economy, none of the living languages can vie with it."

We shall now consider the last branch of the Arian family, commonly called Slavonic—a language spoken over vast tracts of country, on the confines of Asia and Europe, on the threshold between barbarism and civilisation, and as yet without a national literature in any of its numerous branches, though not without its counterfeits of Voltaire and Byron, of Wieland and Göthe:—with powerful resources, and flexible as Greek and Latin; yet all, as it were, without self-respect and self-dependence, always looking abroad and vainly decking itself with the tinsel of foreign countries, instead of gathering strength from within and putting forth without shame the genuine fruits of its own not barren soil. This applies particularly to the modern Russian, for Bohemian and Polish may boast in a certain sense of an ancient national literature and of an advanced civilisation which was crushed by political misfortunes. There are signs also in Bohemia and in parts of Russia, of an awakening national feeling in literature and of a healthy reaction against foreign influences. Windic languages.

It would be better to use Windic as the general name of what is now called the Slavonic branch, Winidae being one of the most ancient and most comprehensive names by which these tribes were known to the early historians of Europe. We have to distinguish again between the Lettic and the Slavonic divisions, and it would be preferable not to use Slavonic in two different senses.

Lettic Division. I. The Lettic division comprises the Lithuanian, the Old Prussian, and the Lettish. The Lithunian, as we had occasion to point out before, is one of the most interesting languages to the comparative philologist, because, though poor in literature—(for the Lithuanian popular songs are all that can be called such in a national sense) — it has retained to the present day some of the most primitive features of Arian grammar. It was once spoken, according to Mielcke, within the limits of East Prussia, in the districts of Memel, Tilsit, Ragnit, Labiau, and Insterburg; and through the division of Poland, more Lithuanian subjects were added to the kingdom of Prussia, so that the number of Prussians, who speak Lithuanian, is now stated at 200,000. But this amount, is diminishing steadily, and in one or two generations Lithuanian will probably have to be counted among the dead languages, like Cornish in England. In Russia, the number of Lithuanians is estimated at 1,282,000.

Prussian. The Old Prussian has been an extinct language since the end of the 17th century. Formerly spoken on the Northern coast, East of the Vistula, it has left no literature behind, except a translation of a catechism.

Lettish. Lettish is the language of Kurland and Livonia, more modern in its grammar than Lithuanian, and standing towards it, not in the relation of daughter to mother, but rather of niece to aunt.

The entire number of persons who speak Lithuanian and Lettish, in Prussia and Russia, is estimated by Safarik at 2,000,000. North of Memel the English fleet will hear Lithuanian and Lettish spoken at Liebau, in the Gulf of Riga. On the northern side of the Gulf, the Lettish is bounded by the Esthonian, a Finnic dialect, which occupies all the rest of the coast as far as Kronstadt and Petersburg. The Lettic as well as the Esthonic population supply a considerable contingent to the Russian navy.

The Slavonic branch is divided again into two great dialects, each represented by a number of national idioms. These are the South-Eastern and Western dialects, and may be distinguished by certain phonetic peculiarities. Slavonic Branch.

I. The South-Eastern dialect comprises:

1. The Russian, divided again into Great-Russian, Little-Russian, and White-Russian.
2. Bulgarian, represented under its most ancient form in the Ecclesiastical Slavonic, and spoken at present in the province of Bulgaria, one seat of the war. The Ecclesiastical Slavonic is the language of the translation of the Bible by Cyrillus in the 9th century, which we have in Mss. of the eleventh. It was formerly considered as the root of all Slavonic dialects, but it is really the parent of the Bulgarian only. This is Safarik's opinion. Micklosich calls the Ecclesiastical Slavonic "lingua Palæo-Slovenica", and Kopitar also considers it as a Carinthian dialect; but neither of these scholars has brought proofs convincing as those by which Safarik establishes the close connection between the present Bulgarian and the language of Cyrillus.
3. The Illyrian, which is a general name for the Servian, Kroatian, and Slovenian. The Servian is written either with Roman or with Cyrillic letters. The former is patronised by the Roman, the latter by the Greek Church. The Slovenian comprises the Windian, Carniolian, Carinthian and Styrian idioms. The Kroatian, according to Safarik, should not be reckoned as a separate language; the provincial Kroatian being but a continuation of the Slovenian, while the language of the Kroats, as spoken on the military frontier, is simply Servian.

II. The Western dialect comprises:

1. Polish.
2. Bohemian or Tchechian, spoken in Bohemia,

Moravia and Hungary, and of which the Slovakian, found in Hungary, is but a less developed remnant.

3. Wendian or Sorbian, as spoken in Upper and Lower Lusatia.
4. Polabian, an extinct language, formerly in existence on the Elbe.

Relation of the South-Eastern and Western Slavonic languages.

Although it is possible to point out characteristic marks by which these two great dialects can be kept separate, still in their grammar and words they differ much less than English and German. People who speak languages belonging to the Western or South-Eastern division, are to a certain extent mutually intelligible. A Bohemian, according to *Safarik*, understands a Slovak of Hungary, a Slovak understands the Polish, a Pole the language of Lusatia. The same applies to Russians and Illyrians: less to the Bulgarians. But even the Russian and the Pole, though belonging to different divisions, have so many words and grammatical forms in common that they do not find much more difficulty in conversing together than Italians and Spaniards. Panslavistic writers maintain that the various Slavonic dialects do not differ more widely than the four principal dialects of the ancient Greek — Attic, Ionic, Doric, and Æolic. As we go back into antiquity, the differences between the Slavonic languages become even less: yet from the ninth century, when we have the first literary documents, the fundamental distinction between South-Eastern and Western dialects is clearly established. A Russian, however, at the present day, can, with some attention, understand the Bulgarian of the ninth century, as fixed in the translation of the Bible, still used in all Russian churches. I shall here give some of these characteristic differences as laid down by *Safarik*. It will be seen that they can be of real importance only for the minutest researches of the philologist, yet as "pièces justificatives" they may find a place here.

I. In the South-Eastern dialects d and t before l are dropped; they are retained in the Western branch.

Ex. Eccles. Slav. орд-ло, ora-lŏ, a plough; Bohem. ora-dło. (cf. ἄρο-τρον, aratrum.) Eccl. Slav. падъ, palŏ fallen, participle of the root pad, to fall, with the termination lŏ; Bohemian padł.

II. In the South-Eastern dialects d and t are dropped before n; they are retained in the Western branch.

Ex. Russian, ВЯНУШІ, Bohemian vadnouti, from the root ВЯД, vad, and нуть, nutě.

III. In the South-Eastern dialects an l is put before every palatal semi-vowel (y), if preceded by a labial; this is not the case in the Western branch (l epentheticum).

Ex. Eccl. Slav. zemly (землꙗ), earth; Polish ziemia. Eccl. Sl. korablyě, (корабль); Pol. and Boh. korab', ship.

Other words by which the difference between an Eastern and Western dialect can be recognized are, according to Dobrowsky, (Bohemian Grammar, iv. and Institutiones, § 1),

SOUTH-EASTERN.	WESTERN
1. raz, razum.	roz, rozum.
2. iz, izdati.	wy, wydàti.
3. peč, moč, noč.	pec, moc, noc.
4. zwiezda.	hwiezda, gwiazda.
5. toj.	ten.
6. Genitive, ago.	ego, eho.
Dative, omu.	emu.
7. ptika.	ptak.

Area occupied by Slavonic languages.

The area at present occupied by the Slavonic race, extends from Asia into Europe, from the Dwina in the East to the frontiers of Germany in the West, from the Sea in the North to the Sea in the South of Europe. Slavonic names of cities and rivers in the interior of Germany, show that these races once were in occupation as far west as the Elbe; and Slavonic dialects are still spoken, though by small and disconnected tribes, in Lusatia, not far from Berlin and Leipzig. But while the Slavonic race has been repulsed in the West, it has extended itself in the East towards Asia, and is now the language of law and civilization in the North of Asia, whence it stretches over to America.

South-Eastern languages. Russian.

The language, politically most important among the Slavonic races, is the **Russian**. It is hemmed in on the West by the Polish, Hungarian, and Wallachian languages. In the North and South it reaches as far as the sea, and in the East it encroaches upon Finnic and Tataric populations. We shall give the geographical limits of the three Russian dialects, that of the **Great-Russians**, the **Little-Russians**, and **White-Russians**, as determined by *Safarik*, on grammatical grounds: because these three originally different races, can at present be distinguished by the pecularities of their dialects only.

Great-Russians.

The Great-Russians inhabit the governments of Moscow, Petersburg, Novgorod, Vologda, Pskov, Tver, Yaroslav, Kostroma, Vladimir, Nizhni Novgorod, Smolensk, Kaluga, Tula, Riazan, Penza, Simbirsk, Orel, Kursk, Voronezh, Tambov, Saratov, and the country of the Cossacks of the Don. The greatest part of the governments of Orenburg, Viatka, Perm, and Kasan, is inhabited by the same race, which daily absorbs more and more the remnants of the Finnic nations, and of the Tatars yet extant in those provinces. A line drawn from Lake Peipus to the mouth of the Don, would very nearly mark the frontier of the Great-Russian towards the Little and White-Russian dialects. Great-Russians are, further, spread over all Siberia, Kamchatka, and the Russian colonies on the north-western coast of America. There are many settlements of the Great-Russians in various parts of ancient Poland, formed under the Polish dominion by the Raskolniks or Russian sectarians, who fled from their country on account of religious persecution. A few of the same kind exist beyond the Danube in the Turkish dominions. The Great-Russian idiom is now the literary and official language of Russia.

Little-Russians.

The **Little Russians** or Russines resemble, in their physical and moral qualities other Slavonic nations more than their namesakes. Their language differs from the Muscovite idiom, and forms, in some measure, a transition between that and Polish. Nestor calls them Polanes, which signifies inhabitants of the fields (Campani), and asserts they are of the same nation as the Lekhs of the Vistula, i.e. the Poles. Their language is said to be one of the finest Slavonic tongues, few equalling its power in the expression of tender feelings, and their literature, though limited to popular songs and ballads, replete with poetical beauties. The Russines inhabit the Russian governments of Poltava, Kharkov, Tchernigov, Kiev, Volhynia, Podolia, and parts of those of Ekaterinoslav, Voronezh, Kherson, Taurida, and Bessarabia, as well as the country of the Cossacks of the Black Sea. In the kingdom of Poland, they occupy parts of the provinces of Lublin and Padlachia. In Gallicia, or Austrian Poland, the circles of Lemberg, Przemysl, Zloczov, Zolkiev, Tarnopol, Brzezany, Sambor, Sanok, Stry, Stanislawow, Kolomea, Czortkow, and in part those of Rzeszow, Novysandec, and Tchernowitz. In Hungary, the greater part of the comitats of Beregh, Unghvar, Ugocza, and Marmaros, and a small portion of those of Zemplin and Szaros. It is the dialect of the South of Russia from Gallicia to the Don. The Rusniaks or Ruthenians in Gallicia, Hungary, and Bukovina speak the Little-Russian dialect: though with some peculiarities.

White-Russians.

The White-Russians occupy the whole of the Russian Governments of Mohilev and Minsk, and the greatest part of those of Vitepsk and Grodno, extending even over a part of those of Vilna and Bialystok. Their dialect was formerly the official language of Lithuanian, and is full of Polish expressions. They are called White-Russians in opposition to the original Russian race, inhabiting the central provinces of Russia which are still called Black-Russia (Czernaja Rusj).

Although the Cossack repudiates the idea of being descended from either the Great or the Little-Russians, he has been proved to be Great-Russian by blood, though considerably mixed with Little-Russian. Köppen (p. 152) accounts for this mixture by the war against the Turks in 1569. The Turks had invested Astrachan, and Czar Johann IV, called on Prince Michajlo Wishnewezkij to assist him. The army of Prince Michajlo was chiefly collected at Tcherkassy in the Government of Kiev, whence the name of Tcherkassian or Tcherkaskian for the Little-Russian peasants on the Don; hence also the name of the chief city in the country of the Don-Cossacks, Tcherkask, founded in 1570, and rebuilt, as Novo Tcherkask in 1805. Antiquities which are found in the neighbourhood attest the former presence of various tribes in this part of Russia. Inscriptions were found here belonging to the Bosporian Kings Rhoemetalkes (132—154 A. D.) and Ininthimaeos (237 A. D.). They were published by Graefe in the Memoires de l'Académie des Sciences de St. Petersbourg; VI. Série; Sciences politiques, T. VII (1844, 3), p. 24. Ancient stone images have been also found in the steppes, and now serve the inhabitants as scarecrows. The races to which these idols belonged, the nations ruled by the Bosporian kings, and in more modern times, tribes even from the Caucasus, have all contributed their share toward the formation of the Cossack, and hence the conflicting opinions as to his real nationality.

Bulgarians. The territory on which Bulgarian is spoken at the present day lies almost entirely within the Turkish dominions; only a small area to the North of the arms of the Danube being under Russian sovereignty. Eastward the Bulgarian is bounded by the Black Sea; from the mouth of the southern arm of the Danube this river forms the northern frontier towards the Wallachians as far as Widin and Florentin, with the exception of the tract between the towns of Tultch and Reni, where the Bulgarian extends across the river towards Russia. The frontier is here indicated by the towns of Ismail, Kalpak, Faltchi, and thence southwards along the river Pruth, which here forms the frontier between Russia and Moldavia, and between the Wallachians and the Bulgarians down to the Danube. From Widin the frontier extends along the Servian territory as far as Prizren (Perserin), and hence southward past the towns of Tettovo, Ochrida, Drenovo, Bilista (or Bichlista) as far as St. Marina; hence the Southern frontier line forms a slight bend round the Gulf of Thessalonica, and thence continues in the direction of the towns of Rupa, Arda, Tchermenti, Adrianople, Tirnovo, and Vasiliko to the Black Sea again. Thus the Bulgarians occupy the greater part of the ancient Moesia, Thracia, and Macedonia, or the present province of Rumelia. The name Bulgarian was transferred to the original Slavonic inhabitants of that country after they were conquered by the Bulgars, an Uralic race, towards the end of the 7th Century. The Slavonic element, however, began soon to prevail over that of the foreign conquerors, and after two hundred years, nothing but the name indicated the barbarous origin of the prospering Bulgarian Kingdom. In the middle of the ninth Century Christianity began to spread over the country and the translation of the Bible by Methodius and Cyrillus was the forerunner of other literary works. This incipient civilisation, however, was destroyed by the inroads of the Magyars in the beginning of the eleventh Century. Before the arrival of the Magyars, the Plawzi and Pechenegs, that is during the ascendancy of the Bulgarian kingdom, the Bulgarian language was spoken beyond its present limits in the countries along the Danube, now inhabited by Magyars and Wallachians. It extended from the Danube to the Pruth and Jager, and beyond to the Karpathian mountains and the sources of the Theiss. When these countries lying North of the Danube were inundated by the Magyars and similar Finnic tribes, the original inhabitants retired below it. The Bulgarian of the 9th Century, the language of the translation of the Bible by Cyrillus, remained the literary language of Russia to the 14th Century, and is still the ecclesiastical language of the Greek-Russian church in Russia, Servia and Bulgaria. It holds the same place in Slavonic philology which Gothic occupies in the history of the German idioms. The spoken Bulgarian, on the contrary, so far as grammatical forms are concerned, is the most reduced among the Slavonic dialects.

Illyria

Illyrian is used as a general name to comprehend the Servian, Kroatian and Slovenian dialects. The name Illyria was revived by Napoleon in 1809. Illyrian implies sometimes the Slovenian and Kroatian, as opposed to the Servian. Religious and political agitation has made "Illyrian" the watchword for the Roman Catholic population of these South-Slavonic countries; "Servian" that of the Greek church; the former using the Roman, the latter the Cyrillic alphabet. Another party, the Panslavistic, allows no difference between Illyrians and Servians, whether in nationality or language. These South-Slavonic dialects are spoken West of Bulgaria, occupying the western half of the peninsula to the Adriatic, while the Bulgarian occupies the eastern part towards the Black Sea.

Area occupied by the Illyrian dialects.

A rough outline of the whole Illyrian territory would be formed by a line drawn from the Adriatic Sea, near the mouth of the Bojana River, to Perserin (Prizren) in Albania, this line being somewhat inclined towards the North. A line from Perserin to Widin on the Danube would separate the Illyrian (here Servian) from the Bulgarian. A line from Widin to Temesvar would divide the Illyrian from the Wallachian; and a line from Temesvar to Klagenfurt from Magyar and German neighbours. A line from Klagenfurt back to Trieste would close the circle within which Illyrian dialects are to be met with. The Adriatic coast is partly occupied by Italian dialects, which encroach upon the Slavonic in the north, but diminish gradually in breadth as we proceed southward.

These frontiers, however, are far too narrow for the national aspirations of what may be called the Young-Illyrian party. The founder of this party is Dr. Ludewit Gaj, the editor of a newspaper which has become the standard of the literary Illyrian language. In Illyria, in Styria, in Dalmatia, in Croatia, Slavonia, and Servia, there existed not long ago about twenty different dialects, and each had in certain localities assumed the dignity of a literary language with its own peculiar orthography. It was in 1835 that Gaj began the publication of his Croatian Newspaper, which originally addressed itself to the provincial Croatians only. In 1836, however, this assumed the title of a National Illyrian Newspaper, appealing no longer to the provincial Croatians alone, but to all who in Dalmatia, Istria, Croatia, Slavonia, Servia, Bosnia, Montenegro, Carniola, Carinthia and Styria spoke the common Illyrian language. "The poorer and less cultivated provincial Croatian, he says, must make room for the rich and harmonious Illyrian language, as spoken by the people and fixed by early writers, and at the same time a more rational orthography must be introduced." This attempt has been successful, and instead of many Croatian and Windian dialects, the Southern Slaves have gained a common national and cultivated language.

Gaj has found many followers, and Agram has become the literary capital of Illyria. Hungarian intolerance has strengthened the unity of his party, which has further a certain political importance. His enthusiastic followers speak of an "Illyria", of which the frontiers are the Adriatic, the Aegaean, and the Black Sea, and which comprises Carinthia, Carniola, Styria, Görz, Istria, the Litorale, Dalmatia, Ragusa, Montenegro, Herzegovina, Bosnia, Serbia, Croatia, Slavonia, the Banat with the South of Hungary, part of Albania, Bulgaria, and even the northern districts of Macedonia. This Illyria, however does not yet exist; in fact the unbounded enthusiasm of its advocates has provoked a natural reaction from the very nations which it meant to embrace. The Servians, particularly, object to the name of Illyrians, and maintain their own nationality, which is supported by a difference of religion (the Servians belonging to the Greek church), and by a difference of alphabet (the Servians adhering to the Cyrillic letters). This natural division between the Illyrians, i. e. the Croatians and Sloventzi on the one side, and the Servians on the other, will prove a strong impediment to the realisation of the Great-Illyrian nationality.

Frontier between the Servians and the Illyrians.

If we make this distinction between Illyrians and Servians, the Illyrians will be separated by a line beginning from the town Monoschtur, at the mouth of the river Lobnitza (Lafnitz) which falls into the Raab, in the Comitat Eisenburg in Hungary. This line extends along that river while it forms the limit between Hungary and Styria, then turns into Styria and Illyria, passing the towns of Radkersburg, Völkermarkt, Klagenfurt, Villach, to Pontafel; thence southward, along the small towns of Resciutta, and Bardo, towards Udine, and then, following pretty closely the course of the Isonzo to the Adriatic sea, it extends along the sea-coast until below Capo d'Istria. Here it takes an eastern direction, passing the towns of Materia, Laas, and the German colony of Gotschze (Hoczewje) to Neustädtel, Mötting, Petrinia, and the mouth of the Unna, which falls into the Save on the Turkish frontier. Hence it recedes northwards past the towns of Novka, Chasma, and Belovar, until it reaches Verücze on the Drave, behind which river it touches the Magyar frontier at Gross-Scigeth. Here it runs west again, past the towns of Breznitz, Kanisa, Lindava (Lendva) and Csesztreg, until it rejoins Monoschtur. The smaller or eastern portion of this territory is inhabited by Kroats or Chorwats, and the larger and western portion by the Sloventsi.

Kroatian. The Kroatian or Chorvatian dialect is chiefly spoken in the Comitats of Agram, Kreuz, and Warasdin, and numerous colonies exist in the western parts of Hungary. The language stands between Slovenian and Servian, more closely allied to the latter, and at present, particularly at Agram, influenced by a small literary party, who endeavour to introduce Slovenian and Cyrillic expressions into the spoken language of the people. Thus the Dual, which according to Berlić is unknown in the spoken language of Kroatia, and exists only in Slovenian, has been introduced into literary works, and terminations are used in the declensions which have a warrant only in the Cyrillic translation of the Bible.

Slovenian. Slovenian, also called Corutanian or Windian, is spoken in the country surrounded by the Adriatic, the Upper Drave and Kroatia. It is the language of a great part of Styria, Carinthia, and Carniola, and reaches into the west of Hungary, the Illyrian coast and part of Istria.

Servian. The territory occupied by the Servians is bordered on the west by the Adriatic from Capo d'Istria to the river Bojana. The southern frontier separating the Servians from the Albanians, extends from the lake of Scutari towards the towns of Rosalia, Ipek, and Jakova, as far as Prizren (Perserin). Here begins the eastern frontier towards the Bulgarians, passing the towns of Morava, Nova Berda, and Nissa, as far as Gurguchevatz, and following thence the Timok, the boundary until it falls into the Danube. The Danube then forms the limit towards the Wallachians, as far as Golubatch, where the line crossing that river extends past the towns of Szaszka, Weisskirchen, Denta, Ritberg, and Temesvar, as far as Arad: then westward along the small towns of Lak, Marienfeld, Kaniza, Topolya, and Mohacz to Scigeth, and along the Illyrian frontier to Capo d'Istria.

This extensive area comprises within the Austrian dominions the southern Comitats of Hungary, the whole of Slavonia, a great part of Kroatia and Carniola, Istria, the Littoral, Dalmatia and the military frontier of Kroatia, Slavonia, and Hungary,—and within the Turkish dominions, the principalities of Servia, Bosnia, Herzegovina, Montenegro, and the ancient Rascia (the territory between Novi Bazar and Nova Berda). The Servian population belongs partly to the Roman Catholic and Greek persuasions, partly to the Mohammedan. There is a sprinkling of Magyars, Germans, Italians, Albanians, Turks, Wallachians, and Rusnyaks over the whole of Servia. On the other hand there are considerable Servian colonies in Hungary and Russia. The most important is that of "New Servia" on the Dniepr, founded between 1751—53. It consists of about 100,000 inhabitants.

According to Vuk Stephanowitch the Servian is divided into three dialects:

1. The dialect of Herzegovina, Bosnia, Montenegro, Dalmatia, Kroatia, and the upper part of Servia, in the district of Matchwa, as far as Maljewo and Karanowatz.

2. The Ressawian dialect, spoken in the district of Branitshevo, on the Resava, in the district of Levatsh, on the Upper Morava, and along the Schwarzbach, as far as Negotin.

3. The Syrmian, spoken in Syrmia, Slavonia, in the Batchka, in the Banat of Temesvar, and in Servia, between the Save, the Danube, and the Morava.

The Magyars and Slovaks call the Servians of the Greek persuasion, Razes, from Rass, the former capital of Servia, now Novi Bazar.

We now come to the Western branch.

Western languages.

The frontier-line of the territory inhabited by the Poles in the north is the coast of the Baltic, from the promontory of Hela, in the gulf of Putzig, along the sea as far as the Lake of Schmolsin; then westward, toward the German nation: at first along the Pommeranian frontier to the neighbourhood of Butow, in the direction of the towns of Jastrow, Wirsitz, Chodzies, Filehne, Meseritz, Lissa, Bojawono, Rawicz, Wartenberg, and Rosenberg; next westward, as far as the mouth of the Neisse, which falls into the Oder below Brieg, and along the river Biala toward Zuckmantel, on the Austrian frontier. Here, after a bend in an easterly direction, it falls in with the frontier of the Bohemo-Moravian dialect, in the neighbourhood of Troppau. The Polish language comes into contact with this dialect from Oderberg along the course of the Oder, down to the Carpathian ridge. Hence the southern frontier extends toward the Slovaks, along the foot of the Carpathians as far as Piwniczna, where the Poprad forms the limit between the three populations of the Poles, the Slovaks, and the Russines. The southern frontier towards the Russines runs through Gallicia, past the towns of Sandec, Biecz, Krosno, Brozozow:—hence the eastern frontier extends straight northwards, past the towns of Przeworzk Lezaisk, Krzeszow, Goray, Turobin, Krasnoslav, Radzyn, Miedzyryc; along the river Zna, towards Biala and Sarnaki; and thence also eastwards along the boundary of the White Russians, in the direction of the towns of Bransk, Tykoczyn, Knyszyn, Stabin, Lipsk, and as far as Grodno. The Niemen forms in part the north-western frontier toward the Lithuanians. From this river it follows the Hansze as far as Seyny, then westward towards Oletzko, near which place it returns to the

Prussian territory, descending by the town of Goldapp to Darkehmen. Hence it takes a westerly course, through the ancient kingdom of Prussia, touched by the German frontier near the towns of Rastenburg, Bischofsburg, and Seeburg; then to the mouth of the Welle, which disembogues into the Drewenz above Neumark. It reaches nearly to the Vistula, but turns south, past the town of Culm, to Thorn. Here it crosses the Vistula, and turns towards the Netze till il reaches Nakel, when, taking a northern course, it accompanies the western side of the Vistula to the point where that river divides. After following the river for several miles, it bends off, below Derschau and before it reaches Dantzig, and ends in the Bay of Putzig. Besides the inhabitants of this territory, all the upper classes in the ancient provinces of Poland are composed of Poles by origin, and of others who became Polonized during the Polish dominion in those parts. The language of Gallicia is Polish.

The old name of the Polish language was Lekhian, spoken in ancient times beyond its present limit, in parts of Pommerania and Silesia now occupied by Germans. At present it exists in two dialects, Polish and Kashubian, —the latter spoken in a small district between Leba and Lauenburg by about 100,000 people. Here the English fleet may hear it on the Baltic coast.

The limits of the B o h e m i a n population may be marked by a line beginning between the towns of Josephstadt and Königshof, which are on the Bohemian side, and Turnau and Semile, on the German. This line runs from the last-named place in a northwestern direction along the towns of Aupa, Böhmisch-Aicha, Leitmeritz, Theresienstadt, Laun, Pilsen, Mies, Bischofteinitz, as far as Klenz; thence it turns in a south-eastern direction along the towns of Winterberg, Krummau, Gratzen, Neuhaus, Moravian-Budweis (Budwitz), Znaym, Lundenburg, as far as Rabensburg, on the river March. Hence to the north-east, touching the Slovaks, in an almost straight line, along the towns Holitsch, Strasnitz, and Wessely, to the Carpathian ridge, where it comes into contact with the Poles of Galicia. Bohemian.

From this point the river Oder forms the frontier as far as Oderberg. Bohemian is spoken in the whole of the district of Troppau. Passing then from Sternberg, along the Sudet mountains, through Moravian-Neustadt, it returns to Königshof. The territory within this line comprehends a space of about 850 German square miles, which, with the exception of few German colonies, is inhabited by a pure Slavonic population.

Another name for the language of Bohemia and Moravia is Tchechian. Some literary monuments of the ancient Tchech language exist, as the song of Libussa of the ninth century, and poems of the thirteenth, exhibiting a much richer grammatical system than the spoken Bohemian. This is divided again into dialects, Horakian, Hanakian, Moravo-Slovakian, Wallachian, and others. Since the beginning of this century a new impulse has been given to the national literature of Bohemia, chiefly by the exertions of Dobrowsky, Safarik, and Palacky. Safarik's works on Slavonic antiquities have acquired a European reputation: they are the chief authority for all that is known of the ethnology, history and language of Bohemia and of the whole Slavonic race.

Slovakian. The language of the Slovaks has retained in its grammar certain original forms which the Bohemian has lost. It is spoken by the Slovaks, who are separated from the Bohemians on the north-west by a line already mentioned. Thence the boundary continues along the Carpathian ridge to the town of Piwniczna, separating the Slovaks from the Poles in Gallicia. From that place it runs through the towns Bordijow, and Humené (Homona), and follows the course of the river Ondava, which parts off the Russines in Gallicia and Hungary. On the south the Slovaks are divided from the Magyars by a line running through the towns Kaschau, Tornala (Torna), Filekovo (Fulek), from the river Eipel as far as Hont; — thence along the towns of Zeviza, Neuhäusel, nearly to Comorn and Pressburg; then following the course of the Danube to the mouth of the river March. The same river, separates them on the West from the Germans. The territory inhabited by the Slovaks extends over fifteen Comitats, of which five are entirely, and the rest principally, occupied by them. There are besides several large settlements of Slovaks scattered over different parts of Hungary.

The last Slavonic dialect is the Wendian, spoken by the Wends of Lusatia, whose number though variously stated, probably does not exceed 150,000. They are the remnants of those Slavonians by whom all that country was formerly inhabited, and whose settlements extended beyond the Elbe to the river Saale. They are called by a general name the Pólabes (from po, near, and Labe, the Elbe). The Wends inhabit the region around the towns of Löbau, Neusalz, Budissin, Camenz, Spremberg, Lübben, Lieberosa, Cottbus and Muskav, forming a kind of Slavonian island in a German sea. Their language is also called Sorbian, and divided into two dialects, each possessing, besides popular songs, translations of the Bible, and other sacred works. Though German is taught now in every school, yet the common people cling to their national dialect and prefer to speak "serski." Wendian or Lusatian.

The following is an estimate of the Slavonic population: Slavonic statistics.

1. Great-Russians (Welikoruski)	35,000,000
2. Little-Russians (Maloruski)	13,000,000
3. White-Russians (Beloruski)	2,700,000
4. Bulgarians (Bolgari)	3,600,000
5. Kroatians (Horwati)	800,000
6. Slovenians (Slovenzi)	1,150,000
7. Servians	5,300,000
8. Poles (Polaki)	9,300,000
9. Bohemians (Czechi)	7,200,000
10. Wends (Syrbi)	150,000
	78,200,000

This gives for the Eastern branch	62,000,000
„ for the Western branch	17,000,000
	79,000,000

According to their religion the Slavonic races were arranged by *Safarik* (in 1842) in the following table: — *

	Greek or Eastern Church.	Greek united with Rome.	Roman Catholics.	Protestants.	Mohammedans.
Great Russians, or Muscovites	35,314,000				
Little Russians, or Malorusses	10,154,000	2,990,000			
White Russians	2,376,000		350,000		
Bulgarians	3,287,000		50,000		250,000
Servians or Illyrians	2,880,000		1,864,000		550,000
Kroats			801,000		
Carynthians			1,138,000	13,000	
Poles			8,923,000	442,000	
Bohemians and Moravians			4,270,000	144,000	
Slovaks (in the North of Hungary)			1,953,000	800,000	
Lusatians or Wends, Upper			10,000	88,000	
" " Lower				44,000	
Total	54,011,000	2,990,000	19,359.000	1,531,000	800,00

According to the States to which they belong, the Slavonic races were arranged by *Safarik* (in 1842) in the following table: —

	Russia.	Austria.	Prussia.	Turkey.	Republic of Cracow.	Saxony.	Tot
Great Russians	35,314,000						35,314
Little Russians	10,370,000	2,774,000					13,144
White Russians	2,726,000						2,726
Bulgarians	80,000	7,000		3,500,000			3,587
Servians and Illyrians	100,000	2,594,000		2,600,000			5,294
Kroats		801,000					801
Carynthians		1,151,000					1,151
Poles	4,912,000	2,341,000	1,982,000		130,000		9,365
Bohemians and Moravians		4,370,000	44,000				4,414
Slovaks in North Hungary		2,753,000					2,753
Lusatians or Wends, Upper			38,000			60,000	98
" " Lower			44,000				44
Total	53,502,000	16.791,000	2,108,000	6,100,000	130,000	60,000	78,691

Political position of the Great Russians.

Numerically as well as politically, the Russians stand at present in the van of the Slavonic races, while formerly the Poles held a place much more important in the political system of Europe. In the sixteenth century the Russian eagle began to try his wings, after shaking

* *Safarik's* figures of population, according to a letter from the Hon. H. Stanley, H. M. Secretary of Legation at Athens, are less correct than those of Ubicini in his Lettres sur la Turquie. May not *Safarik* have been guided by linguistic and ethnological evidence, while Ubicini's figures are based on political statistics?

off the yoke of the Mongolians, who for nearly two hundred years had held Russia in the most cruel vassalage. The first conquests of the Russians were near the Volga:

In 1552, they conquer the countries along the middle course of the Volga.
1554, the Lower Volga.
1577, the Lower Don.
1581, they cross the Ural.
1584, they occupy the middle course of the Ob.
1594—96, they take the countries watered by the Irtis.
1608, the Lower Ob.
1620—30, the Yenisei.

After thus conquering the north, the Russian arms turned to the South and the Caucasus.

In 1630—40 they take the Baikal lake and the Lena-country.
1646, the Behring Straits.
1658, they cross the Southern Siberian mountains, and advance into Mongolia, along the Chinese river Amur. They found Nyer*k*insk.
1690, they take Kam*k*atka, and push along the Aleute islands into America; while in Europe they advance to the Don and Dniepr.
1721, they take the coast of the Finnic Bay and the Gulf of Riga, thus securing the ground on which now stands the capital of the Russian empire, Petersburg.
1743, Karelia taken.
1783, Krimea taken.
1774, Country to the north of the Krimea annexed.
1791, they advance against Tataric tribes as far as the Dniestr.
1802, Georgia is annexed.
1812, Bessarabia conquered.
1813, Daghestan and *S*irwan taken.

1828, Abhasia, Mingrelia, and Araxes-countries taken.

1809, Sweden taken as far as the Bothnian Gulf.

1812, Advance to the Pruth in Wallachia.

1828, the mouth of the Danube secured.

1848, Principalities occupied against revolutionary tendencies.

1853, Principalities occupied as a material guarantee.

1854, Declaration, that Russia does not aim at conquest.

Genealogical tables of the Arian Family.

We have thus completed our survey of the second family of languages, and the following table will give a general view of all the members which can be proved to belong to it. Each column begins with the languages now spoken. These are traced back to their previous stages, wherever literary monuments have been preserved, and are then referred to the different classes, branches, and divisions, which all took their origin from one central language, the language of the Arian ancestors. Since their first separation took place, in times previous to Homer, Zoroaster, and the poets of the Veda, no new roots have been added to the common inheritance of these dialects, no new elements have been created in the formation of their grammar. They have experienced various losses, and compensated them by a skilful application of what they carried away as their common heirloom. All, from Sanskrit to English, are but various forms of the same type, modifications of a language, once formed in Asia we know not and can hardly imagine how, yet a language the existence and reality of which has the full certainty of matters resting on inductive evidence, although it goes back to times when historical chronology borders on the geological eras.

ARIAN FAMILY.

Living Languages.	Dead Languages.	Branches.	Classes.	Division
Dialects of India	Prakrit and Pali—Classical Sanskrit.—Vaidik Sanskrit		Indic	Southern Division.
„ Persia	Parsi—Pehlevi—Cuneiform Inscriptions—Zend		Iranic	
„ Afghanistan				
„ Kurdistan				
„ Bokhara				
„ Armenia	Old Armenian			
„ Ossethi	(Alanian—Sarmatian)			
„ Wales		Cymric	Celtic	Northern Division.
„ Britany				
„	Cornish			
„ Scotland		Gadhelic		
„ Ireland				
„ Man				
„ Portugal			Italic	
„ Spain	Oscan			
„ Provence	Old Provençal — Lingua Vulgaris — Latin			
„ France	Umbrian			
„ Italy				
„ Wallachia				
„ Albania			Illyric (?)	
„ Greece	Κοινή { Doric—Aeolic. Attic—Ionic.		Hellenic	
„ Lithuania				
„	Old Prussian	Lettic		
„ Kurland and Livonia (Lettish)				
„ Bulgaria	Ecclesiastical Slavonic	South-East Slavonic	Windic	
„ Russia (Great, Little, White Russian)				
„ Illyria (Slovenian, Croatian, Servian)				
„ Poland		West-Slavonic		
„ Bohemia (Slovakian)	Old Bohemian			
„ Lusatia	Polabian			
„ Germany	Old High-German	High-German	Teutonic	
„	Gothic	Low-German		
„ England	Anglo-Saxon			
„ Holland	Old-Dutch			
„ Friesland	Old Frisic			
„ North of Germany (Platt-Deutsch)	Old-Saxon			
„ Danemark	Old Norse	Scandinavian		
„ Sweden				
„ Norway				
„ Iceland				

Turanian Family.

The third family is the Turanian. It comprises all languages spoken in Asia or Europe not included under the Arian and Semitic families, with the exception perhaps of the Chinese and its dialects. This is, indeed, a very wide range; and the characteristic marks of union, ascertained for this immense variety of languages, are as yet very vague and general, if compared with the definite ties of relationship which severally unite the Semitic and the Arian. The common origin of some of these wide-spread idioms has indeed been proved with the same accuracy as that of Sanskrit and Greek, of Hebrew and Arabic:—and languages as widely distant as Hungarian and Finnish, have been traced back conclusively to one common source. Large divisions have thus been established, and five linguistic districts, the Tungusic, Mongolic, Turkic, Samoiedic and Finnic, have been surveyed and laid down definitely as portions of one vast kingdom of speech. And after the convergence of these five divisions towards one central point has once been established, it will be difficult to exclude from the same system the other provinces of speech which lie scattered throughout on the map of Asia and Europe.

Character of Turanian or Nomade Languages.

The absence of that close family likeness which holds the Arian and Semitic languages together, becomes itself one of the distinguishing features of the Turanian dialects. They are Nomadic languages as contrasted with the Arian and Semitic dialects, which may be called State or political languages. In the grammatical features of the latter class, we can discover the stamp of one powerful mind, once impressed on the floating materials of speech at the very beginning of their growth, and never to be obliterated again in the course of centuries. Like mighty empires founded by the genius of one man, in which his will is perpetuated as law through generations to come, the Semitic and Arian languages exhibit in all ages and countries a strict historical continuity which makes the idioms of Moses and Mohammed, of Homer and Shakspeare, appear but slightly altered impressions of one original type. Most words and grammatical forms in these two families seem to have been thrown out but once by the creative power of an individual mind; and the differences of the various Semitic and Arian languages, whether ancient or modern, were produced, not so much by losses and new creations, as by changes and corruptions which defaced in various ways the original design of these most primitive works of human art. This process of handing down a language through centuries without break or loss, is possible only among people whose history runs on in one main stream; and where religion, law, and poetry supply well defined borders which hem in on every side the current of language. Thus only can it be explained how, at the present day, the Lithuanian peasant expresses, "I am, esmi," with exactly the same root and the same termination which the poet of the Veda used in India four thousand years ago; and how the numerals which we employ, are the same tokens which passed current among the common ancestors of the Teutons, Greeks, Romans, and Hindus.

The case is widely different with the Turanian languages. Firstly, the area over which they are spoken is much larger than that of the Arian and Semitic dialects. The latter occupy only what may be called the four Western Peninsulas of the great continent of the old world—India with Persia, Arabia, Asia-Minor, and Europe; and we have reason to suppose that even these countries were held by Turanian tribes previous to the immigration of the Arian and Semitic races. To our own times, by far the greater part of the primeval continent remains in possession of the descendants of Tur. But secondly, so far as history can reach back, no lasting nucleus of society or civilization has ever been formed in these vast Turanian wildernesses. Empires were no sooner founded there than they were scattered again like the sand-clouds of the desert; no laws, no songs, no stories outlived the age of their authors. How quickly language can change if thus left to itself without any standard, and kept up only by the daily wants of a savage life, may be seen from the endless variety of idioms in America, or on the borders of India, Tibet, and China. There it has happened that colonies from the same village, settled in neighbouring valleys, became mutually unintelligible after one or two generations. If then we bear in mind that thousands of years must have elapsed since the first separation of the Finnic and Mongolic races, that for a long time these races possessed nothing like a national or sacred literature, such as the Veda in India, or Homer in Greece, but that the scanty conversation of scattered tribes was the only safeguard for words once fixed to a certain meaning, and forms once coined with a certain value, we may understand why among the descendants of Tur we do not find the same clear traces of linguistic consanguinity as in the Arian and Semitic families. A different method must, therefore, be adopted to bring out the few remaining features that all Turanian dialects share in common, and which, though seemingly vague and general, it would be impossible to consider as the result of mere accident. The most necessary substantives, such as father, mother, daughter, son, have frequently been lost and replaced by synonymes in the different branches of this family; yet common words are found, though not with the same consistency and regularity as in Semitic and Arian dialects. The Turanian numerals and pronouns point to a single original source, yet here again the tenacity of these Nomadic dialects cannot be compared with the tenacity of the political languages of Asia and Europe:—and common roots, discovered in the most distant Nomadic idioms, are mostly of a much more general form and character than the radicals of the Arian and Semitic treasuries.

But although we do not find, and cannot expect to find, in Nomadic languages those striking material coincidences by which the common origin of the Arian branches of speech has been proved, we are struck in them by a similarity of form such as it would be difficult to explain without the admission of common blood running in the veins of all Turanian dialects. This requires some explanation.

A reference to the latter stages of the Arian language, may serve to illustrate what is meant by a similarity in form between Turanian languages. The grammatical forms of the Arian languages were fixed but once. Each language, whether Greek or Sanskrit, received them ready made, and preserved them without feeling conscious of the manner in which originally they had been formed. No Roman probably was aware that in amamus, we love, mus was the remnant of a pronoun once attached to the root ama; as little as we suspect that the d in "I loved" was originally an auxiliary verb (to do), added to a root for the purpose of giving it a past sense (I love-did). Most, if not all, of these grammatical forms had become typical before the common Arian speech was broken up into Sanskrit, Greek, and the rest. Now, if in place of adopting these grammatical forms, each language had produced them anew from its own materials, it is clear that the material parts of these new forms might have differed, while the principle on which they were composed might still have been the same. Let us take, for instance, the Future of the Romance languages, the formation of which was explained before. We cannot say that this Future j'aimer-ai, I-to-love-have, had become fixed and typical previous to the separation of the Romance dialects, that is to say, at the time when Latin was no longer classical Latin, but not resolved as yet into Italian, French, or Spanish. If this had been the case, the similarity between the Future in the six Romance languages, would probably be much greater than it is. Besides, we know for certain that in Provençal at least the component parts of this new Future had not yet coalesced, but were understood as meaning "I have to love." Here then we find in the later remodelling of the Latin grammar, a coincidence in form analogous to the coincidences which unite the Turanian languages. Each Romance dialect took its own auxiliary verb "to have," under that peculiar form which it had reached after ceasing to be the Latin "habeo." Hence the materials of which these Futures are formed cannot be said

Morpholog cal coinci dences o Turanian Language

to be the same, nor can they be treated as mere corruptions of one original type. Cantero was never chanterai, nor canterei, a modification of canteraggio. Each Romance dialect formed its Future for itself, but all according to the same principle. And this applies to the Turanian languages. The materials employed by each for the production of grammatical forms are generally taken from its own resources; but the manner of the combination shows a character common to all. To use a homely illustration, the uniforms of the Arian languages are actually made of one and the same piece of cloth and by the same hands, while the uniformity of the Turanian dialects lies not so much in the stuff, as in the cut and make of their dress.

The system of Agglutination.

The most characteristic feature of the Nomadic or Turanian languages has been called 'Agglutination.' This means not only that in their grammars pronouns are glued to the verbs in order to form the conjugation, or prepositions to substantives in order to form declensions. *That* would not be characteristic of the Turanian languages; for in Hebrew as well as in Sanskrit, conjugations and declensions were originally formed on the same principle. What distinguishes the Turanian languages is, that in them the conjugation and declension can still be taken to pieces, and although the terminations have by no means retained their significative power as independent words, they are felt as modificatory syllables, and distinct from the words to which they are added. In the Arian languages the modifications of words, comprised under declension and conjugation, were likewise originally expressed by agglutination. But the two component parts began soon to coalesce, so as to form but one word, liable in its turn to phonetic corruption, rendering it impossible after a time to decide which was the root and which the modificatory termination. The difference between a Turanian and an Arian language is somewhat the same as between composing and reading. The compositor puts the *s* to the end of a word, and looks on the type s in his hand as producing the change of pound into pounds; to the reader the s has no separate existence (except on scientific reflection); the whole word expresses to him the modified idea, and in his perception the same change is produced in penny and pence as in pound and pounds.

Integrity of Turanian roots.

The reason why, in the Turanian languages, the termination appears but slightly united to the body of a word is this, — it was felt essential that the radical portion of each word should stand out in distinct relief, and never be obscured or absorbed, as happens so frequently in the later stages of political languages. The French *âge*, for instance, has lost its whole material body, and is nothing but termination. Age, in Old French, was eage and edage. Edage is a corruption of aetaticum; aetaticum is a derivative of aetas; aetas an abbreviation of aevitas, and in aevum, ae only is the radical portion (the Sanskrit ây-us), containing the germ from which these various words derive their life and meaning. What trace of ae, ar aevum, or aevitas, remains in age? Turanian languages cannot afford to retain such words as *age* in their living dictionaries. It is an indispensable requirement in every Nomadic language that it should be intelligible to many, though their intercourse be but scanty. It requires tradition, society, and literature to maintain forms which can no longer be analyzed at once, nor their formal elements separated from the base.

The Arian verb, for instance, contains many forms in which the personal pronoun is no longer felt distinctly. And yet tradition, custom, and law, preserve the comprehensibility of these veterans, and make us feel unwilling to part with them. But in the evershifting state of a Nomadic society no debased coin can be tolerated in language, no obscure legend accepted on trust. The metal must be pure, and the legend distinct; that the one may be weighed, and the other, if not deciphered, at least recognized as a well-known guarantee.

A Turanian might tolerate the Sanskrit,

as-mi,	a-si,	as-ti,	's-mas,	s-tha,	's-anti,
I am,	thou art,	he is,	we are,	you are,	they are;

or even the Latin,

's-um,	e-s,	es-t,	'su-mus,	es-tis,	'sunt.

In these instances, with a few exceptions, root and affix are as distinguishable as for instance in Turkish:

bakar-im,	bakar-sin,	bakar,
I regard,	thou regardest,	he regards,
bakar-iz,	bakar-siniz,	bakar-lar.
we regard,	you regard,	they regard.

But a conjugation like the Hindustani, which is a modern Arian dialect,

hun, hai, hai, hain, ho, hain,

would not be compatible with the genius of the Turanian languages, because it would not answer the requirements of a Nomadic life. Turanian dialects exhibit either no terminational distinctions at all, as in Man*g*u, which is a Tungusic dialect; or a complete and intelligible system of affixes, as in the spoken dialect of Nyer*k*insk, equally of Tungusic descent. But a state of conjugation in which, through phonetic corruption, the suffix of the first person singular and plural, and of the third person plural are the same, where is no distinction between the second and third persons singular, and between the first and third persons plural, would necessarily lead in a Turanian dialect to the adoption of new and more expressive forms. New pronouns would have to be used to mark the persons, or some other expedient be resorted to for the same purpose. *

Divergence of Turanian Dialects.

But we must not dwell much longer on these general features of the Turanian languages. All we desire to show is the fact that dialects whose grammar has not yet

* For further particulars see the author's Letter to Chevalier Bunsen, On the Classification of the Turanian Languages, London, 1854, in the first volume of Chev. Bunsen's Outlines of the Philosophy of Universal History.

settled down into a solid system, are liable to perpetual changes, and likely to diverge most rapidly if separated for any length of time. A Turanian retains, as it were, the consciousness of his grammar. The idea, for instance, which he connects with a plural is that of a noun followed by a syllable indicative of plurality; a passive is a verb followed by a syllable expressive of suffering. Now these determinative ideas may be expressed in various ways. But in one and the same clan, and during one period of time, one suffix would generally become popular, and be assigned to the expression of a single grammatical category, such as the plural, the passive, or the genitive. Thus, out of large mass of possible formations, a small number only would become customary and technical, leading finally to a scheme of declension and conjugation such as we find in Turkish and Finnish. Different hordes, however, as they separated, would still feel themselves at liberty to repeat the same process; thus forming in their different idioms different phases of grammatical life, which, if confined to a single tribe, would naturally have disappeared without leaving any traces.

In Nomadic languages, therefore, the sudden rise of a family or of a small association may produce an effect which, in political languages, can only be produced by the ascendency of a town or a province, a race or a religious sect. Where so little is fixed, the peculiarities of a rising family may change the whole surface of a language, and the accent of a successful Khán may leave its stamp on the grammar of all the tribes that follow him. When one of the great Tatar chiefs proceeds on an expedition, he, as Marco Polo tells us in the fourteenth century, puts himself at the head of an army of a hundred thousand horse, and organizes them in the following manner. One officer he appoints to the command of every ten men, and others to command a hundred, a thousand, and ten thousand men respectively. Thus, ten of the officers commanding ten men take their orders from him who commands a hundred; of these, each ten from him who commands a thousand; and each ten of these latter from him who commands ten thousand. By this arrangement each officer has only to attend to the management of ten men, or ten bodies of men, and the word of command is spread from the Khán to the hundred thousand common soldiers, after passing through not more than four mouths. This is characteristic linguistically as well as politically.

Turanian Languages approaching to an Arian type.

If a language is once fixed by literary works of a national character, change becomes difficult, nay, impossible without political convulsions. Where Nomadic nations rise to this stage of civilization and political organization, their language, though Turanian in its grammar, may approach to the system of political languages, such as Sanskrit or Hebrew. This is indeed the case with the most advanced members of the Turanian family, the Hungarian and Finnish. Here some terminations have been so much worn out by continual use, and yet not replaced by new syllables, that on this point, the distinction between Turanian and Arian grammar appears to vanish. Yet some characteristic Turian features are always retained: the root is never obscured; the determinative syllables are placed at the end; and the vowels never become so absolutely fixed for each syllable as in Sanskrit or Hebrew. On the contrary, there is a law of harmony, according to which the vowels of each word may be changed and modulated so as to harmonise with the key-note struck by its chief vowel. The vowels in Turkish, for instance, are divided into two classes, sharp and flat. If a verb contains a sharp vowel in its radical portion, the vowels of the terminations are all sharp, while the same terminations, if following a root with a flat vowel, modulate their own vowels into the flat key. Thus we have sev-mek, to love, but bak-mak, to regard, mek and mak being the termination of the infinitive. Thus we say, ev-ler, the houses, but at-lar, the horses, ler and lar, being the termination of the plural.

No Arian or Semitic language has preserved a similar freedom in the harmonic arrangement of its vowels, while traces of it have been found among the most distant members of the Turanian family, as in Hungarian, Mongolian, Turkish, the Yakut, spoken in the North of Siberia, and in dialects spoken on the eastern frontiers of India.

A number of words and roots, common to all Turanian languages, has been collected by Professor Schott in his Essay "On the Tataric Languages."

Tungusic Languages.

It would carry us too far were we to attempt to pass in review all the languages of the Turanian family. We shall only mention those with which the English Army is likely to be brought into more immediate contact. Hence we may dismiss the whole Tungusic branch, which extends from China northward to Siberia and westward to 113°, where the river Tunguska partly marks its frontier. Though Tungusic tribes in Siberia are under Russian sway, they are not likely to appear on the theatre of war. The other Tungusic tribes belonging to the Chinese empire, are known by the name of Man*g*u or Mandshu, a name taken after they had conquered China in 1644, and founded the present Imperial Dynasty. The name Tungus is derived from Donki,* which in their own language means "men," and by this the Tungusic tribes in Siberia call themselves. Other Tungusic tribes speak of themselves as Boyè, which likewise has the original meaning of "people."

Mongolic Branch.

The Mongolic branch also might be passed over for the present, as far as the original seats of the people who speak Mongolic dialects are concerned. These lie near the Lake Baikal and in the eastern parts of Siberia, where we find them as early as the ninth century after Christ. They were divided into three classes, the Mon-

* Another explanation of this name has been suggested by the Hon. H. Stanley, H. M. Secretary of Legation at Athens. He derives it from tungus (طوڭوز), a pig, the tribe of the pig, and remarks that this word is pronounced Domuz at Constantinople, but Donguz or Tunguz in Anadol and Persia.

gols proper, the Buriäts, and the Ölöt or Kalmüks. *K*ingis-khán (1227) united them into a nation and founded the Mongolian Empire, which included however, not only Mongolic, but Tungusic and Turkic tribes.

Origin of the name Tataric. The name of Tatar soon became the terror of Asia and Europe, and it was applied promiscuously to all the Nomadic warriors, whom Asia then poured forth over Europe. Originally Tatar was a name that belonged to the Mongolic races, but through their political ascendency in Asia after *K*ingis-khán, it became usual to call all the tribes which stood under Mongolian sovereigns by the name of Tatar. In linguistic works Tataric is now used in two several senses. Following the example of writers of the middle ages, Tataric, like Scythian in Greek, has been fixed upon as the general term comprising *all* languages spoken by the Nomadic tribes of Asia. Hence it is used sometimes in the same sense in which we use Turanian. Secondly, Tataric has become the name of that class of Turanian languages of which the Turkish is the most prominent member. While the Mongolic class — that which in fact has the greatest claims on the name of Tataric — is never thus called, it has become an almost universal custom to apply it to the third or Turkic branch of the Ural-Altaic division, and the races belonging to this branch have in many instances themselves adopted this name. These Turkic, or as they were afterwards called, Tataric races, were settled on the northern side of the Caspian Sea, and on the Black Sea, and were known as Komanes, Pe*k*enegs, and Bulgars, when conquered by the Mongolic army of the son of *K*ingis-khán, who founded the Kap*k*akian Empire, extending from the Dniestr to the Yemba, and the Kirgisian steppes. Russia for two centuries was under the sway of these Khans, known as the Khans of the Golden Horde. This empire was dissolved towards the end of the 15th century, and several smaller royalties rose out of its ruins. Among these Krim, Kasan, and Astrachan, were the most important. The princes of these empires still gloried in their descent from *K*ingiskhán, and had hence a right to the name of Mongols or Tatars. But their armies or subjects also, who were of Turkish blood, received the name of their princes; and their dialects continued to be called Tataric, even after the tribes by whom they were spoken had been brought under the Russian sceptre, and were no longer governed by Kháns of Mongolic or Tataric origin. It would perhaps be desirable to use Turkic or Hunnic, instead of Tataric, when speaking of the third branch of the northern division of the Turanian family, though a change of terminology generally produces as much confusion as it remedies. The recollection of their non-Tataric, i. e. non-Mongolic origin, remains, it appears, among the so called Tatars of Kasan and Astrachan. If asked whether they are Tatars, they reply no; and they call their language Turki or Turuk, but not Tatari. Nay, they consider Tatar as a term of abuse, synonymous with robber, evidently from a recollection that their ancestors had once been conquered and enslaved by Mongolic, that is, *Tataric* tribes. All this rests on the authority of Klaproth, who during his stay in Russia, had great opportunities of studying the languages spoken on all the frontiers of this half-Asiatic Empire.

The Mongolic conquests.

The conquests of the Mongols or the descendants of *K*ingis-khán, were not confined however, to these Turkic tribes. They conquered China in the east, where they founded the Mongolic dynasty of Yuan, and in the west, after subduing the Khalifs of Bagdad, and the Sultans of Iconium, they conquered Moscow, and devastated the greater part of Russia. In 1240 they invaded Poland, in 1241 Silesia. Here they recoiled before the united armies of Germany, Poland, and Silesia. They retired into Moravia, and having exhausted this country, occupied Hungary. At that time they had to choose a new Khan, which could only be done at Karakorum, the old capital of their empire. Thither they withdrew to elect an emperor to govern an empire which then extended from China to Poland, from India to Siberia. But a realm of such vast proportions could not be long held together, and towards the end of the 13th century, it broke up into several independent states, all still under Mongolian princes, but no longer under one Khan of Khans. Thus, new independent Mongolic empires arose in China, Turkestan, Siberia, Southern Russia, and Persia. In 1360, the Mongolian dynasty was driven out of China; in the 15th century they lost their hold on Russia. In Central Asia they rallied once more under Timur (1369), whose sway was again acknowledged from Karakorum to Persia and Anatolia. But in 1468, this empire also fell by its own weight, and for want of a powerful ruler like *K*ingis-khán or Timur. In *G*agatai alone, the country extending from the Aral Lake to the Hindukush, between the rivers Oxus and Yaxartes, (*G*ihon and Sihon), and once governed by *G*agatai, the son of *K*ingis-khán — the Mongolian dynasty maintained itself, and thence it was that Baber, a descendant of Timur, conquered India, and founded there a Mongolian dynasty, surviving up to our own times as the Great-Moguls of Delhi. Most Mogolic tribes are now under the sway of the nations whom they once had conquered, the Tungusic or Man*g*u sovereigns of China, the Russian Czars, and the Turkish Sultans.

Mongolic Dialects.

The Mongolic language, although spoken (but not con tinuously) from China as far as the Volga, has given rise to but few dialects. Next to Tungusic, the Mongolic is the poorest language of the Turanian family, and the scantiness of grammatical terminations accounts for the fact that, as a language, it has remained very much unchanged. There is, however, a distinction between the language as spoken by the Eastern, Western, and Northern tribes, and incipient traces of grammatical life have lately been discovered by Castrén, the great Swedish traveller and Turanian philologist, in the spoken dialect of the Buriäts. In it the persons of the verb are distinguished by affixes, while according to the rules of Mongolic grammar, no other dialect distinguishes in the verb between amo, am*as*, am*at*.

The Mongols who live in Europe have fixed their tents on each side of the Volga and along the coast of the Caspian Sea near Astrachan. Another colony is found south-east of Sembirsk. They belong to the Western branch, and are Ölöt or Kalmüks, who left their seats on the Koko-nur, and entered Europe in 1662. They proceeded from the clans Dürbet and Torgod, but most of the Torgods returned again in 1770, and their descendants are now scattered over the Kirgisian steppes.

According to Köppen, in his Statistical journey in the country of the Don Cossacks (or Kosaks) (Petersburg), 1852, the Kalmyks form two per cent of the inhabitants of that country, and nearly four per cent of the Cossack army. They are divided into Chutun's, Sotni's (Hundreds), and Uluss's; a Chutun consisting of 10 to 25 Kibitkas or tents. In 1850 there were 3 Uluss's, with 13 Sotni's and 5007 Kibitkas.

Bronewsky, in his history of the Don army, says that the number of the Kalmyks in the country of the Don Cossacks, began to increase about 1699, and that in 1710 the Khan Ajuki undertook to send 10,000 Kalmyks, of the Dürbet clan, to the Don. According to Köppen, however, Ajuki only agreed to allow 10,000 Kalmyks to pass the winter of 1710—11, near the Manytsh and Ssal-rivers, as a safeguard against the inroads of the Don Cossacks who under Nekrassow, had escaped to the Kuban. They probably remained afterwards, and those who were baptized, have been allowed, since 1729, to enter the army on the same footing as the Cossacks. In 1771 a great emigration took place, and many of the Kalmyks went back into their Trans-Uralian steppes; but as late as 1800, the Emperor Paul gave to the Kalmyk's of the Great and Little clans of Dürbet, who had remained or returned, all the land which they had occupied before 1771. It is here, between the Volga, the Sarpa, the Ssal, the Manytsh, the Kuma and the Caspian Sea, that they still lead their nomadic life.

Much more important at the present moment are the languages belonging to the third branch of the Turanian family, most prominent among which is the Turkish or Osmanli of Constantinople. The number of the Turkish inhabitants of European Turkey is indeed small. It is Turkic Languages.

generally stated at 2,000,000; but Safarik estimates the number of genuine Turks in Europe at not more than 700,000, who rule over fifteen millions of people. The different Turkic dialects of which the Osmanli is one, occupy one of the largest linguistic areas, extending from the Lena and the Polar Sea down to the Adriatic.

The three principal dialects of Turkish are, according to Béresin:

1. the *K*agataic or Eastern dialect, spoken in Turkestan and known by some books printed at Kasan;

2. the Northern dialect generally called Tataric and spoken in the Kip*k*ak and Siberia;

3. the Western dialect, best known as the Osmanli, and spoken in the South-East of Europe and Asia minor.

To these should be added, however, as independent branches the dialect of the Yakuts and that of the *K*uvashians.

Turkish or Osmanli.

The Turkish of Constantinople is so full of Persian and Arabic words, that a Turk from the country finds difficulty in understanding his master in town. Yet the real stock of the language has changed so little, that a Turk from Tomsk and Yeniseisk in Siberia is said to be able to understand the Turkish of Constantinople if spoken slowly and distinctly, and without admixture of Persian or Arabic words. A well-educated Turk may speak a whole sentence containing no one word of Turkic origin, and even particles and grammatical terminations, ever the last importations from one language into another, betray frequently a Persian or Arabic origin. Arabic as the language of Mahommed and the Koran would naturally find its way into the language of the people who adopted that religion. As to Persian, this was long the language of the most civilized and most advanced nation in Asia. In the first centuries of the Islam, Persians were the teachers of Arabs, and among the early Arabic authors, many names are found of Persian origin. Persian literature again was the only source whence, in the East, a taste for the more refined branches of poetry could be satisfied, whether through originals or by the medium of translations. In fact, Persian was for a long time the French of Asia, and it is still used there as the language of diplomatic correspondence. Hence many terms connected with literary subjects, or referring to other occupations of a society more advanced in civilization, are of Persian, *i. e.* of Arian origin. A knowledge of Persian and Arabic is therefore invaluable to the student of Turkish.

Ancient Sea of Turkic Tribes.

A list of all Turkic dialects, arranged under three divisions, South-eastern, Northern, and Western, is given at the end of this chapter according to Beresin.

The most ancient name by which the Turkic tribes of Central Asia were known to the Chinese, was Hiung-nu. These Hiung-nu founded an empire (206 B. C.) comprising a large portion of Asia, west of China. Engaged in frequent wars with the Chinese, they were defeated at last in the middle of the first century after Christ. Thereupon they divided into a northern and southern empire; and after the southern Hiung-nu had become subjects of China, they attacked the northern Hiung-nu together with the Chinese, and, driving them out of their seats between the rivers Amur and Selenga, and the Altai-mountains, westward, they gave the first impulse to the inroads of the Barbarians into Europe. In the beginning of the third century, Mongolic and Tungusic tribes, who had filled the seats of the Northern Hiung-nu, had grown so powerful as to attack the Southern Hiung-nu and drive them from their territories. This occasioned a second migration of Asiatic tribes towards the west.

Another name by which the Chinese designate these Hiung-nu or Turkish tribes, is Tukiu. Tukiu is supposed to be identical with Turk, and although the tribe to which this name was given was originally but small, it began to spread in the sixth century from the Altai to the Caspian Sea, and it was probably to them that in 569 the Emperor Justinian sent an ambassador in the person of Semarchos. The empire of the Tu-kiu was destroyed in the eighth century, by the 'Hui-ʿhe (Chinese Kao-*ke*). This tribe, equally of Turkic origin, maintained itself for about a century, and was then conquered by the Chinese and driven back from the northern borders of China. Part of the 'Hui-'he occupied Tangut, and after a second defeat by the Mongolians in 1257, the remnant proceeded still further west, and joined the Uigurs, whose tents were pitched near the towns of Turfan, Kasgar, 'Hamil, and Aksu.

These facts, gleaned chiefly from Chinese historians, show from the very earliest times the westward tendency of the Turkish nations. In 568 Turkic tribes occupied the country between the Volga and the sea of Azov, and numerous reinforcements have since strengthened their position in those parts.

Turkmans. The northern part of Persia, west of the Caspian Sea, Armenia, the south of Georgia, Sirwan, and Dagestan, harbour a Turkic population, known by the general name of Turkman or Kisil-bas (Red-caps). They are Nomadic robbers, and their arrival in these countries dates from the eleventh and twelfth centuries.

East of the Caspian Sea the Turkman tribes are under command of the Usbek-Khans of Khiva, Fergana and Bukhára. They call themselves, however, not subjects but guests of these Khans. Still more to the East the Turkmans are under Chinese sovereignty, and in the southwest they reach as far as Khorasan and the adjoining provinces of Persia.

Usbeks. The Usbeks, descendants of the 'Huy-'he and Uigurs, and originally settled in the neighbourhood of the towns of 'Hoten, Kasgar, Turfan, and 'Hamil, crossed the Yaxartes in the sixteenth century, and after several successful campaigns gained possession of Balkh, Kharism (Khiva), Bukhára, and Ferganah. In the latter country and in Balkh, they have become agricultural; but generally their life is nomadic, and too warlike to be called pastoral.

Nogáis. Another Turkic tribe are the Nogái, west of the Caspian, and also north of the Black Sea. To the beginning of the seventeenth century they lived northeast of the Caspian, and the steppes on the left of the Irtis bore their name. Pressed by the Kalmüks, a Mongolic tribe, the Nogáis advanced westward as far as Astrachan. Peter I. transferred them thence to the north of the Caucasian mountains, where they still graze their flocks on the shores of the Kuban and the Kuma. Their chief clans are the Kasbulat, Kip*k*ak, Mangut, Yedisan, *G*ambulat, Yedikul and Naurus; between the rivers 'Hots and Laba, the Mansur-ogli, and between the Terek and Kuma, the Kara-Nogai, Yedikul, Yedisan, and *G*ambulat. One horde, that of Kundur, remained on the Volga, subject to the Kalmüks.

Another tribe of Turkic origin in the Caucasus are the Bazianes. They now live near the sources of the Kuban, but before the fifteenth century within the town Ma*g*ari, on the Kuma. Bazianes.

A third Turkish tribe in the Caucasus are the Kumüks on the rivers Sun*g*a, Aksai, and Koisu: now subjects of Russia though under native princes. Kumüks.

A grammar of the Turkic or as they are more commonly called, Tataric dialects, as spoken in the Caucasus, was published at Tiflis in 1848 by Makarow. It is written in Russian. An account of it is given by Professor Boehtlingk in the Mélanges Asiatiques, i., p. 127. It comprises the dialects of the Nogáis, the Kumüks of Aderbi*g*an, with others:—showing where they deviate in pronunciation or grammatical peculiarities from the general rules of Turkish or Tataric grammar.

The southern portion of the Altaic mountains has long been inhabited by the Baskirs, a race considerably mixed with Mongolic blood, savage and ignorant, subjects of Russia, and Mahommedans by faith. Their land is divided into four Roads, called the Roads of Siberia, that of Kasan, of Nogai, and of Osa, a place on the Kama. Among the Baskirs, and in villages near Ufa, is now settled a Turkic tribe, the Mes*k*eräks who formerly lived near the Volga. Baskirs.

The tribes near the Lake of Aral are called Kara-Kalpak. They are subject partly to Russia, partly to the Khans of Khiva.

The Turks of Siberia, commonly celled Tatars, are partly original settlers, who crossed the Ural, and founded the Khanat of Sibir, partly later colonists. Their chief Turks of Siberia.

towns are Tobolsk, Yeniseisk, and Tomsk. Separate tribes are the Uranhat on the *K*ulym, and the Barabas in the steppes between the Irtis and the Ob.

The dialects of these Siberian Turks are considerably intermingled with foreign words, taken from Mongolic, Samoïedic or Russian sources. Still they resemble one another closely in all that belongs to the original stock of the language.

Yakuts. In the north-east of Asia, on both sides of the river Lena, the Yakuts form the most remote link in the Turkic chain of languages. Their male population has lately risen to 100,000, while in 1795 it amounted only to 50,066. The Russians became first acquainted with them in 1620. They call themselves Sakha, and are mostly heathen, though Christianity is gaining ground among them. According to their traditions, their ancestors lived for a long time in company with Mongolic tribes, and traces of this can still be discovered in their language. Attacked by their neighbours, they built rafts and floated down the river Lena, where they settled in the neighbourhood of what is now Yakutzk. Their original seats seem to have been north-west of Lake Baikal. Their language has preserved the Turkic type more completely than any other dialect of this third Turanian class. Separated from the common stock at an early time, and removed from the disturbing influences to which the other dialects were exposed, whether in war or in peace, the Yakutian has preserved so many primitive features of Turkic grammar, that even now it may be used as a key to the grammatical forms of the Osmanli and other more cultivated dialects.

Kirgis. Southern Siberia is the mother-country of the Kirgis, one of the most numerous tribes of Turkic origin. The Kirgis lived originally between the Ob and Yenisei, where Mongolic tribes settled among them. At the beginning of the seventeenth century the Russians became acquainted with the Eastern Kirgis, then living along the Yenisei. In 1606 they had become tributary to Russia, and after several wars with two neighbouring tribes, were driven more and more south-westward, till they left Siberia altogether at the beginning of the eighteenth century. They now live at Burut, in Chinese Turkestan, together with the Kirgis of the "Great Horde", near the town of Kasgar, north as far as the Irtis.

Another tribe is that of the Western Kirgis, or Kirgis-Kasak, who are partly independent, partly tributary to Russia and China.

Of what are called the three Kirgis Hordes, from the Caspian Sea East as far as Lake Tenghiz, the Small Horde is fixed in the West, between the rivers Yemba and Ural; the Great Horde in the East; while the most powerful occupies the centre between the Sarasu and Yemba, and is called the Middle Horde. Since 1819 the Great Horde has been subject to Russia. Other Kirgis tribes, though nominally subject to Russia, are really her most dangerous enemies.

The Turks of Asia Minor and Syria came from Khorasan and Eastern Persia, and are Turkman, or remnants of the Selguks, the rulers of Persia during the Middle Ages. The Osmanli, whom we are accustomed to call Turks par excellence, and who form the ruling portion of the Turkish empire, must be traced to the same source. They are now scattered over the whole Turkish empire in Europe, Asia and Africa, and their number amounts to between eleven and twelve millions. They form the landed gentry, the aristocracy, and bureaucracy of Turkey, and their language, the Osmanli, is spoken by persons of rank and education, and by all government authorities in Syria, in Egypt, at Tunis, and at Tripoli. In the southern provinces of Asiatic Russia, along the borders of the Caspian, and through the whole of Turkestan, it is the language of the people. It is heard even at the Court of Teheran, and understood by official personages in Persia. Turks of Asia Minor and Europe

The rise of this powerful tribe of Osman, and the spreading of that Turkish dialect which is now emphatically called the Turkish, are matters of historical notoriety. We need not search for evidence in Chinese annals, or try to discover analogies between names that a Rise of the Osmanlis.

Greek or an Arabic writer may by chance have heard and handed down to us, and which some of these tribes have preserved to the present day. The ancestors of the Osman Turks are men as well known to European historians as Charlemagne or Alfred. It was in the year 1224 that Soliman-shah and his tribe, pressed by Mongolians, left Khorasan and pushed westward into Syria, Armenia, and Asia Minor. Soliman's son, Ertoghrul, took service under Aladdin, the Selguk-Snltan of Iconium (Nicaea), and after several successful campaigns against Greeks and Mongolians, received part of Phrygia as his own, and there founded what was afterwards to become the basis of the Osmanic empire. During the last years of the thirteenth century the Sultans of Iconium lost their power, and their former vassals became independent sovereigns. Osman, after taking his share of the spoil in Asia, advanced through the Olympic passes into Bithynia and was successful against the armies of the Emperors of Byzantium:—and Osman became henceforth the national name of his people. His son, Orkhan, whose capital was Prusa (Bursa), after conquering Nicomedia (1327), and Nicaea (1330), threatened the Hellespont. He took the title of Padishah, and his court was called the "High Porte." His son, Soliman, crossed the Hellespont (1357), and took possession of Gallipoli and Sestos. He thus became master of the Dardanelles. Murad I. took Adrianople in 1362, made it his capital, conquered Macedonia, and after a severe struggle, overthrew the united forces of the Slavonic races, south of the Danube, the Bulgarians, Servians, and Kroatians, in the battle of Kossovapolye (1389). He fell himself, but his successor Bayazeth, followed his course, took Thessaly, passed Thermopylae, and devastated the Peloponnesus. The Emperor of Germany, Sigismund, who advanced at the head of an army, composed of French, German and Slavonic soldiers, was defeated by Bayazeth on the Danube in the battle of Nicopolis, 1399. Bayazeth took Bosnia, and would have taken Constantinople, had not the same Mongolians, who in 1244 drove the first Turkish tribes westward into

Persia, threatened again their newly acquired possessions. Timur had grasped the reins, fallen from the hands of *K*ingis-khán: Bayazeth was compelled to meet him, and suffered defeat (1402) in the battle of Angora (Ankyra) in Galatia.

Europa now had respite, but not long; Timur died, and with him his empire fell to pieces, while the Osmanic army rallied again under Mahomet I. (1413), and re-attained its former power under Murad II. (1421). Successful in Asia, Murad sent his armies back to the Danube, and after long continued campaigns, and powerful resistance from the Hungarians and Slaves under Hunyad, he at last gained two decisive victories; Varna in 1444, and Kossova in 1418. Constantinople could no longer be held, and the Pope endeavoured in vain to rouse the chivalry of Western Europe to a crusade against the Turks. Mahomet II, succeeded in 1451, and on the 29th of May, 1453, Constantinople, after a valiant resistance, fell and became the capital of the Turkish empire.

Four hundred years have since elapsed, and it is now no longer the power, but the weakness of the Turks, which forms the terror of Europe. The vacuum which was created by the decay of the Byzantine empire, in the political system of Europe, filled for a time by the Turks, begins to make itself felt again, and concomitant pressure from all sides has brought on the events we are called to witness.

It is no easy matter to acquire a perfect knowledge of Turkish. In order to speak, to read, and to write it with ease, elegance, and correctness, we must in reality learn three languages, Arabic, Persian, and Turkish, each built on a different system of grammar, the Arabic belonging to the Semitic, the Persian to the Arian, and the Turkish to the Turanian family of speech. But few, even of the most learned Turks, command this full knowledge of their language, no more perhaps than in England possess a knowledge of Latin, Anglo-Saxon, and Norman-French. Divested of its foreign elements, few languages are so easy, so intelligible, and I might almost say, so amusing as Turkish. It is a real pleasure to read the Tnrkish grammar, even without the wish to acquire it practically. The ingenious manner in which the numerous grammatical forms are brought out, the regularity which pervades the system of declension and conjugation, the transparency and intelligibility of the whole structure must strike all who have a sense for that wonderful power of the human mind which has displayed itself in language. Given so small a number of graphic and demonstrative roots as would not suffice to express the commonest wants of human beings: — to produce an instrument that shall render the faintest shades of feeling and thought; — given a vague infinitive or a stern imperative: — to derive from it such moods as an optative or subjunctive, and such tenses as an Aorist or Paulo-post Future; — given incoherent utterances: — to arrange them into a system where all is uniform and regular, all combined and harmonious — such is the work of the human mind which we see realized in "language." But in most languages nothing of this early process remains visible, and we hardly know whether to call them the work of nature or of art. They stand before us like solid rocks, and the microscope of the philologist alone can reveal the remains of organic life of which they are composed.

Turkish Grammar.

But in the grammar of the Turkic languages we have before us a language of perfectly transparent structure, and a grammar whose inner workings we can study, as if watching the building of cells in a crystal beehive. An eminent Orientalist remarked "we might imagine Turkish to be the result of the deliberations of some eminent society of learned men;" but no such society could have devised what the mind of man produced, left to itself in the steppes of Tatary, and guided by its innate laws, or by an instinctive power as wonderful as any within the realm of nature.

Turkish conjugation.

Let us examine a few forms. "To love", in the most general sense of the word, or love, as a root, is in

Turkish sev. This does not as yet mean "to love", which is sevmek, or "love" as a substantive, which is sevgu, or sevi; but it only expresses the general quality of loving in the abstract. This root, as we remarked before, can never be touched. Whatever syllables may be added for the modification of its meaning, the root itself must stand out in full prominence like a pearl set in diamonds. It must never be changed or broken, assimilated or modified, as in the English I fall, I fell, I take, I took, I think, I thought, and many similar. With this one restriction, however, we are free to treat it at pleasure.

Let us suppose we possessed nothing like our conjugation, but had to express such ideas as I love, thou lovest, and the rest, for the first time arising in the mind. Nothing would seem more natural now than to form an adjective or a participle, meaning "loving", and then add the different pronouns, as I loving, thou loving, &c. Exactly this the Turks have done. We need not inquire at present how they produced what we call a participle. It was a task by no means facile as we now conceive it, nor is it possible in every case to trace a process essentially complicated. In Turkish, one participle, corresponding to ours in ing, is formed by er. Sev+er, would, therefore, mean lov+er or lov+ing. Thou in Turkish is sen, and as all modificatory syllables are placed at the end of the root, we get sev-er-sen, thou lovest. You in Turkish is siz; hence sev-er-siz, you love. In these cases the pronouns and the terminations of the verb coincide exactly. In other persons the coincidences are less complete, because the pronominal terminations have sometimes been modified, or, as in the third person singular, sever, dropped altogether as unnecessary. A reference to other cognate languages, however, where either the terminations or the pronouns themselves have maintained a more primitive form, enables us to say that in the original Turkic verb, all persons of the present were formed by means of pronouns appended to this participle sever. Instead of "I love, thou lovest, he loves", the Tataric grammarian says, "lover-I, lover-thou, lover."

But these personal terminations are not the same in the imperfect as in the present.

PRESENT.	IMPERFECT.
Sev-er-im I love	sev-di-m, I loved.
Sev-er-sen	sev-di-n·.
Sev-er	sev-di.
Sev-er-iz	sev-di-k (miz).
Sev-er-siz	sev-di-n·iz.
Sev-er-ler	sev-di-ler.

We need not inquire as yet into the origin of the di, added to form the imperfect; but it should be stated that in the first person plural of the imperfect, a various reading occurs in other Turkic dialects, and that miz is used there instead of k. Now, looking at these terminations m, n·, i, miz, n·iz, and ler, we find that they are exactly the same as the possessive pronouns used after nouns. As in some Italian dialects we have fratel-mio, my brother, and as in Hebrew we can say El-i, God (of) I, *i. e.* my God, the Turkic languages form the phrases "my house, thy house, his house", by possessive pronouns appended to substantives. A Turk says, —

Bâbâ,	father,	bâbâ-m,	my father.
Aghâ,	lord,	aghâ-n·,	thy lord.
El,	hand,	el-i,	his hand.
O'*h*lu,	son,	o'*h*lu-muz,	our son.
Anâ,	mother,	anâ-n·iz,	your mother.
Kitâb,	book,	kitâb-leri,	their book.

We may hence infer that in the imperfect these pronominal terminations were originally taken in a possessive sense, and that, therefore, what remains after the personal terminations are removed, sev-di, was never an adjective or a participle, like sev-er, but must have been originally a substantive capable of receiving terminal possessive pronouns; that is, the idea originally expressed by the imperfect could not have been "loving-I", but "love of me."

How then, could this convey the idea of a past tense as contrasted with the present? Let us look to our own language. If desirous to express the perfect, we say, I have loved, j'ai aimé. This "I have", meant originally, I possess, and in Latin "amicus quem amatum habeo", signified in fact a friend whom I hold dear, — not as yet, whom I *have* loved. In the course of time, however, these phrases, "I have said, I have loved", took the sense of the perfect, and of time past — and not unnaturally, inasmuch as what I *hold*, or *have* done, *is* done; — done, as we say, and past. In place of an auxiliary possessive verb, the Turkic language uses an auxiliary possessive pronoun to the same effect. "Paying belonging to me", equals "I have paid"; in either case a phrase originally possessive, took a temporal signification, and became a past or perfect tense. This, however, is the very anatomy of grammar, and when a Turk says "sevdim" he is, of course, as unconscious of its literal force, "loving belonging to me", as of the circulation of his blood. Leaving, therefore, these analytical niceties, and the earlier stage of the Turanian speech, we proceed to a rapid glance at some of its further developments.

The most ingenious part of Turkish is undoubtedly the verb. Like Greek and Sanskrit, it exhibits a variety of moods and tenses, sufficient to express the nicest shades of doubt, of surmise, of hope, and supposition. In all these forms the root remains intact, and sounds like a key-note through all the various modulations produced by the changes of person, number, mood, and time. But there is one feature so peculiar to the Turkish verb, that no analogy can be found in any of the Arian languages — the power of producing new roots by the mere addition of certain letters, which give to every verb a negative, or causative, or reflexive, or reciprocal meaning.

Sev-mek, for instance, as a simple root, means to love. By adding in, we obtain a reflexive verb, sev-in-mek, which means to love oneself, or rather, to rejoice, to be happy. This may now be conjugated through all moods and tenses, sevin being in every respect equal to a new root. By adding ish we form a reciprocal verb, sev-ish-mek, to love one another.

To each of these three forms a causative sense may be imparted by the addition of the syllable dir.. Thus,

I. sev-mek, to love, becomes IV, sev-dir-mek, to cause to love.

II. sev-in-mek, to rejoice, becomes V, sev-in-dir-mek, to cause to rejoice.

III. sev-ish-mek, to love one another, becomes VI, sev-ish-dir-mek, to cause ourselves to love one another.

Each of these six forms may again be turned into a passive by the addition of il. Thus,

I. sev-mek, to love, becomes VII, sev-il-mek, to be loved.

II. sev-in-mek, to rejoice, becomes VIII, sev-in-il-mek, to be rejoiced at.

III. sev-ish-mek, to love one another, becomes IX, sev-ish-il-mek, not translatable.

IV. sev-dir-mek, to cause one to love, becomes IX, sev-dir-il-mek, to be brought to love.

V. sev-in-dir-mek, to cause to rejoice, becomes XI, sev-in-dir-il-mek, to be made to rejoice.

VI. sev-ish-dir-mek, to cause to love one another, becomes XII, sev-ish-dir-il-mek, to be brought to love one another.

This, however, is by no means the whole verbal contingent at the command of a Turkish grammarian. Every one of these twelve secondary or tertiary roots may again be turned into a negative by the mere addition of me. Thus, sev-mek, to love, becomes sev-me-mek, not to love. And if it is necessary to express the impossibility of loving, the Turk has a new root at hand to convey even that idea. Thus while sev-me-mek denies only the fact of loving, sev-eme-mek, denies its possibility, and means not to be able to love. By the addition of these two modificatory syllables, the number of derivative roots is at once raised to thirty-six. Thus,

I. sev-mek, to love, becomes XIII, sev-me-mek, not to love.

II. sev-in-mek, to rejoice, becomes XIV, sev-in-me-mek, not to rejoice.

III. sev-ish-mek, to love one another, becomes XV, sev-ish-me-mek, not to love one another.

IV. sev-dir-mek, to cause to love, becomes XVI, sev-dir-me-mek, not to cause one to love.

V. sev-in-dir-mek, to cause to rejoice, becomes XVII, sev-in-dir-me-mek, not to cause one to rejoice.

VI. sev-ish-dir-mek, to cause ourselves to love one another, becomes XVIII, sev-ish-dir-me-mek, not to cause ourselves to love one another.

VII. sev-il-mek, to be loved, becomes XIX, sev-il-me-mek, not to be loved.

VIII. sev-in-il-mek, to be rejoiced at, becomes XX, sev-in-il-me-mek, not to be the object of rejoicing.

IX. sev-ish-il-mek, if it was used, would become XXI, sev-is-il-me-mek; neither form being translatable.

X. sev-dir-il-mek, to be brought to love, becomes XXII, sev-dir-il-me-mek, not to be brought to love.

XI. sev-in-dir-mek, to be made to rejoice, becomes XXIII, sev-in-dir-il-me-mek, not to be made to rejoice.

XII. sev-ish-dir-il-mek, to be brought to love one another, becomes XXIV, sev-ish-dir-il-me-mek, not to be brought to love one another.

Some of these forms are of course of rare occurrence, and with many verbs these derivative roots, though possible grammatically, would be logically impossible. Even a verb like 'to love', perhaps the most pliant of all, resists some of the modifications to which a Turkish grammarian is fain to subject it. It is clear, however, that wherever a negation can be formed, the idea of impossibility also can be superadded, so that by substituting eme for me, we should raise the number of derivative roots to thirty-six. The very last of these, XXXVI, sev-ish-dir-il-eme-mek would be perfectly intelligible, and might be used, for instance, at the present moment if, in speaking of the Sultan and the Czar, we wished to say, that it was impossible that they should be brought to love one another.

Our review of the languages of the seat of war in the East might here be closed, because the next branch of the Turanian family, the Finnic, carries us up so far to the north of Europe and Asia, that we may hope no European army will have to march there. But while the army in the South will probably never exchange words with a Finn, many of the inhabitants of the Baltic coast, with whom the fleets will have probably to make acquaintance belong to this division of the Turanian race. And indeed so wide and wayward have been the migrations of this family, that its scattered members — Magyars or Hungarians on the Middle Danube, and Finns and Lapps on the Northern Gulf, touch either extreme on the vast line of the allied operations. We shall therefore add a few words on these nations and their early wanderings.

Finnic Branch.

It is generally supposed that the original seat of the Finnic tribes was in the Ural mountains, and their languages have been therefore called Uralic. From this centre they spread east and west: and southward in ancient times, even to the Black Sea, where Finnic tribes, together with Mongolic and Turkic, were probably known to the Greeks under the comprehensive and convenient name of Scythians. As we possess no literary documents of any of these Nomadic nations, it is impossible to say, even where Greek writers have preserved their barbarous names, to what branch of the vast Turanian family they belonged. Their habits were probably identical before the Christian era, during the Middle Ages, and at the present day. One tribe takes possession of a tract and retains it perhaps for several generations, giving its name to the meadows where it tends its flocks, and to the rivers where the horses are watered. If the country be fertile, it will attract the eye of other tribes; wars begin, and if resistance be hopeless, hundreds of families fly from their paternal pastures, to migrate perhaps for generations, — for migration they find a more natural life than permanent habitation, — and after a time we may rediscover their names a thousand miles distant. Or two tribes will carry on their warfare for ages, till with reduced numbers both have perhaps to make common cause against some new enemy.

During these continued struggles their languages lose as many words, perhaps, as men are killed on the field of battle. Some words (we might say) go over like deserters — others are made prisoners, and exchanged again during times of peace. Besides, there are parleys and challenges, and at last a dialect is produced which may very properly be called a language of the camp, — (Urdu-zebán, camp-language, is the proper name of Hindustani, formed in the armies of the Mogol-emperors) — but where it is difficult for the philologist to arrange the living and to number the slain, unless some salient points of grammar have been preserved throughout the mêlée. We saw how a number of tribes may be at times suddenly gathered by the command of a *K*ingis-khán or Timur, like billows heaving and swelling at the call of a thunderstorm. One such wave rolling on from Karakorum to Liegnitz may sweep away all the sheepfolds and landmarks of centuries, and when the storm is over, a thin crust will, as after a flood, remain, concealing the underlying stratum of people and languages. Geologists tell us that beneath a layer of gravel, granite rocks are often conccaled. And thus when we set aside the family name of Tatar, conferred by the princes of the house of *K*ingis-khán on the tribes of the Black Sea and Siberia, we recognize the tribes themselves as indubitably and purely Turkic.

On the evidence of language, the Finnic stock is divided into four branches, Four Divisions of the Finnic Branch.

The *K*udic,
The Bulgaric,
The Permic,
The Ugric.

The Kudic Branch. The *Kudic* branch comprises the Finnic of the Baltic coasts. The name is derived from *Kud* (Tchud) originally applied by the Russians to the Finnic nations in the north-west of Russia. Afterwards it took a more general sense, and was used almost synonymously with Scythian for all the tribes of Central and Northern Asia. The

The Finns. Finns, properly so called, or as they call themselves Suomalaïnen, *i. e.*, inhabitants of fens, are settled in the provinces of Finland (formerly belonging to Sweden, but since 1809 annexed to Russia), and in parts of the governments of Archangel and Olonetz. Their number is 1,521,515. The Finns are governed by Russia with some moderation, and their country, though apparently more swamp than soil, yields an annual surplus of revenue. The Finns are the most advanced of their whole family, and are, the Magyars excepted, the only Finnic race that can claim a station among the civilized and civilizing nations of the world. Their literature and, above all, their popular poetry bears witness to a high intellectual development in times which we may call mythical, and in places more favourable to the glow of poetical feelings than their present abode, the last refuge that Europe could afford them. These songs still live among the poorest, recorded by oral tradition alone, and preserving all the features of a perfect metre and of a more ancient language. A national feeling has lately arisen amongst the Finns, in spite of Russian supremacy, and the labours of Sjögren, Lönnrot, Castrén, and Kellgren, receiving hence a powerful impulse, have produced results truly surprising. From the mouths of the aged an epic poem has been collected equalling the Iliad in length and completeness, nay, if we can forget for a moment all that we in our youth learned to call beautiful, of a beauty essentially similar. A Finn is not a Greek, and Wainamoinen was not a Homer. But if the poet may take his colours from that nature by which he is surrounded, if he may depict the men with whom he lives, "Kalewala" possesses merits not dissimilar from the Iliad, and will claim its place as the fifth national epic of the world, side by side with the Ionian songs, with the Mahabharata, the Shah-námeh, and the Nibelunge. This early literary cultivation has not been without a powerful influence on the language. It has imparted permanency to its form and a traditional character to its words, so that at first sight we might almost doubt whether the grammar of this language had not left the agglutinative stage, and entered into the current of inflection, with Greek or Sanskrit. The agglutinative type, however, yet remains, and its grammar shows a luxuriance of grammatical combination second only to Turkish and Hungarian. Like Turkish it observes the "harmony of vowels", a feature peculiar to Turanian languages, as explained before.

Karelian and Tavastian are dialectical varieties of Finnish.

The present civilization of Finnland, its schools and university (Helsingfors), its literature and government, are rather of Teutonic than of indigenous growth. But traces of the Finnic character are visible amongst the existing race. A tone of sad resignation, broken by fantastic wildness, runs through their literature, and meditativeness has almost become their national character.

The Esths or Esthonians, neighbouring on the Finns, speak a language closely allied to the Finnish. It is divided into the dialects of Dorpat (in Livonia) and Reval. Except some popular songs it is almost without literature. Esthonia together with Livonia and Kurland form the three Baltic provinces of Russia. The population on the islands of the Gulf of Finland is mostly Esthonian. In the higher ranks of society, however, the national language is hardly understood, and never spoken.

The Esth nians.

Besides the Finns and Esthonians, the Livonians and the Laps must be reckoned also amongst the same family. Their number, however, is small. The population of Livonia consists chiefly of Esths, Letts, Russians and Germans. The number of Livonians speaking their own dialect is not more than 5000.

The Liv nians.

The Laps or Laplanders inhabit the most Northern part of Europe. They belong to Sweden and to Russia.

The Lap landers

Their number is estimated at 28,000. Their language has lately received much attention, and Castrén's travels give a description of their manners most interesting from its simplicity and faithfulness.

The Bulgaric Branch.

We need not dwell on the Bulgaric branch. This comprises the *K*eremissians and Mordvinians, scattered in disconnected colonies along the Volga, and surrounded by Russian and Turkic dialects. Both languages are extremely artificial in their grammar, and allow an accumulation of pronominal affixes at the end of verbs, surpassed only by the Bask, the Caucasian, and those American dialects that have been called Polysynthetic.

The general name given to these tribes, Bulgaric, is not borrowed from Bulgaria, the present seat of war; Bulgaria, on the contrary, received its name (replacing that of Moesia) from the Finnic armies by whom it was conquered in the seventh century. Bulgarian tribes advanced from the Volga to the Don, and after a period, passed under the sovereignty of the Avars, on the Don and Dniepr, advancing to the Danube in 635, they founded the Bulgarian kingdom. This has retained its name to the present day, though the Finnic Bulgarians have long been absorbed by Slavonic inhabitants, and both brought under Turkish sway since 1392.

The Permic Branch.

The third branch also, Permic, concerns us little. It comprises the idioms of the Votiakes, the Sirianes, and the Permians, three dialects of one language. Perm was the ancient name for the country between 61°—76° E. L., and 55°—65° N. L. The Permic tribes were driven westward by their eastern neighbours, the Voguls, and thus pressed upon their western neighbours, the Bulgars of the Volga. The Votiakes are found between the rivers Vyatka and Kama. Northwards follow the Sirianes, inhabiting the country on the Upper Kama, while the Eastern portion is held by the Permians. These are surrounded on the south by the Tatars of Orenburg and the Baskirs; on the north by the Samoiedes, and on the east by Voguls, who pressed ou them from the Ural.

These Voguls together with Hungarians and Ostiakes form the fourth and last branch of the Finnic family, the Ugric. It was in 462, after the dismemberment of Attila's Hunnic empire that these Ugric tribes approached Europe. They were then called Onagurs, Saragurs and Urogs; and in later times they occur in Russian Chronicles as Ugry. They are the ancestors of the Hungarians, and should not be confounded with the Uigurs, an ancient Turkic tribe mentioned before. The Ugric Branch.

The similarity between the Hungarian language and dialects of Finnic origin, spoken east of the Volga, is not a new discovery. In 1253, Wilhelm Ruysbroeck, a priest who travelled beyond the Volga, remarked that a race called Pascatir, who live on the Yaïk, spoke the same language as the Hungarians. They were then settled east of the old Bulgarian kingdom, the capital of which, the ancient Bolgari, on the left of the Volga, may still be traced in the ruins of Spask. If these Pascatir — the portion of the Ugric tribes that remained east of the Volga — are identical with the Baskir, as Klaproth supposes, it would follow that, in later times, they gave up their language, for the present Baskir no longer speak a Hungarian, but a Turkic language. The affinity of the Hungarian and the Ugro-Finnic dialects was first proved philologically by Gyarmathi in 1799.

A few instances may suffice to show this connection: —

Hungarian.	*K*eremissian.	English.
Atya-m,	atya-m,	my father.
Atya-d,	atya-t,	thy father.
Attya,	atya-se,	his father.
Atya-nk,	atya-ne,	our father.
Atya-tok,	atya-da,	your father.
Atty-ok.	atya-st,	their father.

Declension.

	Hungarian.	Esthonian.	English.
Nom.	vér	werri	blood
Gen.	véré	werre	of blood
Dat.	vérnek	werrele	to blood
Acc.	vért	werd	blood
Abl.	vérestöl	werrist	from blood.

Conjugation.

Hungarian.	Esthonian.	English.
Lelem	leian	I find
Leled	leiad	thou findest
Leli	leiab	he finds
Leljük	leiame	we find
Lelitek	leiate	you find
Lelik	leiawad	they find.

A comparative Table of the Numerals of each of the four branches of the Finnic Class will show the degree of their mutual relationship.

	1	2	3	4	5	6	7	8	9	10
*K*udic, Finnish	yksi	kaksi	kolme	neljä	viisi	kuusi	seitsemän	kahdeksan	yhdeksan	kymmenen
*K*udic, Esthonian	üts	kats	kolm	nelli	wiis	kuus	seitse	kattesa	üttesa	kümme
Bulgaric, *K*eremissian .	ik	kok	kum	nil	vis	kut	sim	kändäxe	endexe	lu
Bulgaric, Mordvinian .	vaike	kavto	kolmo	nile	väte	kóto	sisem	kavkso	väikse	kämen
Permic, Sirianian . . .	ötik	kyk	kujim	njolj	vit	kvait	sizim	kökjâmys	ökmys	das
Ugric, Ostiakian	it	kat	chudem	njeda	vet	chut	tabet	nida	arjong	jong
Ugric, Hungarian . . .	egy	ket	harom	negy	öt	hat	het	njolcz	kilencz	tiz

Ascending scale of the Tungusic, Mongolic, Turkic, and Finnic Branches.

We have thus examined the four chief classes of the Turanian family, the Tungusic, Mongolic, Turkic, and Finnic. The Tungusic branch stands lowest; its grammar is not much richer than Chinese, and in its structure there is an absence of that architectonic order which in Chinese makes the Cyclopean stones of language hold together without grammatical cement. This applies, however, principally to the Man*g*u; other Tungusic dialects spoken, not in China, but in the original seats of the Man*g*us, are even now beginning to develop grammatical forms.

The Mongolic dialects excel the Tungusic, but in their grammar can hardly distinguish between the different parts of speech. The spoken idioms of the Mongolians, as of the Tungusians, are evidently struggling towards a more organic life, and Castrén has brought home evidence of incipient verbal growth in the language of the Buriäts and a Tungusic dialect spoken near Nyer*k*insk.

This is, however, only a small beginning, if compared with the profusion of grammatical resources displayed by the Turkic languages. In their system of conjugation, the Turkic dialects can hardly be surpassed. Their verbs are like branches which break down under the heavy burden of fruits and blossoms. The excellence of the Finnic languages consists rather in a diminution than increase of verbal forms; but in declension, Finnish is even more overburdened than Turkish.

The Northern and Southern Divisions of the Turanian Family.

These four branches, together with the Samoiedic, constitute the Northern or Ural-Altaic Division of the Turanian family. The Southern division consists of the Tamulic, the Bhotíya, comprising the Gangetic and Lohitic, the Taïc, and the Malaic branches. These two divisions comprehend very nearly all the languages of Asia, with the exception of Chinese. A few, such as Japanese, the language of Korea, of the Koriakes, the Kam*k*adales, &c. remain unclassed, but in them also some traces of common origin with the Turanian languages have, it is probable, survived, and await the discovery of philological research.

Genealogical Table of the Turanian Family of Speech.

Living Languages.	Dead Languages.	Branches.	Classes.	
Dialects of the *Kapogires* (Upper Tunguska)		Western	Tungusic	Northern Division.
" Orotongs (Lower Tunguska)				
" People of Nyer*k*insk				
" Lamutos (Coast of O'h-otsk)		Eastern		
" Mangu (China)				
" *S*arra-Mongols (South of Gobi)		Eastern or Mongols Proper	Mongolic	
" Khalkhas (North of Gobi)				
" *S*araigol (Tibet and Tangut)				
" *K*osot (Koko-nûr) — Ölöt or Kalmüks		Western-Mongols		
" Dsungar — Ölöt or Kalmüks				
" Torgod — Ölöt or Kalmüks				
" Dürbet — Ölöt or Kalmüks				
" Aimaks (*i. e.* tribes of Persia)				
" Tokpas (Tibet)				
" Buriäts (Lake Baikal)		Northern-Mongols		
" Uigurs		*K*agataic, S. E.	Turkic	
" Komans				
" *K*agatais				
" Usbeks				
" Turkomans				
" People of Kasan				
" Kirgis		Turkic, N.		
" Baskirs				
" Nogais				
" Kumians				
" Kara*k*ais				
" Karakalpaks				
" Mes*k*eryäk's				
" People of Siberia				
" Yakuts				
" People of Derbend		Turkic, W.		
" " Aderbigan				
" " Krimea				
" " Anatolia				
" " Rumelia				
" Yurazes		Northern	Samoiedic	
" Tawgi				
" Yenisei				
" Ostiako-Samoiedes		Eastern		
" Kamas				
" Hungarians		Ugric	Finnic (Uralic)	
" Voguls				
" Ugro-Ostiakes				
" *K*eremissians		Bulgaric		
" Mordvins				
" Permians		Permic		
" Sirianes				
" Votiaks				
" Lapps		*K*udic		
" Finns				
" Esths				

Scattered Languages of the Turanian Family.

Dialects which have become separated from the common stock at an early time, and have grown up without further intercourse, are sometimes carried away by certain individual peculiarities to an extent that effaces every sign of their common and original character. Intercourse with other nations, and a national literature preserve languages from dialectic schisms and the perpetuation of the fancies of individual expression. Language, and particularly Turanian language, is so pliant, that it lends itself to endless combinations and complexities. Even in Turkish, so long under the influence of a literary cultivation, the number of possible forms is endless: and some are actually used in the dialects of Tataric tribes, which the literary Osmanli has discarded. Tribes that have no idea of literature or other intellectual occupations, seem occasionally to take a delight in working their language to the utmost limits of grammatical expansion. The American dialects are a wellknown instance: and the greater the seclusion of a tribe, the more amazing this rank vegetation of their grammar. Probably we can form no correct idea with what feeling a savage nation looks upon its language; perhaps, it may be, as a plaything, a kind of intellectual amusement, a maze in which the mind likes to lose and to find itself. But the result is the same everywhere. If the work of agglutination has once commenced, and if there is nothing like literature or society to keep it within limits, two villages, separated only for a few generations, will become mutually unintelligible. This takes place in America, as well as on the borders of India and China; and in the North of Asia, Messerschmidt relates that the Ostiakes, though really speaking the same language everywhere, have produced so many words and forms peculiar to each tribe, that even within the limits of twelve or twenty German miles, conversation between them becomes extremely difficult. It must be remembered also that the dictionary of these languages is small if compared with a Latin or Greek Thesaurus. The conversation of Nomadic tribes moves within a narrow circle, and with the great facility of forming new words, and the great inducement that a solitary life holds out to invent, for the objects which form the world of a shepherd or a huntsman, new appellations, half-poetical perhaps or satirical, we can understand how, after a few generations, the dictionary of a Nomadic tribe may have gone, as it were, through more than one edition. These few hints I give to show from what point of view we should look upon the relationship between Nomadic dialects: prepared to find but scanty remains of their original vocabulary among tribes who after being severed from the rest, have continued for centuries without literature and without tradition, in the fastnesses of the Pyrenees, the unapproachable valleys of Mount Caucasus, or the solitary Tundras of Northern Europe.

After these preliminary remarks, we proceed at once to a consideration of the Caucasian dialects, one of the outstanding and degenerated colonies of the Turanian family of speech.

Caucasian Languages

The first scholar who supplied information on the languages spoken in the Caucasus, was Klaproth. His travels, undertaken under the auspices of the Russian government, fall in the years 1807 and 1808, and their results were published in several works, as "Travels in the Caucasus and Georgia"; "Archives for Asiatic Literature, History and Languages", and "Asia Polyglotta."

We begin with the first class.

He drew a distinction between the Caucasian tribes, properly so called, who have lived in their present seats from time immemorial; — other tribes now settled there, but known to be later immigrants, the Ossetes, and the Georgians; — and Turkish tribes, the Bazianes and others.

Georgic Branch.

The Georgians occupy the larger portion of the Caucasian territory. Their frontiers are the river Alazani in the east; the Black Sea on the west; the Caucasian mountains on the north; and the river Kur, the mountains of Karabagh, Pambaki, and Kildir in the south. They immigrated from the south-east; and their traditions, framed on Christian models, assign the country south of the Kur, to Karthlos, son of Thargamos, and great-grandson of Japhet, the reputed ancestor of the Georgians.

The Georgians are divided into four branches.

Georgian. 1. The Georgians proper, called also Grusians or Karthu'hli, inhabit Karthli, Kha'hethi and Imerethi, and extend westward to the river Ts'henis-tskali. The P*s*awi and Gudamakari in the high Caucasian mountains, east of the river Aragwa, belong to the same branch.

Mingrelian. 2. The inhabitants of Mingrelia, Odi*s*i, and Guria. Their country is the old Colchis, and their language most closely allied with the Lazian.

Suanian. 3. The Suans, or, as they call themselves, *S*wan (not Shnau), inhabit the southern slopes of the Caucasian Alps, where they rise from the Black Sea and cross the Isthmus from west to east. Their country lies west of the Mount *G*uman-taw, along the rivers Ts'henis-tskali, Enguri, and Egrisi. Part of the Suans are independent; others are under the rule of Mingrelian princes: none as yet subject to Russia. The district of Le*k*kum, on the Ts'henis-tskali, is inhabited by Georgians; also the district of Ra*g*a, in the Rion-basin. Both are governed by Russia. These Georgians are called Imerians, and all the country west of the Mes'hian mountains, goes by the name Imerethi. The eastern tribes of ihe Suans are mixed with Os; and those further east, the P*s*awi, 'Hevsurs, and Thu*s*i, along the sources of the Eastern Aragva, the Alazan, and the Andian Koisu, are mixed with *Kek* tribes, and have lost almost all sign of Georgian descent.

Ptolemy knew the Suans as Suano-Kolchi. Their language is peculiar on many points, if compared with Mingrelian and Lazian: but the coincidences in roots, words, and grammatical forms are sufficiently numerous to give it a place in the Georgian family.

Lazian. 4. The Lazes, in the San*g*akat of Lazistan, belonging to the Pashalik of Trebizond. Their language is spoken along the coast of the Black Sea from the Promontory of Kyemer Burnu to the mouth of the *K*orok. In the south it extends only a few leagues from the coast into the interior, while in the north the Lazian is spoken as far east as the watershed of the *K*orok, and even beyond. At Batum, which belongs to the San*g*akat of Lazistan, the Grusian dialect of Guria is spoken; at Trebizond — Turkish, Greek, and Armenian: but there is no distinct Lazian dialect for Trebizond, as Klaproth asserts, though Lazes from all parts of Lazistan are gathered within that city.

In the Middle Ages there was a powerful Lazian kingdom, comprehending the whole of Imerethi. The Lazes afterwards became subordinate to the princes of Grusia: but when these were conquered by the Turks in 1580, every valley of Lazistan declared itself independent under small princes, who were continually engaged in warfare and mutual depredation. Not quite twenty years ago Lazistan was conquered by Osman Pasha and incorporated with Turkey. The inhabitants are Mohammedans; their alphabet is Turkish; and Turkish is frequently spoken in their valleys.

These four branches speak dialects different, but decidedly cognate, with many varieties in each valley. The dialects differ more in their dictionary than in their grammar. Their grammatical system is throughout identical, and connects the language east and west of the Caucasian watershed, into one family. The mountains that form the Isthmus between the Black Sea and the Caspian Sea, are no barrier between the languages they geographically divide. And on the east the chain rises gently, and opens many passes towards the western coast. It is difficult to say whether Georgic dialects were ever spoken on the coast of the Caspian Sea, but from the river Alazani westward they form an uninterrupted chain across the entire Isthmus. Among them, two, the Lazian and Mingrelian, agree so much both in words and grammar, that they may formerly have been but one language, as French and Italian. The people themselves are fully aware of the great similarity of their idioms, but they would deny all connection with the Suanian. Their relation with this dialect is indeed more distant; not so much, however, as not to disclose the traces of a common family type, when more carefully examined and compared.

Aboriginal Languages. The second class of languages, spoken by the aboriginal inhabitants of the Caucasian territory is divided into three branches,

1. Eastern, or Lesghi.
2. Middle, or Mitsgeghi.
3. Western, or *K*erkessian and Abasian tribes.

Lesghic Branch. Lesghistan, or the country of the Lesghi, also called Daghestan, or the mountain-country, lies between the rivers Koisu, Alazani, and the Caspian Sea. The Lesghi or Leski, are called Lekhi by the Georgians, Leksi by the Armenians, and Leki by the Ossetes, and may therefore be the same as the "Legae" mentioned by Strabo.

The inhabitants of Lesghistan do not call or esteem themselves one people, and according to Klaproth, not less than four different languages are spoken in this small country. These are: —

Avarian Language. 1. Avarian, spoken in the districts of ʻHundsag, or Avar, Käseruk, Hidatle, Mukratle, Ansokul, Karaʻhle, Gumbet, Arrakan, Burtuna, Anzuʻh, Tebel, Tumurga, Aʻhti, Ruthul, *K*ari and Belakan, amongst the Andi, and at Kabu*k*. It is subdivided into various dialects. The frontiers of the Avarian are, the river Aksai on the west; the mountains south of the Aksai, Endery and Tilbak in the north; the rivers Koisu in the east; and the Upper Samur and Mount *S*adagh in the south.

The language of the districts Dido and Unso on the Upper Samur, though mixed with other Caucasian words, belongs to the Avarian division.

Kasikumükian Language. 2. The language of the Kasikumüks, spoken in various dialects in Kara-kaitak end Tabaseran. Its western frontiers are the river Koisu; southern, the river Gurieni; the promontories of Tabaseran and North Daghestan on the east; and the sources of the Osen to the north. On the coast of the Caspian Sea Tatar tribes have settled in considerable numbers, and north of Derbend we find not less than twelve Turkman villages, the Kaitak. Again in the north and east of the Caucasian Isthmus, numerous Tatar settlements exists: dating perhaps from the time of *K*ingis-khán. They belong to the Nogai-Tatar, and in some places preserve that name.

3. The language of Akuska, spoken also in Tsudakara and Kubi*k*i, and in the Alps between the Koisu, the Upper Manas-rivers and the sources of the Buam. Akuskian Language.

4. The language of Kura in south Daghestan. Kurian Language.

The Lesghians are Mohammedans, and like most Caucasians, belong to the orthodox sect of the Sunites. The Islam made little progress in the Caucasus in early times, except on the Eastern coast, which is open to Persian influence, particularly the portion known under the name of Daghestan. It was only when compelled to surrender the Krimea to Russia, and after the fall of Kuban (now *K*ernomoria) before the Czar, that the Porte found it expedient to strengthen its political and religious hold on the people of the Caucasus as a barrier against Russian influence. Since that time several prophets, Mursids or teachers, have risen in the Caucasus and inflamed their flocks against the Giaour and the Muscovite. Their chief object is to establish a feeling of common interest, and of national and religious unity among tribes kept asunder unfortunately by mutual feuds, difference of language, and national prejudices. The name of Mahomet Mansur, taken prisoner in 1791, and never heard of since his confinement in the fortress of Schlüsselburg, the name of Kasi-Mollah, who fell with the fortress of Himri in 1832; of Hamsad Beg, murdered in 1834, and Shamyl, the living hero, rouse dreadful recollections in the minds of Russian officers.

Very little is known of the Lesghic language, and the lists of words given by Klaproth convey hardly any information on the grammatical character of this class of Caucasian dialects. Brosset has lately paid attention to this branch of philology, and collected Avarian songs during his stay at Tiflis. There is reason to suppose that another distinguished member of the Petersburg Academy, M. Schiefner, will take up this subject and prepare a grammar of the Avarian dialect.

II. The language of the Mits*g*eghi, a race sometimes called Kistian, is spoken west and north-west of the Lesghian. Its frontiers are, — in the west, the Upper Mitsgeghic Branch.

Terek; north, the Little Kabardah and the river Sun*g*a; south, the snowy heights of the Caucasus which separates the Mits*g*eghi Proper from the 'Hevsurs, Psawi, Gudamakaris, and from Kha'hethi; eastward, the Upper Ya'hsai and Endery. Some mixed Mits*g*eghian tribes, as the Thusi, live south of the mountains near the sources of the Alazani.

The Mits*g*eghi, or as the Russians pronounce it, Mitshik, are again divided into three branches.

Galgai. The first comprises the Galgai, Halha or Ingus, who call themselves Lamur, *i. e.*, mountaineers. They inhabit the country on the rivers Kumbalei, Sun*g*a and Salgir or Asai.

Karabulak. The second comprises the Karabulak, or Aristoyai, as they are called by the *Kek*entsi: but in their own language named Ars'hte. They live in the valley of the Martan-river.

Kek. The third consists of the *Kek*, or as the Russians name them *Kek*entsi, extending from the Karabulaks eastward to the river Ya'hsai. The name *Kek*, with the Russian termination, *Kek*entsi, is said to be derived from a village where one of the first battles between this race and the Russians took place, and is sometimes, at least by Russians, used as a general name for all Mits*g*eghian tribes.

The languages of these three tribes have a common type, different from the other Caucasian idioms, but approximating in grammar most to the Lesghian dialects, particularly the Kasi-Kumukian and Avarian. This applies, however, more particularly to the grammatical system of the Lesghic and Mits*g*eghic dialects, while their vocabularies offer but few coincidences. On the Sun*g*a the Mits*g*eghi are considerably mixed with Tatars, and several tribes, such as the Borahan, Topli, and Istissu, speak Tataric. Ingus is a name given to some *Kek* clans, east of the Terek, who border on the Karabulaks in the plains. The Ingus were formerly Christians, but are now little removed from heathenism. The rest are Mohammedans, and all have acted a prominent part in the war against Russia.

One of the Mits*g*eghic or Kistian dialects has lately

been analysed by Professor Schiefner of Petersburg, in his article on the Thusch language, published in the Bulletin Historico-Philologique de l'Académie des sciences. He identifies the Thus with the Τοῦσκοι, mentioned by Ptolemy (V, 9.), together with the Δίδουροι, in whom M. Schiefner very ingeniously recognises the neighbouring tribe of the Didos. Some of his remarks on the phonetic and grammatical features of this dialect are of interest. No word in Thus begins with r, a remark which applies equally to the Samoiedian, Mongolic and Tataric languages. If the letter r occurs in the body of a word, any r, occurring in terminations, is changed to l. This feature also is shared by the Mongolic. The final i and u of terminations are frequently placed before the consonant or consonants which they originally followed. For instance, nax, people, Gen. nax-i, or naix; khorth, head, Gen. khorthi or khoirth. Similar changes occur in several branches of the Arian family.

The declension of nouns is carried out by means of postpositions, and the great variety of cases, coupled with the absence of a pure accusative, reminds us strongly of the character of some of the most developed Turanian languages.

The pronouns show traces of similarity with the Abchasian and Tcherkessian, while the vocabulary is said to contain many words borrowed from Georgian. Some words which are described as taken from Greek are probably of later origin, and may have been introduced by the Georgian priests. Professor Schiefner denies any close grammatical resemblance between the Thus and the Georgic dialects, and he is inclined to admit a closer relationship between Mitsgeghic and Lesghic, than between either and Georgic. He throws doubt on Klaproth's opinion that there is a connexion between the Caucasic and Samoïedic languages, but he has not yet arrived himself at any conclusion as to the real relationship between this interesting language and any other class of the great Turanian family.

III. The Western Caucasians are best known to us by the name of Circassians, *K*erkessians or Abas- *Kerkess Branch*

9*

sians. They call themselves Adighé or Addi-ghé, which Dr. Loewe derives from the Circassian Attaghagh, height, and explains it therefore in the sense of Mountaineer. In ancient times their seats were not only in the Western Caucasus but extended within the Krimea; and Arrian, at the beginning of the second century after Christ, mentions Ζύχοι, supposed to be the *K*erkessians on the coast of the Black Sea. According to their own traditions, one of their tribes, the Kabardah, emigrated in the thirteenth century from the Kuban to the Don, and thence to the Krimea: traces of them still exist there in the plains between the rivers Ka*k*a and Belbik. They afterwards returned to the Kuban, and became a powerful tribe under Kabardah princes.

Kerkessians. The *K*erkėssians are by the Ossetes and Mingrelians called Kasa'h, said to have been their name before the Kabardas returned from the Krimea. Kasachia was known to Konstantinus Porphyrogeneta, as the country between Zychia on the Black Sea and the Alanes.

At the beginning of the sixteenth century *K*erkessians inhabited the coast of the Lacus Maeotis, from the Don to the Kimmerian Bosphorus. Thence they were driven back by Russian and Tatar conquests; and the present Cossacks, who are Slavonic, are supposed by Klaproth to be of mingled *K*erkessian and Russian blood.

The name of the *K*erkessians or Circassians on the coast of the Black Sea, by the north-western extremity of the Caucasian mountains, has been known in Europe particularly since 1836, after the capture of the English ship Vixen, and through their resistance against Russia, whose previous operations had been mainly directed against the east of the Caucasian isthmus. Greek writers, however, recognized the *K*erkessians, settled on their present territory, and their name is a corruption of the ancient "Kerketoi." In later times the Greeks place the Zychoi on the coast, and the Kerketoi further inland. At present the *K*erkessians on the sea-coast, and south of the Kuban, distinguish themselves by the name of "Adighé," while those of the interior, in the Kabardah, south of the Malka and along the Terek, are properly called *K*erkessian. The Karbardah was one of the first districts in the Caucasus conquered by Russia. The inhabitants are Mohammedans, and the Adighé also belong mostly to the Islam, though traces of their former Christian and heathen practices still remain among them. The Kabardah, east of the Elburs, south of the Malka, and extending west beyond the Terek as far as the sources of the Sun*g*a, is divided into Great or Western, and Little or Eastern Kabardah. The northern frontier of the Adighé is the Kuban. They inhabit the mountains from the sea to 58° east longitude, and on the northern side of the range, here called the Black or Ahmed Mountains, they extend even to 59° east longitude. The tribes which have maintained their independence are the Nato‘hua*g*, *S*apsu‘h, Abadse‘h, and part of the Mo‘hos and Besle. Subject to Russia are the Bsedu‘h, Hattukai, Temirgoi, and Yegorokoi; all tribes considerably reduced in number.

The Abassians have occupied their present seats on the Black Sea at least since the Christian era. Arrian calls them Abasci, the Georgians Ab‘hasi and their country Ab‘hasethi: the Russians Ab‘has, or *G*igeth. They name themselves Absne. They are divided from the *K*erkessians, on the north, by the river Kapoeti; from the Mingrelians, in the south, by the river Enguri, or, according to Rosen, by the small river Erthi-tskali. Eastward they are conterminous with the Suanes. Some Abassians live between the Upper Kuban, the Kuma, and the Malka. Abassian

The chief Abassian tribes in the northern parts of the Caucasus, and south of the Kuban, lie from east to west; the Besilbai, Midawi, Barrakai, Kasilbeg, *K*egreh, Ba‘h, Tubi, Ubu‘h, Bsubbeh, Abase‘h, and Ne*k*kua*g*a.

The Abassians on the right of the Kuban, as far as Podkumok, are Russian subjects; on the left, near the Little In*g*ik, they are still independent. Named by themselves Tapanta, they are called Baske‘h by *K*erkessians, Alti-Kesek Abasi by the Tatars.

Although Russian troops occupy numerous forts on

the coast, and have there succeeded in subduing some tribes as the Zibeld, yet no stranger, least of all a Russian, can venture many miles away from the coast, for the Abassian tribes are the fiercest of the Caucasus. The Russians hold what they call the Little Abadsa; Abadsa being the Russian name of the country north of the mountain ridge, of which the Little Abadsa is the eastern portion. The Uby'h, a clan of highlanders in the north-west, who have made themselves formidable to the Russians, are probably the same as the Ubi'h or Ubu'h, of Abassian origin. The Abassians are darker than the *K*erkessians. Some call themselves Christian, others Mohammedan.

The following is an approximate statement of the Caucasian population:

*K*erkessians	280,000
Abassians	140,000
Ossetes	60,000
Georgians	50,000
Mits*g*eghians	110,000
Lesghians	400,000
Tatars	80,000
	1,120,000

The following statements with regard to the Circassians are taken from Dr. Loewe's introduction to his Dictionary. Dr. Loewe speaks as an eye-witness, and his accounts therefore deserve attention even where they differ from Klaproth and other authorities.

"The Circassians occupy the territory of the Caucasus situated between the rivers Sotsha and Laba, the lower Kuban and the Black Sea. To this territory belong the following provinces: —

"The province of the Bestiné, situated between the Urup and Khods.

"The province of the Makhot-hi between the Laba and Kars.

"The provinces of the Yegerukaï, the Ademi, and the Temirgoï, situated on the coasts of the rivers

Laba and the Kuban, on the north-western boundaries of the province of the Nagaï.

"The provinces of the S-hane, the Gatyukoï, and the Bs-hedukh, between the Sha.o.ugwasha and the Afips.

"The province of the Abasekh is bounded west by the district inhabited by the Shapsukh; south by the district of the Shapsukh and the Ubykh; east by the Sha.o.ugwasha; north by the provinces of the Gatyukoï and that of the Bs-hedukh.

"The province of the Ubykh, situated between the Shapsukh and the Ds-hig-het-hi.

"The province of the Shapsukh, which is bounded east by the province of Ubykh, west by the province of Natkho-kudash, north by the Kuban, and south by the Pontus.

"The province of the Natko-kuadsh, situated between the Taman, the Kuban, the province of the Shapsukh and the Pontus.

"The province of the Karatshaï, near the sources of the Kuban and the province of the Nagaï.

"The province of the Nagaï, between the Kuban and the Laba."

Since the appearance of Sheikh Manzur (?), the princes and nobles profess the Mohammedan religion, and belong to the sect of the Sunites; but the mass of the people adhere faithfully to their former idolatrous worship. Their principal deities are: —

I. Shiblé, the god of thunder, war, and justice.

II. Tleps, the god of fire.

III. Seostseres, the god of the waters, rivers, and winds.

IV. Sekutkha, the god of travellers, and rewarder of hospitality.

V. Mesitkha, the god of forests.

How then, it may be asked, should a man learn all these languages? Cardinal Mezzofanti, at the time of his recent death, spoke not less than fifty-eight; but even this number would not suffice to carry a man through

Historical recollection connected with the languages of the seat of war all the dialects spoken along the Danube, the Black Sea, the Caspian Sea, and in the Russian Empire at large. And most of these cannot be learned from Grammars, either because none exist; or because they are written in a language which would have to be learned first, as Russian, German, or Armenian. The Caucasus is called by the Persians "the Mountain of Languages," and the diversity of dialects spoken there in every valley has been the chief obstacle to a united resistance on the part of the Caucasian tribes against Russia. The southeast of Europe has indeed long been notorious as a Babel of tongues. Herodotus* (iv. 24) tells us that caravans of Greek merchants, following the course of the Volga upward to the Ural Mountains, were accompanied by seven interpreters, speaking seven different languages. These must have comprised Slavonic, Tataric, and Finnic dialects, spoken in those countries in the time of Herodotus as at the present day. In yet earlier times the South-east of Europe was the first resting-place for the nations who transplanted the seeds of Asia to European soil. Three roads were open to their North-westward migrations. One, east of the Caspian Sea and West of the Ural Mountains, leading to the North of Asia and Europe. Another, on the Caucasian Isthmus, whence they would advance along the northern coast of the Black Sea, and following the course of the Dniepr, Dniestr, or Danube, be led into Russia and Germany. A third road was defined by the Taurus through Asia Minor, to the point where the Hellespont marks the "path of the Hellenes" into Greece and Italy. While the main stream of the Arian nations passed on, carrying its waves to the northern and western shores of Europe, it formed a kind of eddy in the Carpathian Peninsula, and we may still discover in the stagnating dialects North and South of the Danube, the traces of the flux and reflux of those tribes who have since

* An interesting and lucid account of the early inhabitants of Russia founded on the researches of Safarik and others, is found in a pamphlet by Kurd de Schloezer, "Les premiers Habitants de la Russie," Paris, 1846.

become the ruling nations of Europe. The barbarian inroads, which from the 7th century after Christ, infested the regions of civilization and led to the destruction of the Greek and Roman Empires, followed all the same direction. The country near the Danube and the Black Sea has been for ages the battle field of Asia and Europe. Each language settled there on the confines of civilization and barbarism, recalls a chapter of history.

The Ossetian in the Caucasus reminds us of the Scythian Empire in the 7th century before Christ, and of the Median colony of the Sauromatae, then transplanted to the Tanais.

The Greek names of cities on the coast of the Black Sea remind us of their foundation at the same period; when the terror of the Cimmerians had subsided, and their conquerors, the Scythians, had in turn been annihilated by the Medians; 606 B.C. It was then that the name Axine — "the Inhospitable Sea," passed into the Euxine — "the Hospitable." Sinope, destroyed by the Cimmerians, was rebuilt in 632: Odessa was founded in 572, B.C.

Modern Greek, still spoken in Asia Minor and Hellas, recalls the whole history of Greece, the decline of Byzantium, and the latter war of independence.

Wallachian, again, speaks of the Roman Empire, its wide-spread colonies, and its final annihilation by Teutonic and Slavonic armies.

Hungarian transports us to the murderous forays of Attila and his Huns in the 5th century, when it struck roots in soil covered with German, Roman, and Mongolic blood.

The Bulgarian brings back, at least by name, the period when Finnic races founded the Bulgarian Kingdom in the ancient Moesia (635 A. D.). Their name remained; though by the year 800 their language and nationality had been fully absorbed by the Slavonic inhabitants of the country.

At the end of the 12th century the Bulgarian Kingdom was involved in long protracted wars with the Hungarians; and when these two nations, both of Turanian origin, had weakened themselves by successive victories and defeats, a third Turanian race knocked at the gates of Europe, and defeated nations that, united, might have repulsed the Turks of Osman. The Turkish language, now spoken in all the important cities of Turkey, and Asia, regions where its sound was unheard before the 15th century, teaches an historical lesson which should make us pause before we deny to the Turanian race the energy of conquest and the power of organization. While the Turkish memorializes these latest conquests of Tataric tribes in Europe, the Tatar dialects spoken on the Black Sea, in the Dobrudsha, the Krimea, and along the Volga, remind us of the earlier achievements of the armies of *K*ingiskhán and his successors, of the "Golden Horde," and the Mongolian yoke which Russia bore through centuries.

Finally, the Slavonic languages, spoken over so large an area, and in dialects so closely allied, excite an interest not confined to their past alone. The nations that speak them, on the confines of Asia and Europe, may have great destinies to fulfil in the long future; they have means at their command vast as any European nation, and if they can throw out of their system the bastard blood of a Mongolian nobility, and resist the poison of a premature civilization, their history and literature may rise high on the horizon of Europe, and restore to "Slava" its original meaning of "good report and glory".

List of grammars, dictionaries, dialogues, &c.*

The best introduction to a knowledge of the Slavonic languages is Russian. For practical purposes this will be most desirable to officers, and more available than an acquaintance with the minor Slavonic dialects. The following books will be found useful for studying Russian: —

Reiff's Russian Grammar, or Principles of the Russian language for the use of Englishmen, with synop-

* The books here mentioned may be obtained from Williams and Norgate, Henrietta Street, Covent-Garden, from whose catalogues the titles have been taken.

tical tables for the declensions and conjugations, graduated themes or exercises for the application of the grammatical rules, the correct construction of these exercises, and the accentuation of all the Russian words. 8vo., 1853. 4*s.*

Reiff's Dictionary of the Russian, French, German, and English Languages. Square 8vo., 1853. 8*s.*

Dictionary of the Russian and English Languages. 16mo. Leipzig. 3*s.*

Heym (J.), Dictionnaire des Langages Russe, Française, et Allemande, 3 vols. 8vo., Leipzig. 1844. 18*s.*

Hamonière (G.), Dialogues Russes et Français. 8vo. 1816. 3*s.* 6*d.*

It is essential that those who wish to learn Russian should begin by familiarizing themselves with the peculiar system of the Slavonic alphabet as laid down originally by Cyrillus. An account of it has been given in an earlier portion of this work. This alphabet has been one of the greatest barriers between Russia and the intellectual world of Europe, but there is no hope of its being given up at present. On the contrary, it has been the policy of Petersburgh to maintain and to extend it as much as possible.

For Bulgarian, the only available grammar is Kyriak Cankof, Grammar of the Bulgarian Language. Royal 8vo., Vienna, 1852. 5*s.* 6*d.* The grammar is written in German, the Bulgarian words translated in Roman letters. It contains useful exercises and dialogues. There is no modern Bulgarian literature, except a few religious books imported from Russia. In 1840, a Bulgarian translation of the New Testament was printed by the British and Foreign Bible Society. Translations of the Old or New Testament, which exist in almost all languages, will indeed in all cases be found very useful for a first attempt in reading.

A Bulgarian grammar in English was published by E. Riggs, an American Missionary at Smyrna; but whether it is obtainable I cannot say.

For Illyrian, we have Berlic's Grammar of the

Illyrian Languages, as spoken in the Southern Slavonic countries, in Servia, Bosnia, Dalmatia, Kroatia, and by the Illyrians and Servians in Hungary and in the Vojvodina. Agram, 1849. 6*s*. It is written in German, printed in Roman characters, and contains useful dialogues.

The Illyrian Grammar of Babukić was translated into German by Fröhlich. 8vo., Vienna, 1839. 6*s*.

Berlić (A. T.), Grammar of the Illyrian Language as spoken by the Serbians and Kroats. Vienna, 1854. 6*s*.

Richter and Bellmann, Dictionary of the Illyrian and German, and German and Illyrian Languages, for the use of Germans and Illyrians in Croatia, Slavonia, Syrmia, Dalmatia, Bosnia, Servia, Albania, Ragusa, Montenegro, the Herzegovina, the Banat, and Hungary. Vienna, 1839. 15*s*.

Voltiggi (I.), Illyrian, Italian, and German Dictionary and Grammar. Thick 8vo. (610 pp.) Vienna. 6*s*. 6*d*.

Principj Elementari della Grammatica Illirica, premessi al dizionario Italiano, Latino, Illirico, del P. Ardelia della Bella, ed ora di nuovo pubblicati. Ragusa, 1827.

Fröhlich. Dictionary of the Illyrian and German languages. 2 vols. 1854. 10*s*. 6*d*.

Fröhlich. Theoretic and practical Grammar of the Illyrian language. Vienna, 1850. 6*s*.

Illyrian, as we saw, was used as a general name to comprehend all the dialects of the South Slavonians, with the exception of Bulgarian, and, according to some, of Servian. Of the dialects spoken in Servia, Bosnia, Montenegro, Slavonia, and Dalmatia, the Kroatian is perhaps the most independent, yet it is only one dialect of the language common to all Illyrians. Russians learn these dialects with great ease, inasmuch as they resemble Russian more than any other Slavonic language.

Servian.

Wuk Stephanowitsch, Small Servian Grammar, translated into German by Jacob Grimm. 8vo. Berlin, 1824. 2*s*. 6*d*.

Wuk Stephanowitsch, Servian, German, and Latin Dictionary. 8vo. Vienna, 1818. 22*s.*

New Testament in Servian translated by S. Wuk. 8vo. 1848. 9*s.* 6*d.*

Wuk, Servian Proverbs in Servian. Alphabetically arranged. 8vo. 1850. 6*s.*

Milutinovitsch. Songs of the Montenegrians, in Servian. 8vo. 5*s.*

Kroatian.

Gyurkovechky (S.), Kroatian Grammar. 8vo. Ofen, 1825.

Slovenian.

Murko (A. J.), German-Slovenian, and Slovenian-German Dictionary, according to the dialects of the Slovenes in Styria, Carinthia, Carniolia, and the West of Hungary. 2 vols. 8vo. Gratz, 1833. 10*s.* 6*d.*

Kopitar, Grammar of the Slavonic Language in Carniolia, Carinthia, and Styria. 8vo. Laibach, 1808. 5*s.*

Murko, Slovenian Grammar. 8vo. Gratz, 1843. 2*s.* 6*d.*

Weissenthurn (Fr. V.), Saggio Grammaticale Italiano-Cragnolano. 8vo. Trieste, 1811. 6*s.*

The Western Slavonic dialects will be of less practical importance, with the exception perhaps of

Polish.

Frings (M. T.), Polish, French, and German Dialogues. 8vo. Lemberg, 1847. 3*s.*

There is a complete and scientific Polish Dictionary with explanations in German, and a comparison of thirteen other Slavonic dialects by Linde. 6 vols. 4to. Warsaw, 1707—14. £ 6, 16*s.* 6*d.* Though it could hardly obtain a place in the Library of an officer, it deserves to be mentioned here as a classical work in Slavonic philology.

Mongrovius, Polish-English, and English-Polish Dictionary. 2 vols. Royal 8vo. Berlin, 1851. 20*s.*

Schmidt (M.), Dictionnaire portatif. Polonais et Français. 16mo. Leipzig, 1847. 3*s.*

Bohemian.

Cebusky (A.), Grammar of the Bohemian Language. 8vo. Vienna, 1854. 2*s*.

Bible in Bohemian. 8vo. 1833. 14*s*.

Dictionary, Bohemian and German. 16mo. Leipzig. 3*s*.

Slovakian.

Dianiska (K.), Slovakian Grammar (with Dialogues and Selections). 8vo. Vienna, 1850. 4*s*.

There is another Slovakian Grammar by Bernolak, 1790; a dictionary, 1825, and a translation of the Bible, 1829.

A tabular arrangement of the four principal Slavonic dialects was published by Fröhlich, comprehending Bohemian and Polish, Illyrian and Russian. Vienna, 1847. 8vo. 4*s*.

Classical works on the Slavonic languages in general, are —

*S*afarik (P. J.), Slavonic Antiquities, translated into German. 2 vols. 8vo. 1853. 15*s* 6*d*.

*S*afarik, History of the Slavonic Language and Literature. 8vo. Ofen, 1826. 10*s*. 6*d*.

*S*afarik, Slovansky Narodopis (Slavonic Ethnology). Praze, 1849. 8vo.

It is hardly necessary to give a list of grammars and dictionaries for acquiring a knowledge of German, Danish, and Swedish; as any foreign bookseller will supply them.

In the case of the Romance languages also, it will be sufficient to mention the grammars and dictionaries for Wallachian. These are —

Alexi (J.), Grammatica Daco-Romana sive Valachica. 8vo. Vienna, 1826. 3*s*. 6*d*.

Blacewicz (T.), Grammar of the Daco-Romanic, Moldavian or Wallachian Language. 8vo. Lemberg, 1844. 4*s*. In German, with modern Cyrillic types. Both grammars contain dialogues.

Theoklist Schoimul. Theoretic and practical Pocket-Grammar of the Romaic or Wallachian language, written in German, and printed with modern Cyrillic types. Vienna, 1855. 2*s*.

Lesicon, Romanescu, Latinescu, Ungarescu, Nemtescu; *i. e.*, Wallachian, Latin, Hungarian, and German. 4to. Budae, 1825. Scarce.

Vaillant (J. A.), Vocabulaire Français-Roumain et Roumain-Français. 8. Boucoureshti, 1840. 6*s*.

Vaillant (J. A.), Grammaire Roumane à l'usage des Français. 8. Boucourest, 1840.

For Modern Greek, a grammar that can be recommended is —

Corpe (H.), An Introduction to Neo-Hellenic, or Modern Greek, containing a guide to its pronunciation and an epitome of its grammar. 8vo. London, 1851. 5*s*.

A Translation of the Bible into Modern Greek has lately been issued from the University Press at Oxford.

Deheque (F. D.), Dictionnaire Grec-Moderne et Français. 12mo. London, 1825. 5*s*.

Lowndes. Modern-Greek and English Dictionary royal 8vo. Corfu. 21*s*.

For a study of Albanian, little assistance can be derived from books. The latest and most comprehensive work on Albania is —

Hahn (J. G. von), Albanian Studies. Thick 4to. Jena, 1854. £ 1. 10*s*.

The first part contains geographical and ethnographical notices, travels in Albania, description of customs and manners, researches on the origin of the Albanians, an account of the Albanian alphabet, and a history of the the country. The second part gives a grammar of the Toskian dialect, Toskian and Geghan poems, proverbs, phrases, stories; and lastly, a dictionary, Albanian-German, and German-Albanian. An extract of this work might be useful. The best grammatical compilation is to be found in —

Xylander (I. v.), The Language of the Albanians or Skipetars. 8vo. Frankfort, 1835. 4*s*. 6*d*. (In German.)

An excellent account of Albania is given by —

Leake (W. M.), Researches in Greece. London, 4to. 1814.

And Hobhouse (J. C.), Journey through Albania, &c. 4to. London, 1813.

The great desideratum during the present war will no doubt, be a knowledge of Turkish. Most officers will probably be satisfied if they are able to speak by interjections and gestures, and succeed in making a Turk understand that they want a horse, or provisions, or directions for the road in a country not advanced to signposts. This can be learned from dialogues, and even without a knowledge of the Turkish alphabet. By far the best book for this purpose is —

Bianchi (C. X.), Le nouveau Guide de la Conversation en Français et en Turc. It is so arranged, that in learning the dialogues by heart, students acquire the grammar without being aware of it. An abridgment of this book, in English, would be invaluable. The Turkish should be transcribed, however, so as to suit English pronunciation.

Another work which will answer this purpose is —

Le Dragoman Turc. — Regime sanitaire, Monnaies, Vocabulaire, Grammaire. 12mo. Paris, 1854. 2*s*. 6*d*. brds.

A pocket Dictionary of the English and Turkish languages (the Turkish being expressed in English characters, with guide to the correct pronunciation), by W. G. Sauerwein is now in the press and will be very shortly published.

Those, however, who have taste and leisure to study Turkish should make themselves, first of all, acquainted with the Turkish alphabet, whatever has been said to the contrary by our "special correspondents". It is true, no doubt, that by means of transcription in Roman characters the grammar can be learned, without a previous knowledge of the alphabet; but in the long run more time is lost than saved by this. The Roman alphabet is no doubt better adapted to express the sounds of the Turkish language than the Arabic alphabet now used by the Turks, in which even when the vowels are written, as they invariably are in the *K*agataic dialect, three signs must suffice to express eight different vowel-sounds. But until this great alphabetical revolution is accomplished — until the Turks condescend to write their language in those signs which in time must and will be the alphabet of the whole world, any one who wishes to acquire a competent knowledge of Turkish should begin with the alphabet, and impress the declensions and conjugations on his memory, in their Turkish dress. Else he will find that when he comes to read, his Romanized verbs will not answer to their Turkish originals. Then the whole must be learned again; with the discovery that by this double proceeding the learner has weakened and confused what ought to be the most distinct in his memory, "les premières impressions de la grammaire Turque." Soldiers know best that in storming a fortress it does not answer to leave the detached works untaken; though at first they may seem to offer no resistance to advance, they are sure to open fire when least expected.

When the alphabet is once mastered, the pronunciation of Turkish is comparatively easy. It is true that vowels are generally omitted in writing, but they are frequently indicated at the beginning of words, and in open syllables. Besides there are certain rules which make up for this omission of vowel-signs and which are of great assistance to the student of Turkish.

There are two classes of vowels, called sharp and flat. A (in psalm), O (in note), U (in flute), I (in ravine) are sharp. Ä (in date or Väter), Ö (in König, peu), Ü (in Güte, une), Ï (in yield) are flat. As the vowels of every word must be either all sharp or all flat, the knowledge of the vowel of one syllable is generally sufficient to indicate the vocalisation of the whole word. There are certain consonants which only admit of sharp or flat vowels, and hence in many words there is one consonant which indicates whether the word is to be pronounced so to say, in a sharp or flat key. This law of the harmony of vowels which pervades the Turkish and other Turanian languages, and which was first fully explained by Viguier, would in most instances render all vowel-signs except one superfluous. Intercourse with natives however, is the only means to acquire the proper pronunciation of Turkish, of which neither transcription in Roman, nor in the still more difficult Armenian or Greek characters can give an adequate idea. In the Turkish grammar of D. Alexandrides and in his Modern-Greek and Turkish Glossary the accent of Turkish is marked according to the Greek system; the Armenians mark the accent in their transcriptions only where it seems to be irregular. Some scholars maintain that there is no accent at all in Turkish, others that it is always on the last syllable as in French. The distinction between long and short vowels also is of little consequence in Turkish. —

Redhouse (J. W.), Grammaire raisonnée de la Langue Ottomane. Royal 8vo. Paris, 1846. 13*s.* 6*d.* (Best; but why not repeated in English?)

Boyd (Charles), The Turkish Interpreter, or a New Grammar of the Turkish Language. Paris, 1842. 8*s.* 6*d.*

Pfizmaier (A.), Grammaire Turque, ou developpement de trois genres de style, l'Arabe, le Persan, et le Tartare. 8vo. Vienna, 1848. 15*s.* 6*d.*

A very useful book is:

Dieterici. Chrestomathie Ottomane, précedée de tableaux grammaticaux et suivie d'un glossaire Turc-Français. 8vo. Berlin, 1814. 4*s.* It contains an easy explanation of the grammatical principles of Turkish, and extracts chosen with a view to exhibit the genuine Turkish style of literature.

Mirza A. Kazem Beg, Derbend-Nameh, or the History of Derbend; Turkish and English. 4to. St. Petersburg, 1851. 10*s.* 4*d.*

By the same author we have the only grammar of the different Tataric dialects which deviate from the Turkish standard. It is written in Russian, but a German translation has made it more accessible. The translation is not, however, altogether satisfactory.

General Grammar of the Turco-Tataric Language,

by Mirza A. Kazem Beg; translated by Dr. Julius Th. Zenker. Leipzic, 1848. 8vo. 12*s*.

The same author has a complete Chrestomathy of the Turco-Tataric Dialects ready for the press. Among his published works "the history of the Khans of the Crimea" Kasan 1832, printed from a unique MS. might at the present moment prove of more general interest.

The dialect of the Tatars of Kasan can be studied in an elementary book, published by Wakhabof, one of the masters of the Military School of Kasan. It contains specimens, dialogues and songs in the Tatari of Kasan, with Russian translations. Of still greater importance is a similar small book, containing proverbs, dialogues and fables in the dialect of the Tatars of the Crimea, published at Kasan by Krym-Khowadja, teacher at Simpheropol. A few specimens of the Turkish as spoken in the Caucasus, are given by Bodenstedt in the Journal of the German Oriental Society. Vol. V. page 245.

A Tataric translation of the New Testament has been printed at Astrachan.

Specimens of Eastern Tataric dialects are to be found in Quatremère's Chrestomathies Orientales.

For a thorough knowledge of Turkish, a previous acquaintance with Persian and Arabic is invaluable. A useful Persian Grammar is Meerza Mohammad Ibraheem's Grammar of the Persian language. 8vo. London, 1841. 21*s*.

On Persian dialects there is an Essay by Beresin Recherches sur les dialectes persans, the second part of his Recherches sur les dialectes Musulmans. The Persian dialects which he examines and of which he gives specimens, are the Gilek, Tati, Talyshi, Mazandarani, Gebri and the Kurdian of Chorasan and Mosul.

For the spoken Arabic, there is

Mouhammad Ayyad el Tantavy, Sheikh. Traité de la langue Arabe vulgaire. 8vo. Leipzic, 1850. 6*s*.

The most scientific grammar is still Sylvestre de Sacy's Grammaire Arabe à l'usage des élèves de l'école spéciale des langues Orientales vivantes. 2 vols. 8vo. Paris, 1831. £ 2. 10*s.*

The following may also be recommended, Schier, Grammaire Arabe. 8vo. Dresden, 1849. 12*s.*

Caspari, Grammatica Arabica in usum Academicorum: accedit brevis Chrestomathia. 8vo. Leipzig, 1848. 6*s.*

Of Tungusic, Mongolic, Samoïedic, and Finnic languages, it would be superfluous to recommend grammars and dictionaries, as none of them, I suppose, will be chosen for practical study. Perhaps an exception might be made in favour of Hungarian, which has lately attracted more attention, and of which English grammars and dictionaries may be procured.

Frereych (E.), Hungarian and English Dialogues, for the use of Travellers and Students. 8vo. Pesth, 1851. 2*s.*

Csink, Complete Practical Grammar of the Hungarian Language, with Exercises, Selections from the best Authors, and Vocabularies; to which is added a Historical Sketch of Hungarian Literature. 8vo. boards. 1854. 8*s.*

We now come to the last cluster of languages, the dialects spoken in the Caucasian Babel. Here the difficulties are greatest, and the means of acquiring a knowledge of the languages proportionably small. Not one of these numerous dialects has found as yet an English grammarian, and few have been reduced to a grammatical system by any grammarian. Klaproth's "Asia Polyglotta" gives considerable lists of words which, as a beginning, would be found useful; but in the few cases where his collections have been checked by later travellers, they have not always proved accurate and satisfactory. This applies particularly to the Georgian, and its cognate dialects, Lazian and Mingrelian. Here we have since Klaproth, the works of Brosset and Rosen —

Brosset, L'art liberal, ou grammaire Géorgienne. 8vo. Paris, 1834. 10*s.*

Brosset, Eléments de la langue Géorgienne. 8vo. Paris, 1837. 12*s.*

Klaproth (J.), Vocabulaire et grammaire de la langue

Géorgienne. 8vo. Paris, 1827. 16*s*. Other works on the Caucasus by Klaproth are, "Travels in the Caucasus;" "Description of the Russian Provinces between the Caspian and Black Sea," Berlin, 1814, 12*s*; and "Asia Polyglotta," 4to, and atlas folio. 24*s*.

Tschubinof, Dictionnaire Géorgien-Russe-Français, 4to. Petersburg, 1840. 34*s*.

Of the Lazian, Mingrelian, and Suanian, grammatical outlines were published by Rosen in the Transactions of the Berlin Academy, 1846. 4to. 2*s*.

The same author has given a grammar of the Ossetian (4to. 1846, 5*s*.), the only Arian dialect spoken in the centre of the Caucasus; and one more complete has since been published by

Sjögren, Ossetian Grammar, with a short Ossetian-German and German-Ossetian Vocabulary. Petersburg, 1844. Thick 4to. 12*s*.

Of the remaining dialects spoken between the Caspian and the Black Sea no grammars can be procured, as the Russian Government, so liberal in other respects in its support of linguistic studies, has not thought fit to encourage a study of these mountain idioms. Military interpreters and translators of the Caucasian army are educated at Novo-Tcherkask, in the country of the Don Cossacks, where Arabic, Tataric, Avarian and Tcherkessian dialects are taught at the Imperial Gymnasium. At the gymnasium of Stawropol also, Tataric and Tscherkessian form part of the educational system. (Köppen, p. 253.) Grammatical notices and short lists of words may indeed be found scattered through the Transactions of different Academies, in Klaproth's works, in Adelung's Mithridates, 4 vols, 8vo., 35*s*; in Balbi's Atlas Ethnographique, in Bell's Journal of a Residence in Circassia, £ 1, 12*s*, and similar publications; but all that could be extracted thence, as of practical use, might be brought into a very small volume. Rosen's grammatical notices of the Ab'hasian dialect are found in the Transactions of the Berlin Academy, and give an idea of the *K*erkessian, of which the Ab'hasian is but a variety. A grammar and dictionary of *K*erkessian were published by L'Huilier, Odessa, 1846; written in Russian.

A Circassian Dictionary has lately been published by Dr. Loewe. 8vo. 21*s*. It consists of two parts, English-Circassian-Turkish, and Circassian-English-Turkish. The words were collected by Dr. Loewe from the mouth of the natives.

Chora-Beg-Mursin-Nogma in St. Petersburg is said to have composed a Grammar and Dictionary of the Kabardian language; see Loewe's Circassian Dictionary, p. 4.

Another work which deserves to be mentioned here is

F. Bodenstedt, Die Völker des Kaukasus, of which a second edition has just been published. It contains much useful information on the history, the geography and the social state of the Caucasian countries, and is written in a pleasant style.

The southern neighbour of these Caucasian languages, the Armenian, of Arian extraction, has met with a better fate. Besides grammars and dictionaries in other languages we have here, both in English —

Aucher (P.), A Grammar, Armenian and English. 8vo. Venice, 1832. 6*s*.

Aucher (P.), Dictionary, English and Armenian, with the assistance of J. Brand. 2 vols. 4to. Venice, 1821. 1821. 24*s*.

Of the Kurdian language neither grammar nor dictionary can be procured without difficulty. There is

Maurizio Garzoni, Grammatica e vocabulario della lingua Kurda. Rome, 1787.

Some interesting articles on Kurdian were published by Rödiger and Pott, in the "Zeitschrift für die Kunde des Morgenlandes. Vol. III & IV.

The works here specified may be had by applying to Williams and Norgate, 14, Henrietta-street, Covent Garden, London. The prices, as marked above, have been taken from their Catalogues.

THE END.

Map to illustrate
PROFESSOR MAX MÜLLER'S "SUGGESTIONS"
for the assistance of Officers in learning the
LANGUAGES OF THE SEAT OF WAR
IN THE EAST.
Drawn by Augustus Petermann.
1854.
BLACK SEA
ADRIATIC SEA
CASPIAN SEA
Sea of Azov
SERVIAN
BULGARIAN
ALBANIAN
GREEK
TURKISH
KURDIAN
GREAT RUSSIAN
SLOVENIAN
POLISH
EXPLANATION of the COLOURS